SOCIAL LEADERS
AND PUBLIC PERSONS

SOCIAL LEADERS
AND
PUBLIC PERSONS

*A Study of County Government in
Cheshire since 1888*

BY

J. M. LEE

OXFORD
AT THE CLARENDON PRESS
1963

Oxford University Press, Amen House, London E.C.4

GLASGOW NEW YORK TORONTO MELBOURNE WELLINGTON
BOMBAY CALCUTTA MADRAS KARACHI LAHORE DACCA
CAPE TOWN SALISBURY NAIROBI IBADAN ACCRA
KUALA LUMPUR HONG KONG

PRINTED IN GREAT BRITAIN

PREFACE

THIS book is a one-man survey of a large county, based on research in local libraries and conversations with councillors and officials. Its methods are therefore more limited than those of intensive urban studies. My colleagues at Manchester University who helped Professor A. H. Birch in the production of *Small Town Politics* would have needed far greater resources than the voluntary labour of students which they used, if they had turned their attention to the wider fields of county government, and far greater specialist assistance in the analysis of returns, if they had used the same tools of questionnaire and interview. Their methods could have been applied to county affairs, and could have led to a common basis of comparison between town and country politics. There has not yet been any attempt to mount such a large-scale operation. In the meanwhile, this study tries to achieve a workable frame of reference for county council affairs which may help future research.

My aim throughout has been to provide a basis in local history for the work on systems of local social status which several sociologists in recent years have produced from their study of towns and villages.[1] My analysis in terms of social leaders and public persons corresponds in some degree to their distinction between 'traditional' and 'non-traditional' social status, but I have avoided any attempt to link the transformation of leadership in local affairs with a formal treatment based on more precise definitions of social class, such as those provided by the National Census.[2] All the experiments which I made to use such definitions historically seemed unsatisfactory.

At the risk of being repetitive, I have summarized the principal arguments of the book in the introduction and conclusion to Parts II and III which should be read in conjunction with Chapter 7 in order to follow the main lines of thought. Large parts of the remainder must inevitably be more interesting to those who have access to the same sources of information, and are able to 'read between the lines'. Some of my informants provided me with material which might have

[1] D. E. G. Plowman, W. E. Minchinton, and Margaret Stacey, 'Local Social Status in England and Wales', Appendix, pp. 195–202, *The Sociological Review* (1962), x (2), pp. 161–202.

[2] L. J. Sharpe, 'Elected Representatives in Local Government', *British Journal of Sociology* (1962), xiii (3), pp. 189–209.

been better used in a novel—perhaps the natural medium for county affairs—rather than in a work of political science. A novelist can disclaim that his characters bear any resemblance to persons living or dead. My chief difficulty, particularly in Part III, has been to illustrate a thesis of contemporary history with a few living examples when so many of my characters can be immediately identified. Some parts were rewritten several times to avoid personal embarrassment. I hope that the criticisms made by those who were kind enough to read my drafts have produced a text reasonably free from error. For any remaining mistakes, I must alone be responsible.

The production of this book was made possible by the generous co-operation of members of Cheshire County Council. The Chairman and Vice-Chairman kindly agreed to allow the chief officers to give me all the help they could. I am extremely grateful to the Clerk, Mr. A. C. Hetherington, and the other heads of departments, and particularly to Mr. Stephen Brown, the Chief Assistant Solicitor, who was appointed to act as my mentor. The labour of piecing together all the available historical material was made lighter by the assistance of the County Archivist at Chester Castle, and by the willing help of the staff of Manchester Central Reference Library who placed at my disposal one of their carrels, where most of Part II was written.

My greatest debt is to Professor W. J. M. Mackenzie, who had sufficient confidence in my ability to turn from local history to political science. He has given me an excellent apprenticeship in making this change of profession. Time and again he read through the manuscripts which I placed on his desk, and gave me the necessary encouragement to continue. My thanks are also due to other colleagues at Manchester University who read and criticized certain chapters, Dr. W. H. Chaloner, Mr. H. J. Perkin, and Professor T. S. Willan. Professor A. H. Birch gave me the benefit of his expert advice, and Mr. B. Keith-Lucas was most generous in helping with the preparation of the final text.

It is hard to thank adequately all those in the public life of Cheshire who have made a contribution to the study which follows—sometimes unknowingly by a chance conversation in the members' dining-room at County Hall! I am particularly grateful to Alderman H. J. S. Dewes, Alderman W. A. Gibson, Mr. Tinker (the Deputy Treasurer), and Mr. Armitage (the Deputy Director of Education) for their words of advice; and to Mr. Arthur Worsley and Mr. Arnold Kenyon for their insight into Manchester politics before 1929. Lady Chorley

kindly constructed Table 2 (p. 41) from her memories of Alderley
Edge; and the County Planning Officer and his staff were good
enough to make themselves responsible for the maps (facing pp. 8
and 119) and the end paper. The three typists who laboured in difficult conditions to make a decent copy from my manuscript, Mrs.
Pountney, Miss Davies, and Mrs. Beck, deserve all possible praise,
and my wife, who bore the burden of proof-reading, helped me over
all the extra difficulties caused by a year's leave of absence in Africa.

J. M. L.

Makerere College
Kampala, Uganda
23 February 1963

CONTENTS

LIST OF TABLES

LIST OF DIAGRAMS

LIST OF MAPS

PART I

INTRODUCTION

1

THE GOVERNMENT OF THE COUNTRYSIDE

COUNTY councils have never made much impact upon the minds of the electorate. Nobody at the time of their creation in 1888 wished to endow these new public bodies with a defined social purpose, and they had merely the negative virtue of providing a reasonable alternative to the rule of the justices of the peace. There was no organized pressure group working in their favour. After Joseph Hume's Bill of 1836, there were a large number of attempts to establish 'county boards', but the back-bench M.P.s sponsoring these projects received little encouragement from successive governments. The magistrates themselves were not anxious to have certain administrative duties removed from their shoulders and in most counties were persuaded only with great difficulty to remain in public life under the new conditions. Irate country gentlemen, such as Sir John Dorington in Gloucestershire, wrote long and bitter letters of complaint to the Prime Minister, Lord Salisbury, prophesying the dreadful consequences which would arise from the introduction of representative democracy into rural areas. Even the Radicals, who hoped that great improvements would follow the enfranchisement of agricultural labourers in 1884, found little cause for satisfaction in the creation of local authorities where the influence of the landed gentry might continue to predominate. Perhaps the only groups in rural areas to welcome the Local Government Act of 1888 were the village elders of Wales, the small shopkeepers and members of Nonconformist chapels, who were waiting for a convenient opportunity to overthrow the power and influence of the Anglican gentry. Members of

Parliament were primarily concerned with the designation of county boroughs in urban areas.

The tradition of popular indifference to county council work has continued, broken only by occasional outbursts of virulent abuse. The councillors have been regularly accused of retaining a 'feudal' air which belonged to the landed gentry; the officials have been in danger of personal attacks on their character for alleged acts of 'bureaucratic tyranny'. A great deal of the comment upon county administration has been ill-informed. Both the ignorance and the criticism may be due to a fundamental fact of geography that the majority of administrative counties do not correspond to natural communities of interest. Within the boundaries of a single county there may be a large number of settlements which look towards towns in other counties for their work, their leisure, and their information. The most favourable press reports which county councils have ever received were written in the days when county newspapers were read by 'county society', which was composed of the leading families of landed gentry. The Act of 1888 was intended to establish a dual system of local government, one system for the urban areas, county boroughs, and another system for the rural areas, county councils—with district councils added later. But this was a division which frequently did not correspond to the situation in local politics.

The principal irony of this antithesis was that the largest and best-known county council governed the most important urban area. London County Council provided the prototype for government in the large conurbations. Following the principle of a single all-purpose authority for Greater London, the President of the Local Government Board in 1888 proposed the creation of a new administrative county from the area which had hitherto come under the jurisdiction of the Metropolitan Board of Works. The L.C.C. was compelled to share its responsibilities with the new metropolitan boroughs which were created in 1899, and therefore required to experiment with a system of two-tier government. Other large cities, such as Birmingham and Manchester, extended their boundaries by absorbing adjacent urban districts in order to meet the demands for supplying adequate local services, but this process of expansion was not permitted to continue indefinitely. By the time the Royal Commission on Local Government in the Tyneside Area had reported in 1937, it was academically respectable to regard some form of urban county government as the most suitable system for conurbations. The Boundary Commission of 1945-9 regarded the possibility of 'continuous county government' with some favour; the Royal Commission on Local Government in Greater London in 1960 brought the L.C.C. solution up to date in its proposals for a Council for Greater London; and the Local Government Commission for England in 1962 suggested the creation of a Tyneside County Council. The debate about urban government became centred on the division of functions between a county authority and its constituent districts.

Was there ever any foundation for making a distinction between urban areas and rural areas? Were there any rural areas which were able to reject the suggestion that their administrative affairs should be joined to those of the nearest large town? Having made this dichotomy, the government was unable to propose a single all-purpose unit as the only kind of local authority. Should county councils outside the conurbations be liquidated and their constituent districts be reorganized into larger regions? The Local Government Act of 1958 has divided the country into special review areas, which are the conurbations, and general review areas, which contain all other parts. The latter will certainly continue to be the sphere of traditional county government; the former will provide opportunities for a new kind of organization. What will be the resources of the more ancient county authorities if they lose wealthy residential areas to new county boroughs or urban county councils?

Local history has been largely a subject for towns and villages, because they are extremely convenient units to examine. But there is a real need to explore the evolution of county government, and although county councils have not all evolved according to the same pattern, the best way to do it is to take a single county, unnatural and inconvenient though it may be, and make a thorough survey of the influences which have effected the development of the county council.

The disappearance of the 'country party'

The main task of this book is to discover who goes into local politics and why. It seeks to find an answer within the context of county government and in terms of the social and economic changes which have affected the life of the countryside. Its main thesis is that the present nature of county politics can only be understood by examining the causes of one important social transformation—the disappearance of the 'country party' from English politics—and by studying the functions which county councillors perform in relation to the conventions of government formerly determined by the landed gentry and magistrates. Most of the work in this field has been concerned with urban communities. Local government has been rightly regarded as a subject which relates primarily to the public health of the town—drains, sewerage, preventive medicine, and the regulation of housing. During the nineteenth century the greater part of the population of this country came to live in towns. But the county councils of England and Wales, created in 1888, have been given considerable powers in municipal boroughs and responsibility in other large urban areas. At the National Census of 1961 only just over 13½ millions in a total population for England and Wales of 46 millions lived in county boroughs. The dual system of local government, which divides the country into independent authorities, the county boroughs, and into boroughs and district councils which remain subordinate to the counties, owes its origin to social and class distinctions. The antagonism between large urban and rural authorities is the legacy of 'country party' politics. The dispute about the relative merits of single-tier and two-tier systems of government is not entirely a question of administrative convenience; it represents an important piece of English social history.

County government by country gentlemen was perhaps the purest example of oligarchy to be seen in England. Membership of the governing class could be easily defined. The 'country party' was constituted from those with the necessary property qualification who could secure the nomination of the lord-lieutenant to be chosen as a justice of the peace. The historian of eighteenth-century England is familiar with the political role of the county magistrates, the gentlemen and freeholders of the shire. They did not 'go into local politics' in the modern meaning of that phrase. Local politics, by definition, were those affairs which concerned their interests. What then happened to the 'country party' in the nineteenth century? Who replaced the landed gentry as political leaders? What kind of people become present-day county councillors and county officials? To account for the disappearance of the 'country party' calls for an exercise in local history.

The process of change which this book describes has two distinct phases. Neither of them should be regarded too rigidly as a definite period of time, limited by certain historical events; each of them should rather be considered as a stage in the transformation of political leadership. They are both essential to the history of the professionalization of government, and in the following chapters they correspond to Part II and Part III, which have been called respectively 'Social Leaders' and 'Public Persons'. The first phase was marked by the introduction of businessmen and industrialists into the county magistracy. Justices of the peace for the county always included those who made their wealth in the towns, but usually only after the latter had acquired an estate and begun to live the life of country gentlemen. The significance of nominations to the bench in the late-nineteenth century was that they included for the first time men who continued to trade or manufacture. Candidates for election at the first county council elections in 1889 were drawn from the new county society created by the fusion of landed and business interests. Such men may be conveniently described as 'social leaders', a term used by the publishers of county directories for those who possessed sufficient social standing, sufficient time, and sufficient money to participate in the work of local authorities or voluntary societies. The second phase was marked by the vast increase in the number of duties which the central government expected local authorities to perform, particularly after the Education Act of 1902 and the Local Government Act of 1929, and by the need for professional experts in administration. Technical improvements and industrial reorganization removed social leaders from the public service, and their functions were gradually taken over by full-time officials and those who were willing to accept office for its own sake, collecting large numbers of public offices, not because of their social standing, but because of the connexions they had established with various local interest groups and political parties. Such people, both men and women, may be called 'public persons', a term coined by a research group at the London School of Economics, to describe local politicians who are active in a large number of public bodies and private associations.[1]

The two terms, social leader and public person, appear over and over again in the following chapters in order to lay emphasis upon one central theme, the disappearance of social standing as the sole criterion for public service. The essential difference between a social leader and a public person is that the former can surrender public office and still retain his social standing, while the latter acquires social status by taking up 'public life'. In fact, the public person gives the

[1] *Public Administration*, xxxviii (Summer, 1960), pp. 157–72.

impression of one who has turned the business of being a social leader into a recognized profession. Just as the social leader acquired the habits of living like a landed proprietor without possessing a proprietor's independence from the business of making money, so the public person acquired the custom of representing all different kinds of local interests without having the wealth to offer subscriptions to their funds. The transformation of political leadership in county government—from the landed gentleman through the social leader to the public person—was part of a much larger process which drew the whole of society into an increasing series of professional organizations. This book is concerned with the effect of professionalism on the idea of representative democracy. The social leader might fairly have been held responsible to the electorate for the policy of a local authority, but the public person was more and more dependent upon the advice of full-time professional experts, the county officials who were paid to keep abreast with the flood of legislation and administrative memoranda and who were themselves important people in public life. The decline in the importance of social standing in local government was accompanied by an increase in the amount of attention paid to professional standards and technical competence.

Several eminent contemporaries towards the end of the nineteenth century recognized the rise of the professions in local government and acknowledged that the process of professionalization was naturally more rapid in the towns than in the countryside. County government was transformed not from within but by the pressures of urban development. Josef Redlich, who published his great work, *Local Government in England*, in 1903, emphasized that the work of the new boards and councils had increased the personal participation of citizens in public administration, but went on to point out how the introduction of trained staffs of paid officials had brought technical skill for the first time into the conduct of local affairs. Both the increased participation and the technical skill were primarily urban phenomena, and in the tradition of writings on municipal socialism, developed particularly by Sidney and Beatrice Webb, they have been the subject of some serious academic study. E. S. Griffith's classic two-volume work, *The Modern Development of City Government*, was published in 1927, but there is no equivalent authority on county affairs. The impact of the towns upon the government of the countryside had not advanced far enough in 1927 for sufficient material to be available. Each phase in the transformation of county leadership required an act of urban aggression. In 1897 T. H. Sweet Escott in *Social Transformation of the Victorian Age* emphasized that the creation of county councils would not have been successful if it had been tried before 1888 because their success depended upon the activity of a new class of person from the towns who had settled in the countryside, as neighbours of the resident gentry. He believed that local government reform had promoted 'a wholesome fusion of classes'. It is not the purpose of this book to determine how wholesome this fusion has been, but to describe the process at work. Social leaders arose from a class of wealthy 'commuters'. Public persons arose from the second wave of suburban settlement, the building of large numbers of housing estates in the 1920's and 1930's. There are still several counties which have not fully experienced the second phase of the transformation. But the likely pattern of their evolution is clear. The disappearance of the 'country party' is part of the process of urbanization; it takes place wherever urban standards of health and comfort have come to prevail.

The desirability of Cheshire

The county of Cheshire, which is the subject of this study, provides many excellent examples of the effects of urbanization. It has, for example, since the middle of the nineteenth century, been compelled to come to terms with the two great conurbations of Merseyside and South-East Lancashire and to live beside them as peaceably as possible. Its history includes all the tensions which have been generated by the rise of the 'great towns'. The rivalries between Liverpool and Manchester and their suburban satellites have had a profound effect upon the county's industrial development since the first railways were constructed. The 'great towns' attracted large numbers of people by providing them with employment. The great expansion of the population of Cheshire, from 192,000 in 1801 to 644,000 in 1881, took place in the towns of the county. Even after the county boroughs of Birkenhead, Chester, and Stockport were taken out of the administrative county in 1889, the population continued to increase, particularly in the suburban areas along its northern boundary. The numbers living inside the administrative county have risen from 597,000 in 1901, to 921,000 in 1961.[1] As if the whole county had been tipped sideways, the greater part of its population has flowed towards the

---

[1] Dorothy Sylvester and Geoffrey Nulty, *The Historical Atlas of Cheshire* (1958), pp. 43–49 give maps of population and industry, 1801–1951.

banks of the Mersey which used to mark its northern limit all the way from Wallasey in the west to Manchester in the east. The County Development Plan in 1952 illustrated this concentration of population diagrammatically by following the course of three lines.[1] The first, an east–west line following the northern boundary of the county, represented a belt of territory which rarely exceeded more than five miles in width but which contained more than 60 per cent. of the county's population. The second and third, both north–south lines which are not exactly parallel but which tend to converge towards the south, represented two other belts of territory, again comparatively narrow, which contained the bulk of the remaining population and industry. The second ran through Northwich and Crewe; and the third through Macclesfield and Congleton. They divided the county into its three agricultural regions; the whole of south-west Cheshire including Delamere Forest and the Peckforton Hills; the area of the Congleton and Bucklow Rural Districts; and the hilly region in the east. Although Cheshire is well known for its agricultural products, particularly its milk and its cheese, it is far from being a predominantly rural county.

The distribution of industry has been governed to a large extent by river navigation, canals, and the railways. The shipbuilding industries of Birkenhead, the soap and chemical manufacture of Port Sunlight, and the oil refineries of Ellesmere Port depend upon the tidal waters of the Mersey. The building of the Manchester Ship Canal, which was opened in 1894, extended the operation of many factories between Runcorn and Salford. The industries of the Weaver valley, which runs northwards into the Mersey, have depended on the historic processes of manufacturing salt. This is the origin of the tremendous manufacturing empire established by Imperial Chemical Industries. But the Weaver valley was also followed by the Trent–Mersey canal in 1766, and by the railway from Birmingham to Liverpool in 1837. Crewe was one of the most important railway junctions in Britain. The county was therefore able to exploit all its natural advantages.

Another feature of Cheshire is what can only be described as the longevity and persistence of its county families. The county has been called the 'seed plot of gentility'. There were a few great landed

---

[1] Cheshire County Council, *Development Plan: Part 2* (1952), p. 18. The map opposite brings the map given in the Development Plan up to date. The concentration of population on the northern county boundary has been increased.

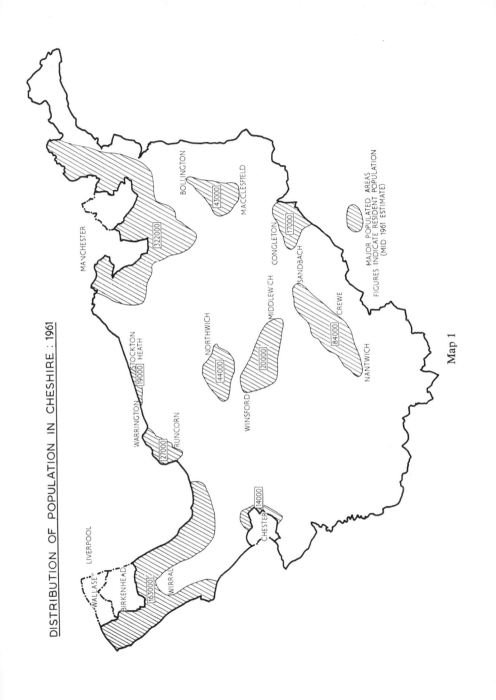

DISTRIBUTION OF POPULATION IN CHESHIRE : 1961

Map 1

MAJOR POPULATED AREAS
FIGURES INDICATE RESIDENT POPULATION
(MID 1961 ESTIMATE)

LIVERPOOL

WALLASEY

BIRKENHEAD

163000

WIRRAL

RUNCORN

27000

WARRINGTON

STOCKTON
HEATH

19000

MANCHESTER

322000

BOLLINGTON

43000

MACCLESFIELD

CONGLETON

17000

SANDBACH

MIDDLEWICH

NORTHWICH

44000

WINSFORD

20000

CREWE

84000

NANTWICH

CHESTER

14000

magnates resident in the county, like the Duke of Westminster at Eaton Hall, the Earl of Stamford at Dunham Massey, and Lord Stanley at Alderley Park,[1] but also a great number of lesser gentry whose fine Georgian houses are particularly noticeable in the eastern half and the north-central area west of Knutsford. Most of the great country houses have been abandoned during the twentieth century, and many of the well-known family names, like Legh of Adlington, Legh of High Legh, or Leicester-Warren of Tabley, have only been preserved in the present generation through changes of name authorized by Royal Licence. Yet the surviving families and the surviving houses have managed to convey the impression that the traditional county society which provided the members of the 'country party' is still important in local politics. The fascination of Cheshire lies in the meeting and merging of the landed interest with the business interest of the new industries. It lies in the separation between large agricultural areas and heavy concentrations of industry. It lies in the fact that in spite of its rapid industrial development the county still contains many 'desirable' places in which to live.

Problems of methods and materials

This book sets out to explore the county of Cheshire with a view to understanding the shift in political influence which has taken place since 1888. It is not intended to write the history of the County Council as such but to use the County Council as a focus for drawing attention to social and political change. The effects of a single county administration are the only factors which link together all the communities, families, and industries to be found within its historic boundaries. The establishment of the County Council in 1889 and its work during the first seventy years of its existence provide the material for the study of politics at the local level which may yield many more questions than it is possible to answer. The chief difficulties arise from the great mass of paper work which the development of local government has created.

Various studies of local authorities have tended to ignore the value of modern administrative records for the political historian by concentrating on the outlines of local government law or recounting only the details of school buildings, road mileage, hospitals, and health services. This study of Cheshire is not meant primarily to discover how efficient the County Council has been in administering

[1] See Map 2, facing p. 119.

the services which the law has laid upon it. The aim is rather more ambitious. It is intended to make some contribution towards a better understanding of the doctrine governing 'local democracy'. So many of the disputes about local government have not looked at the history of a particular authority and asked the obvious questions about its composition and the relations between councillors and officials. Who goes into local politics and why? The period which separates the Local Government Act of 1888 from that of 1958 is clearly one during which ideas about the nature of 'local democracy' have been radically changed by social circumstances. Everyone knows that the orthodox doctrine of elected representatives deciding policy and paid officials executing orders no longer fits the facts of local government. A new interpretation is needed to take account of recent social changes.

In a study of this kind the main stumbling block is the difficulty of measuring social change. The historian is frequently compelled to use the vocabulary of the generations he is studying or to invent his own jargon. Words change their meaning and social categories like 'gentleman', 'company director', or 'clerk' are the most difficult to standardize. Each National Census has successively used a different index of social classes. Very few statistical analyses of social change throw light on political history, and the categories of orthodox Marxist theory are hardly subtle enough to explain the minor snobberies of English provincial life which play such a large part in local politics.

The subject also by its very nature involves a change in the type of material which is available. Before the 1920's there was a great deal of published work on local affairs, either in the form of pamphlets and family memoirs or in the form of handbills and scurrilous news-paper reports. During the 1930's the provincial press developed its present 'tabloid' character and replaced verbatim accounts of politi-cal meetings with descriptions of voluntary societies and mass enter-tainments, because it was the latter which interested the bulk of its readers. Before 1920 there was a considerable amount of correspon-dence which had survived in the muniments of country houses to illuminate the dark patches of political intrigue. The break-up of the large *ménage* of the landed aristocracy and the increased use of the telephone has removed from the historian the valuable source of private letters. In studying the period from 1888 to 1958 one is aware that the sources available are continually changing.

The two halves of this book have therefore been written from different sources; the first half, dealing with social leaders, is based on the abundant published material which they themselves produced. The second half, dealing with public persons, could not have been produced without the co-operation of their leading examples, the chief officers of the County Council. This division into two is inherent in the nature of the subject.

PART II

SOCIAL LEADERS

INTRODUCTION

THE main impetus for local government reform during the nineteenth century came from the needs of the growing urban areas. The ideals which inspired political action developed from the hope that each town would benefit by the public service of the ablest men in the community. Each ambitious borough might receive amenities for the improvement of urban life such as parks, swimming-baths, wash-houses, and libraries, through the generosity of worthy benefactors who saw fit to invest the profits of industry in their fellow citizens, but there could be no effective safeguard for maintaining the standards of public health without the corporate action of the whole municipality. Who should represent the town and take charge of municipal policy? It was natural that the more prosperous business people should be elected to the town council which acted as trustees for the welfare of the whole body of the inhabitants. After the middle of the nineteenth century all thinking about the means of securing sufficiently able candidates for public service as elected members of a local authority was dominated by the conception of the generous benefactor, who not only provides gifts from his own private pocket but also devotes a considerable amount of his time and energy to 'public life'.

This urban ideal ran parallel with the even older tradition of the countryside—*noblesse oblige*—the work of the independent country gentleman. The county magistrate was not in fact obliged to take up his administrative duties; many did not trouble even to take the oath which qualified them for sitting on the bench. But each county was administered by the few who behaved conscientiously, either through a regular attendance at petty sessions in the neighbourhood of their homes, or through the political and family connexions which imposed a close association with Quarter Sessions and its committees.

A combination of urban ideals and rural conventions produced the image of the social leader which appears in the following pages. The basic issue of local politics described in Part II was the need to make more widespread an urban standard of living. As far as Cheshire was concerned the 'great towns' of Liverpool and Manchester and their immediate neighbours set the possible level of attainment. Those who came to settle in the country, particularly after the building of suburban railway lines between 1860 and 1875, expected new local authorities to provide some of the benefits of the town in more salubrious surroundings. The social leader was essentially a local politician who was prepared to meet these demands either by extending the range of his private generosity or by acting with his fellows to promote corporate action. He was an *entrepreneur* who achieved his ends either through personal risks or through the limited liability arrangements of joining his fellow councillors. The distinction between private enterprise and public works was frequently blurred whenever the possibilities were discussed for providing better living conditions.

The following two chapters examine the influence of the 'great towns' upon government in the countryside and describe the behaviour of social leaders in representative institutions, particularly the new county council created by the Local Government Act of 1888. One of the peculiarities of social conditions in the late nineteenth century was the question of allegiance to local authorities. For instance, did the Manchester businessmen who settled in Cheshire think of themselves as 'Cheshire people'? No examination of social leadership should overlook the fact that the possession of money alone did not bring its owner into 'county society'. The latter may have been expanded by the addition of businessmen who began to acquire the same habits of leisure as the gentry, but not all the social leaders of the towns made the necessary personal adjustment. The urban *élite* was usually a homogeneous group of merchants and manufacturers. But the *élite* of the countryside during the late nineteenth century became a series of ill-defined groups which shaded off one into the other. The criteria of acceptability to 'county society' had originally been laid down by the landed gentry who were themselves altering their habits. The transformation of 'county society' under the influence of the 'great towns' involved something of a merger between the landed and business classes. The question of allegiance to Cheshire, like the traditional distinction between town and country, was placed on a different social footing.

2

SETTLEMENT AND SOCIAL ORGANIZATION

THE influence of the 'great towns' was most apparent in determining the main lines of communication. Liverpool and Manchester promoted the first railways to cross the Cheshire countryside. Technological developments not only raised the standard of living in urban areas, but also created a completely new system of transport, which profoundly altered the way of life in rural parts. The predominance of social leaders in the work of local government arose from a particular kind of settlement and social organization which was peculiar to the age of the railways. This chapter sets out to examine the impact which the new opportunities of transport had upon the political life of the county of Cheshire. The 'age of steam' transferred power from the old-fashioned country gentleman to the new social leader. If the gentry wished to retain their political influence they were required by the new social situation to adapt their code of behaviour. In fact, those landed gentlemen who came to terms with the new industrial society gradually transformed the nature of county society, and it was this transformation which provided the basis for county government by county council.

The most important period of social change was between the 1840's and the 1880's, the period between those two important events in the political history of the landed interest, the Repeal of the Corn Laws in 1846 and the Irish Home Rule Crisis in 1886. By the late 1840's and early 1850's the influence of the main railway lines was being felt in the countryside, and between 1865 and 1870 the most important suburban lines around Liverpool and Manchester were laid down. The combination of horse-tram and ferry-boat was a form of transport peculiar to the Wirral. But the railways provided the opportunity for large numbers of people, particularly the wealthier section of the community, to live some distance from their place of work. When the Cheshire County Council held its first meeting in 1889, all the councillors were aware of the fact that they had seen during the previous twenty or thirty years great changes in their mode of living. The settlement and social organization of the county before 1889 determined the task facing the new County Council.

Cheshire possesses an extremely good symbol of the 'age of steam' in local government. The railway town of Crewe, which arose where the main lines from Liverpool, Manchester, Birkenhead, and Birmingham all met in the fields of the parish of Church Coppenhall, became the meeting-place for the discussion of county affairs (see map at end). The Crewe Arms Hotel, which could be entered from the station platform, provided a committee room of both Quarter Sessions and the County Council for over a century. The Finance Committee of Quarter Sessions was meeting there in the early 1850's, and the committees of the County Council did not abandon this practice until 1957. From 1842 onwards Crewe Railway Station was the most accessible place in the county.

Government by Quarter Sessions

The administrative machine of the county was expanded to meet the requirements of the railways and the newcomers which they brought. More magistrates were placed on the bench and the size and arrangement of petty sessional divisions were adjusted to keep pace with the developments in areas of increasing population. It is not true that Quarter Sessions were totally unresponsive to the changing industrial conditions. The justices of the peace included some extremely adaptable people. Their efforts were so successful that the creation of an elected county council did not appear such a revolutionary step to take. Those magistrates who responded quickly and readily to the new situation became the leaders of the new county society and carried over from Quarter Sessions to the new County Council something of the code of behaviour established by the landed gentry. The code of behaviour 'suitable for a gentleman' can disguise a great variety of social changes.

The office of lord-lieutenant was supreme in the county because he was responsible for nominating magistrates. The Prime Minister appointed the lord-lieutenant from among the peers in the county who supported his own party, but the nomination of magistrates was usually a matter of established convention among recognized county families rather than a matter of straight political patronage. Nominations to the bench only became controversial after the magistrates had been deprived of their administrative powers. The lord-lieutenant frequently nominated his own political opponents to the bench. It was advisable to maintain good relations between political parties because the next vacancy in the lieutenancy might be given to an opponent of the previous holder. Each lord-lieutenant tended to retain the office until his death. Two lieutenants presided over the affairs of Cheshire during the crucial period of social change, the first Lord Egerton of Tatton from 1868 until his death in 1883, and the first Duke of Westminster from 1883 until his death in 1898. Egerton was a Tory, and Westminster a Whig grandee, who broke with Gladstone in 1886 and turned Unionist. Cheshire Quarter Sessions met alternately at Chester and at Knutsford, usually in the presence of the lord-lieutenant and of the clerk of the peace whom he appointed.[1] These two gatherings of men from the west and east sides of the county represented all those who possessed sufficient social standing to be considered worthy of a place on the bench. To be a justice of the peace was an honour and not necessarily a duty. According to the parliamentary returns of 1853, there were 556 justices in the commission of the peace for Cheshire, but only 176 had taken the oath which qualified them to act.[2] Even fewer would take an active part in political life. The county was governed by the conscientious magistrates who regularly attended one of the fourteen petty sessions into which it was then divided, and by those 'political' families which associated themselves with the work of Quarter Sessions.

Industrial expansion and population growth made their mark upon this system in two obvious ways: first, in the need to appoint more magistrates to keep pace with the work of executing justice in rapidly developing areas; and second, in the adaptation of administrative boundaries for greater efficiency. The figures available suggest that the number of active magistrates was doubled between 1846 and 1886 from 75 to 150.[3] The total number of those qualified to act continued to increase. There were 296 in 1887 and 355 in 1897. Quarter Sessions altered the boundaries of the petty sessional divisions to meet the new situation while the boundaries of parliamentary constituencies continued to follow the ancient hundred boundaries of the shire. Between 1870 and 1878 three entirely new petty sessional divisions were created in areas where the population had greatly increased: the Altrincham division for new Manchester suburbs; the Leftwich division for the salt-producing area around Northwich; and the Chester Castle division for the urbanized villages around Chester.[4] By 1891 the divisions of Hyde, Stockport, and Altrincham

---

[1] After the Act of 1888 the appointment was made by the Standing Joint Committee.   [2] H.C. 558 (1852–3), lxxxviii, p. 329.
[3] H.C. 356 (1888), lxxxii, pp. 12–16.
[4] H.C. 447 (1870), lvii; H.C. 398 (1878), lxiv.

had over thirty magistrates each, and the Wirral forty-three.[1] The magistrates from industrial areas could make their influence felt on Quarter Sessions. It was considered a victory for urban interests in the 1860's when the Cheshire boroughs, under the leadership of Sir Edward Watkin, secured representation on the board of trustees which administered the navigation of the River Weaver on behalf of the county.[2] Sir Edward, who became the chairman of three railway companies and a director of ten others, had been placed in the commission of the peace on his election as M.P. for Stockport in 1864. Each of the towns clamoured for the attention of the magistrates. Crewe, which agitated for its own commission of the peace, felt that many county magistrates had a prejudice against it, because it presented a challenge to the nearby ancient market town of Nantwich,[3] but elsewhere the tradition of Quarter Sessions was to appoint new magistrates in the most populous and industrial areas. Even in 1848 more than a sixth of the total number of qualified justices were required to sit in the Hyde petty sessions, the most industrialized division of the whole county.[4]

There was no part of the countryside which remained outside the influence of the great towns. Liverpool and Manchester were too close for the county to be unaffected. The attitude of J. H. Leche of Carden Park, four miles north of Malpas, who remained in the commission of the peace from 1849 until his death in 1903, was an exception. He declared in the 1860's that he was a Protectionist and that he was not going to change because a lot of men were making money.[5] But few of his contemporaries in a lifetime of tremendous change preserved such purity of conscience or found consolation in such consistency. To have been born a Protectionist and to have lived a Protectionist were not sufficient reasons to die a Protectionist. As Leche admitted, a lot of men were making money. The great problem in examining the transformation of the 'country party' in local politics is to understand the merging of the landed and business interests. On the one hand, city merchants and company directors became county justices and adopted the habits of country gentlemen; on the other hand, landowners and farmers invested in town property and commercial enterprise. Two themes of social history run side by side.

[1] County Council Year Book (1891).
[2] Select Committee on Taxation, H.C. 353 (1870), viii, Q. 5332.
[3] Chaloner, Crewe, pp. 135–8, 172.
[4] Orders of Quarter Sessions (printed by Chester Courant, 1848).
[5] B. H. Brown, The Tariff Reform Movement: 1881–95 (1943), p. 143.

One is the theme of the great towns 'making money'; the other is the theme of the countryside which provides the social ideals of manners and modes of living.

By the 1880's the composition of Quarter Sessions reflected the fact that a new county society had been created. But the appearance of government by the landed gentry was retained. The family names which appeared among the signatures on Quarter Sessions orders in the 1840's were still there in the 1880's. The aristocratic landowners still played a leading role in county affairs. How was it that Quarter Sessions could be so flexible to the needs of industrial populations and yet the same families should appear to hold the reins of power? One of the most important distinctions to bear in mind when studying social change in the countryside is that made by contemporaries between the great magnates or county patrons and the resident gentry or squires.[1] Men of the latter class, like J. H. Leche, were not in a strong position to resist the inroads which the influence of the towns made on their way of life. Whereas the former class, with their town houses in London and, in some cases, large areas of urban property, had already come to terms with the new methods of transport and new means of leisure. Whenever the status of an *élite* class is threatened it is always the poorer members who shriek the loudest against the dilution of power and the debasement of standards. The minor public schools denounce Eton's liberality; non-commissioned regulars regret war-time commissions to conscripts. In the late nineteenth century the gentry who lived on the profits of their estates and on those alone were the most likely to suffer by the changes which the railways brought about. By the 1880's the patrons who governed county politics were beginning to think in the same terms as the new industrialists and professional people.

More than a quarter of the total area of the county belonged to the great political patrons, and not to the gentry: 26·9 per cent. in 1872-3 was in the hands of seventeen landowners, only four of whom were without a town house in London (see Table 1). The resident gentry with over 1,000 acres each numbered forty-two, but they possessed only 16·9 per cent. of the total land available. Only five of these had a town house in London. The thirteen people who had a large estate in the county as well as a London house and a London club constituted the ruling

---

[1] Cf. the distinction made by H. R. Trevor-Roper, *The Gentry* (Economic History Review Supplement, 1952), between 'official gentry' and 'mere gentry', the *court* gentry and the *country* gentry.

group in Cheshire's political life; all of them were peers. The Duke of Westminster came first in the county's order of precedence. Gladstone's decision in 1874 to promote the Marquess of Westminster

TABLE 1

Cheshire Landowners: 1872–3[1]

Landowners	1 Total	2 Total number with a London house	3 Total number with a London club	4 Total acreage in Cheshire belonging to this group	5 Percentage of total area of county in column 4
1. Resident in the county with estates in all counties totalling					
(a) over 6,000 acres .	17	13	14	163,649	26·9
(b) over 3,000 acres .	16	4	7	61,693	10·1
(c) over 1,000 acres .	26	1	9	41,571	6·8
Total residents . .	59	18	30	266,913	43·8
2. Non-resident in the county but with over 1,000 acres there					
(a) maintaining a house in Cheshire for seasonal visits; .	10	5	5	41,114	6·8
(b) those without a house. . . .	19	6	8	45,445	7·4
Total non-residents .	29	11	13	86,559	14·2
Grand Total . .	88	29	43	353,472	58·0

gave the Grosvenor family the distinction of receiving the last territorial dukedom to be created outside the Royal Family. Next came the Marquesses of Cholmondeley—with their cousins the Lords Delamere—the Earls of Stamford, the Lords Crewe, Combermere, Legh of Lyme, Stanley of Alderley, Tollemache, and Egerton of Tatton. Most of these families married into families of a like kind in other counties, but a few of them were closely connected with the

[1] Parliamentary Papers [C. 1097–I] (1873), lxxii; the acreage figures have been taken from the corrections made on the parliamentary returns in John Bateman, *The Great Landowners of England* (London, 1879).

families of resident gentry. Those family circles which bridged the gap between the county magnates and the resident gentry, such as the relations of Lord Egerton of Tatton and his distant cousins, the Grey-Egertons of Oulton Park, were the core of the 'country party' and included many of the leading members of Parliament and many magistrates and county councillors (see Diagram I). The second Lord Egerton of Tatton caused some embarrassment to himself and others in 1894 by taking the widow of the Duke of Buckingham as his second wife. This action, which was stepping outside his normal sphere, enabled him to claim a promotion in the ranks of the peerage from a barony to an earldom which he received in 1897. The political history of Cheshire before 1885 could be written around the activities of the local peerage and the leading landed families, Delves-Broughton, Bromley-Davenport, France-Hayhurst, Grey-Egerton, Egerton-Warburton, Cornwall-Legh, and Legh of Lyme. The only important nomination borough in the county was the city of Chester itself, which remained in the patronage of the Grosvenor family of Eaton Hall from 1690 until 1885 when its parliamentary representation was reduced from two members to one.[1] The Grosvenors were the principal defenders of the 'Whig' interest. The industrial towns were to some extent in the hands of the chief manufacturers. Members of the Brocklehurst family who were silk manufacturers had an interest in representing Macclesfield in Parliament, just as the principal shipbuilders, John Laird and David MacIver, represented Birkenhead. But before 1885 the county divisions, which were based upon the ancient hundred boundaries, maintained the tradition of sturdy 'independence' supported by the landed gentry. The parliamentary representation of the county was increased from two to four in 1832, from four to six in 1868, and from six to eight in 1885, and throughout this period the members were almost exclusively drawn from the leading 'independent' or 'Tory' families of Egerton, Legh, and Tollemache. In 1868 the four sitting members for the northern and southern divisions were returned for the new western and mid-Cheshire divisions. The two new members for the eastern division belonged to the same family group, W. J. Legh and E. C. Egerton. These arrangements were only altered by the political conditions introduced with the extension of the franchise and by the influence of developing industrial areas. Of the new single-member county constituencies

[1] There are a large number of poll books and other Chester election material in the Eccleston Estate Office of the Duke of Westminster.

C.C. = County Councillor

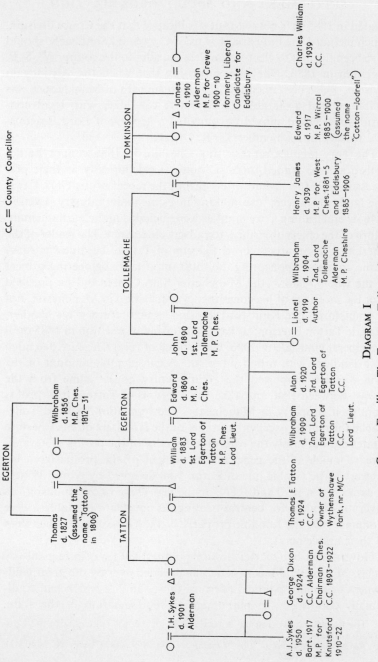

DIAGRAM I

County Families: The Egerton–Tollemache Connexion

created in 1885, it is not without significance that the Crewe division, which included the industrial towns of Crewe and Sandbach, should have been the first to elect a complete outsider to the county, W. S. B. McLaren in 1886. Nor is it surprising that when the Altrincham division, which contained the wealthiest suburbs of Manchester, was unable to find a suitable Conservative candidate with local connexions in 1892, it should have invited a nephew of Lord Beaconsfield to become its member, C. R. Disraeli.

The Tory families representing Cheshire in 1886 cannot be described as 'the landed interest' quite as categorically as their predecessors in 1846 who had voted against the repeal of the Corn Laws. The landowners were also making investments in industry. Even in 1846 several leading Tory families were included in the parliamentary return of the chief subscribers to railway companies. The leader of the Cheshire Conservatives, Lord Egerton of Tatton, became chairman of the company sponsoring the most important engineering project of the whole region—the Manchester Ship Canal; and he presided over the meetings of his constituency association in Manchester, not in Knutsford. The Knutsford division, which returned his brother, Alan de Tatton Egerton, to Parliament from its creation in 1885 until the Liberal landslide in 1906, was a piece of rural Cheshire defended by a landlord with urban interests.[1] A considerable amount of the money which supported the great country houses came from the towns. Between 1846 and 1886 the Egertons of Tatton drew profits from their property in Manchester. The reputation of Lord Tollemache for renting excellent cottages to the labourers on his Cheshire estates did not imply the careful husbandry of the profits of agriculture so much as the generous investment of the profits from his brewery.[2] The Gothic pile of Eaton Hall designed by Alfred Waterhouse between 1870 and 1884 for the first Duke of Westminster, its cavernous boilers for central heating, its courtyard of stables, were monuments to the London property of the Grosvenors rather than to their arable acres.

Government by Quarter Sessions in the 1880's was in fact rule by a class of successful business people presided over by the great landowners or county political patrons, those families which had traditionally controlled the parliamentary representation of the shire.

---

[1] The Knutsford division has a very full set of records belonging to the Conservative Association.

[2] *Royal Commission on the Housing of the Working Classes* (C. 4402–I), pp. 561–2, 565–7 (1884–5), xxxi.

The biographical dictionary, *Walford's County Families* for 1879, provides an excellent guide to the new county society and shows the extent to which businessmen from the towns had penetrated the preserves of the landed gentry. It listed over 250 families for Cheshire, of whom 235 were resident. Barely a hundred of these are clearly identifiable as gentlemen with a considerable landed estate, and at least 73 are manufacturers or merchants. The magistrates on the bench were probably recruited in roughly the same proportion. Of the two hundred-odd families which made up the *élite* of the county, 83 men belonged to a London club (30 resident landowners with over 1,000 acres and 53 others), and 30 maintained a London house (18 resident landowners with over 1,000 acres and 12 others).[1] Therefore 53 gentlemen had only the club as a *pied-à-terre* in London. Those with metropolitan connexions were more important in local politics than the gentry who stayed on their estates. It is significant that the four landowners with more than 6,000 acres in 1872–3 who did not maintain a London house, Sir Richard Brooke, Sir Henry Delves-Broughton, Col. France-Hayhurst, and Col. Egerton-Warburton, were the least active in party political affairs. County members of Parliament of necessity acquired houses in the capital. Those manufacturers who followed the pattern laid down by the great political patrons became more and more important.

The pattern of residential settlement

The businessmen who became members of the new county society were responsible for promoting the railways which governed the course of rural development. Rivalries between the 'great towns' determined the main lines of communication. The chief factor which made Crewe junction the most accessible place in Cheshire was the success of Liverpool over Manchester. The construction of the Grand Junction line, opened in 1837, from Birmingham through Crewe and Warrington to join the Manchester and Liverpool railway, was an enterprise which favoured the industrial interests of Liverpool. Once established the 'Liverpool party' was able to frustrate the construction of an independent line from Manchester to Birmingham, and to ensure that the 'Manchester party' could only establish communication with the south by joining the main line at Crewe. The London and North Western Railway Company was formed in 1846

[1] See Table 1, p. 19.

to amalgamate the lines from Liverpool, Manchester, Birkenhead, and Birmingham which all met at Crewe.[1] The new town which sprang up there was a reminder that forces outside the county were changing its economic structure.

The tidal water of Merseyside and the existing trade of Liverpool provided suitable conditions for the development of industry in western Cheshire. The Wirral peninsula before 1840 was largely a barren sandy landscape which gave excellent hunting country for the merchants of Liverpool who followed the hounds, but it was of no great commercial value.[2] The rise of Birkenhead, like the rise of Crewe, depended to some extent upon the success of Liverpool.[3] The shipbuilders of Birkenhead provided the ships for its ocean-going trade. The high costs of railway transportation and the advantages of immediate shipment brought other industries to the coasts of the Wirral. In 1889 William Lever brought his soap factory from Warrington to Port Sunlight;[4] in 1896 John Summers and Company brought their steel works from Stalybridge to Hawarden Bridge near Shotton.[5] The Manchester Ship Canal, opened in 1894, which was in a sense Manchester's reply to Liverpool's previous success with the railways, brought great industrial possibilities to the northern boundary of Cheshire. The concentration of factories by the side of the canal secured by the company which purchased Trafford Park near Manchester in 1896[6] had its equivalent on a smaller scale for Cheshire in the expanding suburbs of Altrincham and Warrington.

The pattern of railways laid down by the L.N.W.R. was not radically altered before 1860. But between 1860 and 1875 a complicated network of suburban lines was constructed, principally under the auspices of the Cheshire Lines Committee, an inter-group organization formed in 1865 which ran the lines from Manchester to Warrington and Manchester to Chester via Northwich.[7] The Manchester South Junction and Altrincham Railway, opened in 1849, allowed the fashion for moving out of Manchester to grow apace. But even before the railway was constructed, several Manchester

---

[1] Chaloner, *Crewe*, pp. 14–26; see map at end.
The principal books on the Wirral are E. Rideout, *The Growth of Wirral* (1927); J. E. Allison, *The Mersey Estuary* (1949); *Merseyside* (British Association, 1953).
[3] C. R. Fay, *Round About Industrial Britain: 1830–1860* (1952), pp. 86–100.
[4] Charles Wilson, *History of Unilever*, i. 37.
[5] W. H. Scott and others, *Technical Change and Industrial Relations* (1956), p. 38.
[6] T. H. G. Stevens, *Some Notes on the Development of Trafford Park* (1947), p. 6.
[7] R. Prys Griffiths, *The Cheshire Lines Railway* (1947).

businessmen had bought land from Lord Stamford in Altrincham and Bowdon, built houses, and travelled daily to work by the swift packet boats on the Bridgewater Canal. Hyppolite Taine in his *Notes sur l'Angleterre* described Bowdon in the 1860's as 'a sort of public villa, with the splendid park which Lord Stamford throws open for the enjoyment of the multitude'.[1] By the 1860's the houses of Manchester merchants were also scattered over the hillside of Alderley Edge which is thirteen miles on the railway line from Manchester London Road.[2] The exodus from Liverpool was a slower process because of the inconvenience of taking the ferry across the Mersey; it was accelerated only by the opening of the Mersey railway tunnel in 1886 linking Liverpool and Birkenhead. The first tramway had been opened in 1860 to carry the Liverpool businessmen from Birkenhead Park to Woodside Ferry. After 1886 the suburban railway lines were extended: new lines from Hoylake to Parkgate and from Birkenhead to Neston were opened in 1896.[3] The authorities recognized the tremendous importance of railways which allowed businessmen to live in the country. In 1881 Lord Egerton explained to the Select Committee on the Highway Acts that it was the policy of Quarter Sessions to consider any road leading to a railway station as a main road which should be repaired at the expense of the county. No area had complained of neglect because 'there is hardly any part of the county which is not crossed by some railway'.[4]

The local government of the county was greatly affected by the arrival of a new class of people, those who had invested in the pleasures of country living without taking on the responsibilities of the traditional land-owning classes. There was a considerable distinction between those who acquired small estates in the traditional way by which wealth purchased gentility, and those who acquired a few acres of park land on which they erected a house in the hunting-box style. All over the county from the 1880's onwards new houses were erected in a neo-Tudor style which was considered a good imitation of the native half-timbering and which was used, for instance, by the Duke of Westminster in improving the shopping streets of Chester and by W. H. Lever in housing his workers at Port Sunlight. The merchants either designed a completely new house or

[1] H. Taine, *Notes sur l'Angleterre* (2nd ed., 1872), p. 294.
[2] In 1961 called 'Manchester Piccadilly Station'.
[3] D. Sylvester and G. Nulty, *Historical Atlas of Cheshire* (1958), gives maps of railway development.
[4] *Report of Select Committee on Highway Acts*, H.C. 371 (1881), x, Q. 3493.

reconstructed whatever they found in a more fashionable manner. C. J. Galloway, a Manchester engineer, built a house called Thorney-holme at Knutsford in 1885;[1] Ralph Brocklebank, a retired Liverpool shipowner, rebuilt Haughton Hall in 1891–2.[2] Burton Manor, which was one of the last country houses to be reconstructed in the grand manner, was completed in 1904 for the third son of Mr. Gladstone.[3]

The flight from the towns meant the improved sanitation of the countryside. Those who established new country residences after 1860 were often responsible for setting up the first local boards under the provisions of the Public Health Act of 1858. The different dates at which this Act was adopted in rural areas provide some index of the rate of suburban development. The local boards at Altrincham and Bowdon were naturally established before 1858, but many minor boards, like those of Lymm and Tarporley, owe their existence to a few individuals who wished to improve the amenities of the country place in which they had chosen to live. The borough of Bebington originates from a local board established in 1859 by Joseph Mayer, a Liverpool jeweller and great philanthropist.[4] In 1866 the coming of the railway gave the village of Neston the ambition to govern itself; a local board was established in 1867. The chairman of its health committee in 1878 announced that they had recently spent about £10,000 on improvements: 'We wish it to become a place of resid-ence.'[5] Some of the merchants improved at their own expense the villages in which they settled. Duncan Graham, a merchant in the South American trade at Liverpool, about 1870 paid for water to be piped to Willaston.[6] The pattern of minor local government authori-ties was considerably determined by the presence or absence of the new class of people who had moved from the towns or by the presence or absence of private philanthropy.

After 1860 the countryside had in one sense to be preserved arti-ficially from the licence and wealth which the profits of industry had assured. When Alfred Rimmer visited Rostherne Mere in 1887 he was surprised to see that it was the same as it had been on his pre-vious visit in 1852.[7] He had expected to find the lake surrounded by the villa residences of Manchester 'merchant princes'. The owner of

[1] *Manchester Faces and Places*, v. 57–59.
[2] E. Driver, *Cheshire, its Cheese Makers, etc.* (1909), p. 296.
[3] *Kelly's Directory of Cheshire* (1939), p. 67.
[4] W. Lowndes, *The Story of Bebington* (1953).
[5] *Royal Commission on Noxious Vapours* (C. 2159) H.C. (1878), xliv, *Q.* 11387.
[6] *Chester Chronicle*, 12 Jan. 1901, p. 6.
[7] A. Rimmer, *Rambles Round Manchester* (1890), p. 191.

Rostherne, Lord Egerton of Tatton, was obviously unwilling to sell land for this kind of development which was so close to his family seat, Tatton Hall. Both the first and second Lord Egerton contributed to remodelling the village of Rostherne to make it a 'model village'. The luscious grasslands of Tatton Park, like those of Eaton and Crewe Hall, give the impression that the leading families could afford to remain aloof from the determination of those who wished to establish themselves as country gentlemen, with a stake however small in the lands of the county.

Improvements in transport also made the lanes of the countryside accessible to the casual visitor. After 1860 Cheshire was expected more and more to function as a 'lung' for the great towns, to provide light and air for their workers on occasional week-end trips. Before the railways were built the workpeople from the mill towns like Hyde and Stockport spent their free time walking the lanes of the district. The railways and the horse-drawn charabanc extended the range of these escapades. By the 1890's, for example, a young artisan in Warrington could take his family by rail to picnic in the hills above Helsby and Frodsham; he could manage a cheap trip to New Brighton beach on his Saturday half-day. The railways also increased the importance of Chester as a shopping and tourist centre. The Chief Constable reported in 1897 that at least a quarter of a million visitors and sightseers came to Chester during the summer months, including many Americans.[1] The social gatherings in Chester during the Race Week in June were of long-established importance in the county, but it was the railways and the horse-drawn buses which made possible vast congregations of people reaching 100,000. F. L. Olmstead, one of the first American tourists in Chester, was extremely surprised by the 'continual and universal beer drinking' which he found on a visit made about 1850.[2] The authorities were certainly troubled by the effects of travelling for amusement upon the operation of the licensing laws. The special committee of Cheshire Quarter Sessions which investigated the matter in 1891 was disturbed by the difficulty of defining the term 'bona fide traveller', who could legitimately ask for refreshment at an inn. Several magistrates were anxious to limit the definition in order to exclude the large parties from Manchester who were in the habit of coming out to Lymm and Alderley Edge on

[1] Royal Commission on Liquor Licensing Laws, Evidence III (C. 8694), p. 46 (1898), xxxvi.
[2] F. L. Olmstead, Walks and Talks of an American Farmer in England (1852), p. 148; cf. George Borrow, Wild Wales (1868), pp. 5–6, 9.

a Sunday, and the omnibuses which carried the workers of Crewe into adjoining towns.[1] The improvement in transport by rail and by road which permitted the middle classes to live away from their places of work at the same time emancipated the working classes in their leisure hours.

The railways therefore produced two new local phenomena which were in the twentieth century to call for legislation and regulation— the use of land for residential building and the use of land for recreation. The countryside was no longer the preserve of the 'landed interest', the country gentleman, and the tenant farmer, nor was the value of land to be conceived solely in agricultural terms. The industrial revolution of agriculture was at hand. Although by the 1870's Cheshire farmers had quickly abandoned the cultivation of early potatoes because of competition from Cornwall and France, they turned to specialization in various kinds of vegetables and fruit for marketing in Liverpool and Manchester. They claimed that the high cost of railway freight charges made it difficult to compete with imported foodstuffs. Thomas Rigby, secretary of the Cheshire Chamber of Agriculture, showed an American cheese to a meeting of the Over Agricultural Society in 1862 and warned them that American produce would soon be able to drive Cheshire cheese from the market.[2] The farmhouse production of cheese was in many cases altered to suit new market conditions by shortening the length of time required for ripening from over a year to a few months.[3] But the introduction of factory methods was not popular. By 1881 there were only three cheese factories in Cheshire, one of which was sponsored by the Duke of Westminster for his own tenantry.[4] But the Chamber of Agriculture did its best to promote agricultural education, and in 1886 a private company began the Dairy School at Worleston. All the agricultural interest could do was to prepare itself to meet the challenge of rivals in the use of land. Few farmers protested. The most vociferous complaints were made in the Weaver valley against the vapours of the chemical works at Runcorn and the salt-boiling pans at Northwich and Middlewich. But they were directed rather against the harm caused to health and desirability of residence rather than against the effects of industry as such. In evidence before the Royal Commission on Noxious Vapours in

[1] *The Quarter Sessions of Cheshire and the Law of Licensing* (1891), p. 47.
[2] T. Rigby, *Cheshire Farming: its Past and Future* (1862), p. 32.
[3] V. Cheke, *The History of Cheese-making in Britain* (1959), p. 238.
[4] *Royal Commission on Agriculture* (C. 3096), pp. 917–23, H.C. (1881), xvii.

1878, Sir Richard Brooke gave lurid details of the damage caused to the trees and pastures of his estate at Norton Priory by fumes from Runcorn, but the presence of industry had greatly increased the value of his rent roll. Falk, the proprietor of the Meadow Bank Salt Works, claimed that farmers should adjust their crops to utilize the smoke; he had himself grown good crops of wheat and turnips in the fields beside his works.[1] The production of salt and the maintenance of agriculture were completely compatible.

Local politics were dominated by a discussion of the wonderful possibilities for new development which came from the railways and the growth of towns. Henry George came from America to preach the gospel of land nationalization in 1883. Joseph Chamberlain and the more radical members of the Liberal party were advocating the provision of smallholdings by local authorities.[2] Some dreamed grandiose plans for the residential settlement of the working classes. Sydney Evershed, M.P. for Burton, for instance, was advocating that the labouring classes should be taken from the towns and rehoused in pairs of cottages on plots of land in the country, close to main line railway stations, in the manner already adopted by wealthier people.[3] In all these speculations lay the prospect of reforming the local government system. If village life was to continue, parish councils were necessary. If the agricultural labourer was to be re-educated in new industrial techniques, he should be given the vote and allowed to elect representatives from his own class. The Local Government Act of 1888 came after the railways and the new pattern of settlement had transformed the opportunities open to an efficient system of local authorities.

The merging of the landed and business interests

The effects of developments in industry and transport on the personnel of local politics can best be seen by comparing the composition of Quarter Sessions at the time of the repeal of the Corn Laws in 1846 with the composition in the period which immediately preceded the reform of local government by the Acts of 1888 and 1894. It would be difficult to compare the groups of regular attenders at Quarter Sessions for each of these dates; but it is comparatively easy to examine the lists of those who were qualified to attend, namely all magistrates sitting in each of the petty sessional divisions.

[1] *Royal Commission on Noxious Vapours* (C. 2159), H.C. (1878), xlix.
[2] J. L. Garvin, *Life of Joseph Chamberlain*, i. 388–9, 549.
[3] *The New Review* (1889), i. 596–600.

These names alone give some indication of the changes which took place during the forty years before county councils were created.

The property qualification required of justices of the peace by an Act of 1744 did not limit the choice of candidates for the bench to those who derived a considerable income from a large landed estate. The increased value of land for industrial development made a few acres in a convenient place sufficient qualification. As an increasing number of names were added to the commission of the peace between 1846 and 1886, a much greater proportion of the total consisted of industrialists, mill-owners, bankers, and businessmen. Even in 1846 many magistrates in the petty sessional divisions near Stockport, Hyde, and Warrington were occupied in the business of those towns although they may have lived in country mansions. The Daresbury division, for instance, included a brewer, a file-manufacturer, and two bankers from Warrington; the Hyde division included several members of well-known families in the cotton-spinning trade, Ashtons, Cheethams, and Sidebothams.[1] After 1860, the number of mill-owners in the county commission of the peace was greatly increased: Sir Thomas Bazley and William Armitage in Altrincham; Col. C. J. Howard in Stockport; Col. Brocklehurst in Prestbury; Nathaniel Buckley and Ralph Bates in Hyde. The names which were added to the commission during the 1860's and 1870's, while the second Marquess of Westminster and the first Lord Egerton of Tatton were lords-lieutenant, represent the most important revolution in county society, the merging of the landed and business interests. Perhaps the most extreme case of a successful merger was the bench of the Daresbury division which in 1886 was very similar in composition to the boards of directors for two of the principal Warrington companies, Greenall's Brewery and Parr's Bank. But in all petty sessional divisions the same developments were taking place. William Laird, the Birkenhead shipbuilder, had in 1846 been one of the few industrialists on the bench of the Wirral division, whereas in 1886 over a third of the forty magistrates were working daily in the commercial life of Birkenhead and Liverpool.[2] By the time the County Councils Act was passed in 1888 the differences between the social origins of magistrates were matters for subtle distinction.

The men placed in the commission during the year 1888 itself included those from old-fashioned county families: T. W. Legh, later

1 *Orders of Quarter Sessions* (printed by *Chester Courant*, 1848).
2 H.C. 356 (1888), lxxxii, pp. 12, 16.

Lord Newton, C. S. Roundell of Darfold Hall, O. M. Leigh, and H. E. Wilbraham. But there were several belonging to the new class of men. In the Wirral division two names added to the commission were those of J. S. Harmood Banner, a Liverpool accountant and the chairman of Pearson and Knowles Iron Company, Warrington, and of Thomas Brocklebank, a Liverpool banker and shipowner. The Northwich division received W. L. Chew, a Manchester solicitor.[1] The last meeting of Quarter Sessions before the new County Council was elected in January 1889 was not attended by a large number of magistrates who were industrialists. But the presence of John Brunner, the alkali manufacturer, and William Laird, the Birkenhead shipbuilder, was alone sufficient to remind the gentry that the new county society could not be ignored.[2] All the changes which had taken place in the main body of magistrates might not have been reflected so strongly in the composition of Quarter Sessions committees or in the regular attendance at Chester or at Knutsford. But it would be wrong to suppose that the leading county families who remained in positions of influence were unwilling to compromise with new social conditions. The Duke of Westminster, who as lord-lieutenant was choosing magistrates from various positions in society, knew that government by landowners alone was no longer possible.

The rise of the great towns and the expansion of industry had clearly weakened the predominance of the Anglican Church, represented in local government by the squire and the parson. Cheshire was a county well supplied with churches and a tradition of government by the parish vestry. The association of the Established Church with the government of the county seemed apparent in the arrangement of services at Chester Cathedral about 1850. F. L. Olmstead, the American tourist, was disgusted to find that the seats under the organ loft were occupied indiscriminately by unofficiating clergy and military officers in uniform: the governor of the castle, Lord Grosvenor (as colonel of the militia), Lord de Tabley, and others.[3] He thought that this intermingling of the clergy with the military represented local government by the Anglican gentry. By the 1870's Protestant Nonconformity had established itself alongside the Establishment. Even in 1851, at the time of the Census, only just

[1] *Crewe and Nantwich Observer*, 6 Nov. 1909.
[2] *Chester Chronicle*, 5 Jan. 1889.
[3] F. L. Olmstead, *Walks and Talks of an American Farmer in England* (1852), p. 152.

over half the people of Cheshire who attended services on the morning of Sunday, 30 March, were members of the Church of England. Fourteen per cent. were Wesleyan Methodists and nine per cent. Roman Catholics; the rest completed a whole range of Protestant denominations. The Wesleyan Methodists had considerable support in rural areas; the Primitive Methodists were particularly active in the agricultural parts of the south and west between Nantwich and Chester; but the Roman Catholics were largely confined to the urban areas of Birkenhead in the west and of Stockport and Hyde in the east.[1] Between the censuses of 1851 and 1871 the Nonconformists improved their position in the towns. In 1873 the *Nonconformist* claimed that in all the great centres of population the Church of England was no longer the real Established Church. Of all the large boroughs in Cheshire which this magazine surveyed, only Stalybridge possessed a larger number of seats in Anglican churches than could be supplied in the churches and chapels of other denominations.[2] The whole subject of the religions census was extremely controversial, but it seems likely that the Church of England in Cheshire did not keep pace with industrial expansion as efficiently as Nonconformity. The rule of the Anglican gentry required adaptation.

Col. Egerton-Warburton of Arley Hall gave one of his tenants notice to quit in 1893 because the latter would not accept the condition that all tenant farmers on the estate should be members of the Church of England and do personal service in the yeomanry cavalry. His action aroused a storm of protest at the Cheshire Farmers' Club meeting against the dictation of landlords by the 'three C's': three questions requiring a positive answer—Are you a Conservative? Are you a Churchman? Will you join the cavalry? Tenancy agreements on the Arley estate might still require boon work and yeomanry service, but their enforcement did not meet with general approval.[3] By the 1890's the tenant was not expected to have the same opinions as his lord.

The difference of religious belief was in fact one of the chief hindrances to the merging of the landed and the business interests. The distinct social inferiority of Nonconformity occasionally led those who were successful in business to return to the Church of England, just as the rising railway managers in the L.N.W.R. hierarchy at

[1] *National Census (1851) Religious Worship* [1690], p. cxcviii.
[2] *The Nonconformist*, 23 Oct., 6 Nov., 4 Dec. 1872, 8 Jan. 1873.
[3] *Chester Chronicle*, 25 Feb. 1893, p. 8; 4 Mar. 1893, p. 5; 18 Mar. 1893, p. 8; 25 Mar. 1893, p. 2; *Hansard*, 4th ser. IX. col. 14444.

Crewe tended to abandon their chapels for the Established Church on gaining promotion. The Anglican Church in Crewe was under the patronage of the railway company. Christopher Kay, a salt manufacturer who had attended the Congregationalist Church at Over in his youth, died in 1907, the greatly revered churchwarden of Davenham.[1] Nonconformity was a form of protest against the predominance in local politics of the Anglican gentry. Whenever the landed families adapted themselves to come to terms with new social conditions, Nonconformity lost something of its political significance.

Some of the leading industrialists who rose to prominence in Cheshire during the second half of the nineteenth century were Nonconformists: they were also to a large extent Liberals. The image of the Conservative party became linked with the economy of landed estates and tenant farming; that of the Liberals with the new industrial empires of salt, soap, and cotton. W. H. Lever, the soap manufacturer of Port Sunlight, and James Watts of Abney Hall, a Manchester warehouseman, were both Congregationalists and both the leaders of the Liberal party in their own area of the county. W. B. Brocklehurst, the Macclesfield silk manufacturer, and Sir John Brunner, the founder of Brunner Mond Chemical Works at Winnington, were both Unitarians and Liberals. The wealth created in these new industries provided the Liberal party with its sources of patronage, just as the landed gentlemen paid subscriptions to the Conservatives. The nature of management in these industries permitted a paternalist relationship between employer and employee which was similar to that between landlord and tenant. Brocklehurst's business did not become a limited company until 1906; it did not advertise until 1911![2] Sir John Brunner's political career was based upon the successful management of a local industry, and his entry into politics appeared to be a natural extension of his managerial activities. Brunner and Mond acquired the site of their factory at Winnington near Northwich in 1873; they formed a limited company in 1881; and by 1885 Brunner was representing Northwich in Parliament. In 1891 he secured the establishment of the Northwich Salt Compensation Board, a joint authority which is empowered to levy a rate in order to provide funds for the compensation of property owners who suffer from subsidence. His generosity to local associations was extensive. He presented a free library to Northwich

---

[1] *Chester Chronicle*, 22 June 1907, p. 2.
[2] Mary Crozier, *An Old Silk Family: 1745–1945* (1947), pp. 35–39.

D

and Guildhalls to Runcorn and Winsford. The chains of office used by the chairmen of three urban district councils (Northwich, Runcorn, and Middlewich) were presented by him to mark the Jubilee of 1897.[1] The freedom of private enterprise on this scale involved more than the production of goods. The rivalry between Levers of Port Sunlight, Crosfields of Warrington, and Brunner Mond Co. over the production of alkalis for the manufacture of soap involved the future welfare of their workpeople. Each firm was the fatherly benefactor of its employees, and it is sometimes hard to see the difference between the concern of the Duke of Westminster for his tenants and that of W. H. Lever for his workmen. Crosfields had recreation clubs, brass bands, choirs, dramatic societies, evening classes, P.T., and swimming instruction, and even a company of Volunteers which had a fortnightly camp every year.[2] The landlords and industrialists might be on opposite sides in politics or religion, but their ideals of social welfare were surprisingly similar.

The merging of the landed and business interests was a process consciously aided by social activities which were non-denominational and non-political. Freemasonry was certainly an important agent to this purpose, but a very difficult one to assess. The great increase in the number of masonic lodges in Cheshire during the late-nineteenth century and the inauguration of the Cheshire Masonic Benevolent Institution in 1893 were certainly indications that the craft of masonry provided a sense of belonging to the county among all those classes who could afford to join.[3] Alfred Ingham in his *Cheshire: Its Traditions and History* in 1920 saw fit to emphasize the influence of freemasonry with a special chapter. H. K. Aspinall, the Birkenhead brewer and amateur historian, in 1903 linked the craft with a sport which took account of neither religion nor politics: 'Hunting, I always think, closely resembles the wonderful institution of freemasonry; in that it so frequently engenders a lifelong intimacy.'[4] Prowess in the hunting-field attracted the attention of county society and several strangers came into the county for the purpose of following the hounds. The London merchant banker Baron von Schröder bought a house in Cheshire about 1868, became a magistrate in 1876,

---

[1] For Brunner see especially J. M. Cohen, *Life of Ludwig Mond* (1956), pp. 138, 155, 157ff.; J. H. Cooke, *Diamond Jubilee in Chester* (1899), pp. 275–80.
[2] Charles Wilson, *History of Unilever* (1954), chap. ix; *The Improvement of Work People of Jos. Crosfield etc.* (Warrington, 1903).
[3] John Armstrong, *History of Freemasonry in Cheshire* (1901), pp. 204–5.
[4] H. K. Aspinall, *Birkenhead and Its Surroundings* (1903), p. 222.

and was high sheriff and returning officer at the time of the first county council elections in January 1889. He was a well-known follower of the Cheshire hounds.[1] The Volunteer movement through its camps and exercises, like freemasonry and hunting, provided the opportunities for social intercourse which avoided ideological differences. The Earl of Chester's Regiment of Yeomanry Cavalry remained to a large extent under the control of the great country houses. Its two principal squadrons were named after Tatton Hall, the seat of Lord Egerton, and Eaton Hall, the seat of the Duke of Westminster; and were commanded by Lord Egerton's brother and by the Duke's second son.[2] But the Volunteer Regiment in 1915 was raised by a committee which included all the various industrial interests of the county.[3] Soldiering and sport gave all those who wished to participate some common standards of manners. By 1900 the activities of county society had little in common with those of 1840. It was sometimes hard to distinguish between the habits of an industrialist and banker, like 'Fitz' Brocklehurst, a Liberal and a Unitarian, who insisted on spending three months in every year shooting in Scotland, and those of the younger sons of Anglican Army families, like the Grey-Egertons or the Wilbrahams. Social distinctions between the 'upper classes' and the 'middle classes' engaged in production or trade remained; but they were becoming much more difficult to recognize. The middle classes had extended their activities to cover the whole range of county affairs.

The Public Schools assisted the process of standardizing upper-class manners. The Nonconformist businessman or industrialist before 1870 was almost certainly excluded from sending his sons to the great schools of England and to the universities. Quite a large number of the sons of professional men in Cheshire attended Owens College in Manchester. But after 1870 conditions in the educational world were certainly changing. Compare, for example, the careers of James Watts, born 1804, and his grandson, James Watts, born 1878. The former was a Manchester businessman, trained in a tradition of Congregationalism and Liberal politics, who built Abney Hall, near Cheadle, from the tremendous profits of a warehouse trade in fancy goods. He was Mayor of Manchester and entertained the Prince Consort on his visit to the Art Exhibition in 1857. His education

---

[1] *Crewe Chronicle*, 23 July 1938.
[2] F. Leary, *Earl of Chester's Yeomanry Cavalry* (1898), pp. 216 ff.
[3] E. J. W. Disbrowe, *History of Volunteer Movement in Cheshire* (1920).

was of the simplest. But his grandson was sent to Winchester and New College, Oxford, rowed for his college at Henley and did all the smart things expected from his generation, even to the extent of taking an American wife! Although nominally Anglican, a large number of the great Public Schools from the 1880's onwards accepted boys from traditionally Nonconformist families. The publication called *Cheshire Leaders: Social and Political*, which appeared in 1896, is an excellent illustration of the importance given to a Public School education by that generation of leaders in Cheshire politics, the first generation of post-Arnoldian Public School men who had been to school in the 1870's and 1880's when the doctrines of 'muscular Christianity' were first expounded. The entry, for instance, describing Alderman T. H. Sykes, who went to Rugby, includes a long peroration on the 'incalculable influence for good upon our whole national life' exercised by the Public Schools.[1]

One political event was more important than all others in uniting the landed and business interests in a common cause. Gladstone's decision in 1886 to grant Home Rule to Ireland upset the pattern of local political patronage. The lord-lieutenant, the Duke of Westminster, the principal Whig landowner in the county, declined to take office in Gladstone's government, and came out as a Unionist, proclaiming his joy 'at the Union of all classes for maintaining the Empire in its whole and undivided strength'.[2] The Duke exerted his influence over his borough of Chester which had always considered Gladstone to be one of its own worthies because of the proximity of Gladstone's country home at Hawarden in Flintshire; Gladstone's birthday was a regular festival for the local Liberal party. The Duke secured financial control of the *Chester Courant*, a local newspaper, to act as the journal of his interest, and offered to subscribe to the *Manchester Examiner and Times* which was being established as a Unionist journal for the north-west.[3] At the General Election of 1886 the Duke demonstrated the power of his patronage. Walter Foster, the sitting member for Chester who remained loyal to Gladstone, was defeated by the Conservative and Unionist candidate who now received the Duke's support. The Liberals rather maliciously reported that the Duke had removed from Eaton Hall his portrait of Gladstone by Sir John Millais. Although the Duke continued to send

---

[1] *Cheshire Leaders: Social and Political* (1896), p. 75.
[2] B.M. Add. MSS. 44179, ff. 22–23; 44337, ff. 385–6.
[3] Chatsworth House, Devonshire Papers, 340·2250.

flowers to Gladstone on his birthday and was chairman of the appeal for a national memorial on his death, after 1886 their political alliance was at an end; and the majority of Liberal landowners in Cheshire followed the Duke's leadership. James Tomkinson of Willington Hall, the Liberal candidate for Eddisbury, wrote to Gladstone that he was the only member of the 'landed interest' in Cheshire who had not followed the Duke of Westminster.[1]

The issue of Home Rule for Ireland brought into county politics all the burning issues of the day. It threatened the rights of property owners by bringing those of Irish landlords into question; it proclaimed the right of the mass electorate to a popular franchise; it suggested an extension of the powers of the Church of Rome. On all these counts the landowners and businessmen of Cheshire, as elsewhere, tended to take the Unionist part. In Cheshire the matter was fought out particularly fiercely in the new constituency of Northwich which covered the salt-producing towns of the Weaver valley. Sir John Brunner of the chemical works at Winnington had won the seat for the Liberals in 1885 against W. H. Verdin, a Conservative salt manufacturer, but had lost in the crucial 'Home Rule' election of 1886 to Robert Verdin, his brother. The latter's sudden death in 1887 caused a by-election which attracted national attention and focused county opinion upon the new allegiance of the House of Grosvenor, because the Unionist candidate against Sir John Brunner was the Duke of Westminster's third son, Lord Henry Grosvenor. After a Liberal victory in 1887, both Sir John and his son sat for Northwich undisturbed until 1918, in spite of good Unionist candidates in 1895, 1906, and 1910. But the Unionists continued to make forays into Sir John's little kingdom. The Duke of Westminster in 1892 presided at a Unionist demonstration in Northwich Market Hall when Mr. Balfour, who had journeyed from London specially for the meeting, aided a large gathering of local gentry to make a presentation to Mr. Smith-Barry, the squire of Marbury Hall. The latter (who had over 20,000 acres in Ireland) was founder of the Cork Defence Union and had carried on a great struggle with the Irish Land League.[2] His stake in Cheshire was comparatively small but his troubles brought the issue of Ireland into the heart of this constituency.

It is not surprising that after 1885 Liberal victories should have

[1] B.M. Add. MSS. 44498, ff. 114–15.
[2] *Chester Chronicle*, 25 June 1892, p. 8; *Chester Courant*, 29 June 1892, p. 7.

been more likely in some county constituencies, Conservative victories in others. The constituency of Northwich was almost designed to contain the industrial empire of Sir John Brunner. The redistribution of parliamentary seats in 1885 was the first in the county of Cheshire to recognize that the increasing size of the electorate made political success to some extent dependent upon social and industrial factors. When the parliamentary representation of the county was increased from two to four in 1832 and from four to six in 1868, the constituency boundaries were taken from the ancient hundreds of the shire. But the 'country party' realized that political conditions were going to be very different in 1885. Lord Egerton of Tatton, the leader of the Cheshire Conservatives, in November 1884 wrote to Sir Stafford Northcote: 'It will be fatal to our interests if some of the towns above 10,000 are not taken out of my old constituency of Mid-Cheshire.'[1] He proposed a Northwich constituency covering the salt towns of the Weaver valley, a Crewe constituency to include Crewe, Nantwich, and Sandbach, and a Macclesfield constituency to include Macclesfield and Congleton. Sir John Brunner's proposals for the redistribution of seats were very similar to Lord Egerton's.[2] He was as anxious to secure divisions which the Liberals could win, as Lord Egerton was to isolate the Liberals by making concessions. The arrangement of eight county constituencies in 1885, if the rather unpredictable division of Hyde is excluded, confined the industrial areas to three divisions (Northwich, Crewe, and Macclesfield); and left two suburban divisions (Altrincham and Wirral) and two rural divisions (Eddisbury and Knutsford), in all of which the Conservative party could hold its own.

Social and political ideals

The settlement and social organization of the county were therefore regularly taken into account by the party managers after 1885. They were recognized factors in anticipating voting behaviour. It was no longer possible to rely on the followings of great political patrons because the secret ballot prevented the total commitment of voters to one party or the other. Politicians were instead led to consider more closely the boundaries of electoral divisions and to ponder upon the possible effects of different timings of elections. The parliamentary constituencies of the county reflected the social change which had taken place during the previous forty years.

[1] Christ Church, Oxford: Salisbury Papers.
[2] Bodleian Library, Gough Adds. Ches. 8° 54e/5.

The chief issue in local politics was the demand that the democratic ideals which were coming to predominate in the organization of national government should also be transferred to the field of local government, and that the democratic institutions of the towns should be extended to the countryside. The Franchise Act of 1884 gave the vote to the agricultural labourer, and the Local Government Act of 1888 enfranchised the householder in country districts, just as the 1835 Act had applied this privilege in all municipal boroughs. The political atmosphere was filled with promise. The Roman Catholic priest of Runcorn at the Diamond Jubilee dinner of mid-Cheshire authorities in 1897 concluded his speech with a rousing peroration: 'We are all aiming to attain one great object, namely, the uplifting of the masses out of the lethargy in which they have been living for years, and give them a better understanding of their own entities, whereby they might become nobler members of society.'[1] These sentences received rapturous applause because they represented a challenge to the aristocratic principle that local government was to be controlled by the upper classes. But this challenge could not be made effective until the lower classes not only had the vote but also supplied the candidates for election.

One of the most important consequences of the merging of the business and the landed interests had been in fact to perpetuate the ideal of public service by the gentleman amateur. To all intents and purposes social standing remained the principal criterion of acceptability for service with a local authority before 1914, although there may have been variations in social worth according to its size and importance. County councils were by convention socially superior to rural districts, and boroughs to urban districts. The new county society, created by the changes of settlement and social organization in the late-nineteenth century, corresponded to the administrative needs of the new authorities. It was less exclusive, recruited on a much broader basis than the society of landowners, and therefore contained within itself different levels of respectability. Representatives of the 200-odd Cheshire families listed in *Walford's County Families* for 1879 would not all have been acceptable to the company assembled at the George Inn in Knutsford every winter. The committee which issued the invitations to dance at these assemblies was composed from the leading families of gentry, Egerton, Legh, Warburton, Dixon, Smith-Barry, Tabley, &c. George Dixon of Astle Hall, chairman

[1] J. H. Cooke, *Diamond Jubilee in Cheshire* (1899), p. 279.

of the County Council and a leading member of the Knutsford Assembly Committee in the 1880's, no doubt helped to draw the lines above the names of many of his fellow councillors.[1] The removal of a fairly clearly defined distinction between the landed gentry and other prosperous people did not get rid of the importance of social standing in local government; it merely led to greater refinements in the calculation of one's social position.

A good index of the different degrees of social leadership was the number of commissions in county regiments at the outbreak of the First World War. For instance, how far did the sons of Manchester business people who had settled in Cheshire retain a sense of allegiance to the Manchester Regiment, and if they did not, how far were they acceptable to 'county society' for taking up a commission with the Cheshires? The following table shows a selection of young men at the beginning of the First World War who came from Alderley Edge, a village in which the Manchester merchant classes had settled. All chose to join the Manchester Regiment. They continued to think of themselves primarily as Manchester people. The same sentiments affected those who lived even deeper in the countryside and were considered socially superior to the Manchester 'colony' at Alderley Edge. Thomas Blatherwick, for instance, and F. B. Merriman (later Lord Merriman),[2] the barrister, both of Knutsford, joined the Manchesters. Wilfrith Elstob, whose father was Vicar of Siddington and Capesthorne, followed the same course of action because he had been to Manchester University and was friendly with the Worthingtons at Alderley Edge, although some others from the villages around who also had close associations with Manchester, such as J. M. Salisbury of Knutsford or Geoffrey Sparrow of Over Alderley, managed to secure commissions in the Cheshire Regiment. By 1914 the Cheshire Volunteers included a great many industrialists from the towns who were the mainstay of the new county society. While members of the old-fashioned gentry families, such as William Bromley-Davenport and Lord Arthur Grosvenor, still commanded the battalions recruited in farming districts, the commandant of the Northwich battalion was the engineer to the Weaver Navigation, that of the Stockport battalion was the managing director of a bleaching works, and that of the Altrincham battalion was a leading Manchester

---

[1] John Rylands Library, Bromley-Davenport papers, Knutsford County Assembly Minute Book.
[2] *The Times*, 19 Jan. 1962.

yarn agent and former Liberal M.P.[1] War itself was nevertheless one of the most powerful forces in lessening the importance of social standing in local government. The new county society never recovered the pre-1914 values after 1918, and it seems almost fitting that A. W. Boyd, one of the leading Cheshire naturalists and ornithologists after

TABLE 2

Alderley Edge Officers in 1914–18

Name	Battalion	Father's occupation
1. *Manchester City (16–23)*		
'*K*' *Battalions*		
E. G. Agnew . . .	20th	Solicitor
T. W. Crewdson . . .	20th	Cotton
J. S. Gemmell . . .	20th	(not known)
P. Godlee	18th	Calico printer (uncle)
A. Heywood . . .	19th	Doctor of medicine
E. L. Heyworth . . .	17th	Cotton
R. Hobkirk . . .	18th	Cotton
J. J. Payne	16th	Architect
F. G. Ross . . .	20th	Cotton
J. H. Worthington . .	16th	Architect
T. R. Worthington . .	22nd	Architect
2. *Manchester Territorials*		
H. C. L. Heywood . .	6th	Doctor of medicine
C. S. Worthington . .	6th	Architect

the war, should have followed the conventional career of a merchant's son from Rugby School, to Oxford, a commission in the Lancashire Fusiliers, and a place in the business of a Manchester yarn agent.[2] Such a man who could 'fall into Cheshire speech unconsciously'[3] epitomized the new county society in which there were many distinctions of status.

The principle of social standing as the sole criterion for public service ran the risk of being debased by the indifference of the newly arrived or of being neglected through the carelessness of the old-established families. Even before 1914–18 there were signs that the new county society was growing away from the traditions of its worthy predecessor. Clarke Aspinall, the Liverpool solicitor who settled in Bebington in the 1850's, made harsh criticisms of the Wirral commuters who followed him. He had little sympathy with 'that

[1] E. J. W. Disbrowe, *History of Volunteer Movement in Cheshire* (1920), p. 90.
[2] *Manchester Guardian*, 19 Oct. 1959.   [3] *The Times*, 12 Nov. 1960.

hybrid class which is too genteel to be helpful, and too vulgar to use the opportunities of its position for anything but self indulgence'.[1] In order to acquire the status of social leadership the merchant was required to behave like a 'gentleman'. There was no better model of 'what every country squire should be' than Duncan Graham, the first permanent chairman of Cheshire County Council, who was the head of Graham, Rowe and Co., South America merchants, Liverpool. He settled in the village of Willaston about 1860, endowed the church, erected a vicarage, and made generous subscriptions to the National School and Village Institute.[2] His wealth was clearly not a matter of 'self-indulgence', but those who did not settle in the Wirral until after 1900 had hardly the same opportunity of 'playing the squire', and were consequently more indifferent to the importance of their social duties.

Perhaps a greater threat to the established pattern of behaviour than this indifference was the alteration in the standard of manners which opportunities for travel had brought to the upper classes. The next generation of young aristocrats which followed the period of social change wrought by the railways were accustomed to new habits of leisure; and were emancipated from the routine of the London season and country house responsibilities. The age of the motor-car and the private yacht, the week-end in Paris and the polo season at Monte Carlo, did not breed the solid worth which the great political patrons of the previous generation had expected. For the future of local politics in Cheshire there was something foreboding in the image of the young Duke of Westminster (born 1879) and Lord Rocksavage (born 1883), the heir to the Marquess of Cholmondeley and 'the most beautiful of all the young men of his day',[3] driving a red Mercedes around the country houses of England.[4] The families which had traditionally influenced the politics of the county gained from the new situation by being able to extend the scope of their operations and to join a national or metropolitan élite rather than a local one. The small country-loving families of squires living on their own estates who did not have the necessary financial backing were of course the first to suffer unless they came to terms with trade and industry. The gentry could no longer follow the leadership of the great political patrons because the latter had ceased to be interested

---

[1] Walter Lewin, *Clarke Aspinall* (1893), p. 186.
[2] *Chester Chronicle*, 12 Jan. 1901, p. 6.
[3] Diana Cooper, *The Rainbow Comes and Goes* (1958), p. 80.
[4] Fifth Duke of Sutherland, *Looking Back* (1957), p. 64.

primarily in local affairs. It is not surprising that contemporaries considered the increasing number of divorce cases as a sign of the degeneration of the leading county families. In 1879 C. H. Poole of Marbury Hall, who was educated at Eton and Christ Church and belonged to the exclusive Tarporley Hunt Club, lost his wife to the third Viscount Combermere. By 1906, when Sir Philip Grey-Egerton of Oulton Park divorced his young American wife, 'county society' had become accustomed to these actions. The second Duke of Westminster became estranged from his first wife in 1911. The traditional leaders of the county were able to disregard local opinion. J. H. Cooke, when he was reviewing the achievements of Victoria's reign in Cheshire, noted not only that the sports and amusements of the people had been revolutionized by steam, but also that the steam age had brought new dangers: 'dress, luxuries, incessant novel reading, gambling, outside as well as inside Monte Carlo, Stock Exchange transactions turning over a million a day, trades unions, syndicates, strikes, lock-outs, croakers, and agitators'.[1] The value of social standing in local politics in these conditions was in danger of being debased.

[1] J. H. Cooke, *Diamond Jubilee in Cheshire* (1899), p. ix.

3

LOCAL GOVERNMENT BY ELECTION

THE first county council elections in 1889 did not introduce a change in administrative methods, or even a shift in political power, but they provided an opportunity for all classes in the community to recognize the social revolution which had taken place during the previous forty years. The Public Health Act of 1848, the Local Government Act of 1858, and the Public Health Act of 1872 were far more important in establishing the administrative framework by which counties are governed than the Local Government Act of 1888. The Acts of 1848 and 1858 made possible the creation of local boards of health and local government districts which brought a new standard of living to the small towns and villages of the countryside; and the Act of 1872 established a fundamental division between urban and rural sanitary districts which gave the new urban authorities a sense of pride and exclusiveness. The Act of 1888 ensured that geographical counties would survive as administrative units, but while the impetus of local government remained with the new urban authorities, and while the public health of rural districts continued in the hands of the boards of guardians which maintained the poor law, the county councils which the Act created were only of minor administrative importance. Fresh legislation was required to increase the range and scope of their duties. The real significance of the Act of 1888 was to place the county authority on the same social footing as all the other local authorities—borough councils, local boards of health, school boards, and boards of guardians. All these public bodies were open to the processes of democratic election, and the social leaders of all the communities in the shire were able after 1888 to put themselves forward as candidates for service with the county authority. Many of the new county councillors may have rightly considered that their local urban councils had a prior claim upon their attentions. The Act of 1888 brought the counties into line with the general pattern of democratic self-government evolved in the towns, but it is one of the ironies of county administration that some county councillors have continued to be bound by the horizon of their own localities, in spite of the fact that new legislation has transformed the nature of the work for which the county authority is responsible.

The chief difficulty in understanding the effect of elections upon county government is not so much a question of assessing the influence of party politics, but rather one of analysing the distinctions which continued to be made between town and country. If both county and urban authorities accepted the principle that the best political leaders were to be drawn from that class in the community which had the most to contribute, why was there a natural antagonism between county and borough? What was the essential difference between the 'county society' and the *élite* of the towns? The answer to these questions lies in the fact that the new county council was composed from various *élites* scattered throughout the county, and did not possess the homogeneity which a certain social exclusiveness and recognized code of behaviour had given to Quarter Sessions. The county council was an aggregate drawn from different communities and social classes, including members of 'county society' and certainly basking in the reflected glory of the commission of the peace. While 'county society' survived, the divergent tendencies of other groups within the county were conveniently disguised.

It can easily be shown that the county council retained some of the social prestige enjoyed by Quarter Sessions, partly because rural divisions often elected the landed gentry, and partly because aldermen were chosen from the great political patrons of the shire. But the development of the county council cannot be measured in terms of social status alone. It must be somehow related to the gradual disappearance of the 'country party' as a whole. Slowly and almost imperceptibly, the great political families which had represented the county in Parliament loosened their local ties and adopted new habits of life which were made possible by swifter means of transport. This process was not completed until after the First World War. When landowners were faced with the choice of giving up either a town house or a country house, they were frequently compelled by the force of economic circumstances to prefer a suburban house within easy distance of London. In fact, the disappearance of 'county society' to some extent threatened the cohesion of the county as an administrative unit. Its historic boundaries had made political sense while some social leaders thought of themselves as Cheshire rather than as Altrincham or Macclesfield, Bowdon or Congleton. The newly elected County Council in 1889 was able to retain the allegiance of its members through a sense of belonging, however remotely, to 'county society'. This allegiance was natural when new members had already met each other at social gatherings—dinners, parties, or hunt meetings—but when more and more members came to know each other only through the work of the local authority and when permanent officials became more strongly identified with the image of the county than the gentry themselves, it was clear that the era of the public person had displaced that of the social leader.

Urban ambition and county prestige

The prototype for a local authority in the nineteenth century was urban, but the Quarter Sessions continued to enjoy greater social prestige. The Acts of 1888 and 1894 were not revolutionary in conception; they merely extended to the countryside the principle of an elected all-purpose council which had been established in urban areas. Local government was after all a matter of drains, lighting, and paving, subjects which were imperative in urban areas, and not a matter of political ideologies. Every urban sanitary district or local board of health was formed to provide an efficient supply of water and light, and an efficient removal of refuse for its own community, but the appetite growing on what it feeds, each authority wished to extent its scope. There was an undisguised ambition in every urban authority to achieve the status of a borough with its charter and mayor.

The prestige of county politics before 1888 rested upon the right of the magistracy to be consulted whenever wider interests than those of a particular locality were affected. The justices, for instance, were obviously concerned with any attempt to promote a local Act of Parliament. Their natural superiority was embodied in what contemporaries described as the *ex officio* principle—the right of magistrates to be *ex officio* members of other authorities. In 1835 the body of aldermen was retained in the reformed corporations of boroughs as a group of co-opted members chosen by the council who were in theory to maintain the continuity of tradition which might otherwise be upset by a landslide in the annual elections. Many Conservatives in 1888 agitated for the election of aldermen to the new county councils, and in spite of the doubts entertained by prominent members of Lord Salisbury's government, the 'aldermanic principle' was incorporated in the Act. But the 'aldermanic principle' in boroughs and counties should not be confused with the *ex officio* principle as it was applied to the boards of guardians administering the poor law and to the highway boards repairing the roads. Here those magistrates who resided within the area governed by the board were *ex officio* members of it; they could therefore attend meetings when they wished to influence policy, and otherwise allow the elected representatives to carry on the day-to-day administration. The first Lord Egerton of Tatton, the lord-lieutenant, was accused in 1875 of appointing a single magistrate in the area governed by the Stockport Board of Guardians simply in order to swing the vote one way on an extremely crucial issue.[1] A good example of this system at work could be seen in the highway boards which were constituted by Quarter Sessions in 1863. The county was divided into forty-two highway districts governed by boards of elected waywardens, one from each parish. The magistrates fixed the highway rate and were *ex officio* waywardens for the district in which they lived.[2] Those who feared the new county councils were secretly hoping that the *ex officio* principle would apply to these new bodies. The second Lord Egerton's suggestion that Quarter Sessions should be directly represented on the County Council was really an attempt to perpetuate the *ex officio* principle which had been successfully incorporated into the Poor Law Amendment Act of 1834 setting up boards of guardians, and not the 'aldermanic principle' incorporated into the Municipal Corporations Act of 1835 reforming the old corporations.

The County Councils Act of 1888 was therefore in a sense the revenge of the towns against the country gentlemen who, since the fifteenth century at least, had been interfering in the business of the boroughs. The counties were saddled with the same constitution as the municipal boroughs. County aldermen were to be elected by the county council. If the magistrates wished to retain a substantial number of aldermanic seats, they had to win a majority of the places in the council by election. The Duke of Westminster, lord-lieutenant in 1888, appealed to some of the younger magistrates to offer their services to the new elected bodies.[3]

The most likely candidates for a new county council were those who had already submitted themselves for election to smaller authorities, whether they were magistrates or not—the established social leaders of an existing community. The introduction of elections into

---

[1] *Stockport Chronicle*, 17 Dec. 1875.
[2] *Return of Highway Boards*, H.C. 315 (1863), 1.
[3] *Chester Chronicle*, 7 Apr. 1888, p. 2.

county government emphasized the obvious fact that the most important unit in local politics was the town, local board, or vestry. Quarter Sessions were primarily concerned with licensing, the police, and roads and bridges. The magistrates had the prestige which attached itself to social superiority, but the real business of local politics was concerned with the desire to expand the public services of the towns.

Outside the municipal boroughs of Birkenhead, Chester, Congleton, Macclesfield, Stalybridge, and Stockport, there were twenty-five local boards governing the urban areas of Cheshire in 1868, the majority of which had been formed in the previous decade.[1] Macclesfield and Stockport boroughs also possessed local boards of health which governed areas extending outside their municipal boundaries, perhaps the first case of 'urban aggression' which the county might note. Runcorn was governed by a body of Improvement Commissioners established under a local Act of 1852. From these local boards the urban authorities of Cheshire developed, either by amalgamation with existing boroughs or by the growth of population and industry which qualified them to petition for borough status. Three of the wealthiest local boards, Newton Heath, Oxton, and Tranmere, were absorbed into Birkenhead. But after Stalybridge in 1857, only four other districts in Cheshire succeeded in acquiring borough status during the nineteenth century: Birkenhead and Crewe in 1877, Hyde in 1881, and Dukinfield in 1899. Wallasey, a rapidly developing urban area adjacent to Birkenhead, did not become a borough until 1910.[2] Each of these new boroughs in turn applied for another symbol of municipal status, its own commission of the peace. To have its own bench of magistrates gave a town some independence from the jurisdiction of county magistrates, and a sense of release from the tutelage of county administration. All the new nineteenth-century boroughs were successful in receiving a grant of this privilege, except Dukinfield, which had to be content with remaining a separate petty sessional division of the county. Its application for a commission of the peace in 1900 was refused.[3]

Politics in the urban areas before the First World War varied primarily in the extent to which the party organizations of the Conservatives and the Liberals succeeded in capturing the largest number

[1] *Return of Local Boards*, H.C. 489 (1867–8), lviii.
[2] *Return of Authorities*, H.C. 333 (1888), lxxxvi, gives the rateable value of urban districts at the time of the County Councils Act.
[3] Public Record Office, H.O. 45/9758/A61764.

of seats at election time. In all the populous urban areas there was a straight fight between the two main parties. The Cheshire boroughs about 1888 were largely in the hands of a substantial majority for the Liberal party, except Birkenhead and Wallasey in the west and Stalybridge in the east, where the power of the Conservatives could not be shaken. The chief interest of urban politics before the First World War was the weakening of the strength of the Liberals, which by 1914 remained unimpaired only at Crewe where the traditional party struggle of Conservative and Liberal was soon to be abandoned in favour of a common front against Labour. The most radical changes of party control were in Stockport. The Liberals lost their control in 1904 to the Conservatives who retained an over-all majority until 1929. It is clear from examining the declining importance of the Liberal party in borough politics that it stood for different ideals in different places.[1] The Labour party did not succeed in gaining many seats until after 1920. Very few local boards escaped the influence of party politics, with the possible exception of those which were primarily formed to govern the smarter residential districts such as Lymm, Neston, and Tarporley.

The principal elections in rural areas were those for the boards of guardians which administered the poor law. There were eleven unions in 1888 which were wholly within the boundaries of the administrative county; the parts of Cheshire where the poor law was administered by boards of guardians, which belonged to the unions of other counties, were small and chiefly concentrated in the industrial area of the north-east. Here party politics may also have played a part, but they did not necessarily interfere with the working of the principles of county government. The *ex officio* element of magistrates might never have cause to interfere, just as the landowners might never exercise their right to vote. Both landowners and ratepayers were allotted a plurality of votes according to the size of their holdings or assessments. John May told the Select Committee on Local Taxation in 1870 that although the board of guardians had always contained two political parties, not a single absentee landlord in the Macclesfield Union had made a claim to vote since it was formed in 1836. The landowners in each political party confined themselves to supporting their 'friends' at election time, and the *ex officio* guardians, the local magistrates, rarely attended meetings.[2] Provided the

---

[1] Election results have been taken from newspapers, especially the *Manchester Guardian.*   [2] *Report of Select Committee on Taxation*, H.C. 353 (1870), viii.

administration was efficient and their interests were respected, the landed gentry were prepared to allow party politics full freedom.

The Radicals who opposed the rule of the 'landed gentry' in country districts were particularly anxious to preserve the administration of school boards established under the Elementary Education Act of 1870, precisely because these local boards did not embody the *ex officio* principle. School boards were completely 'democratic bodies' consisting of elected representatives with powers to levy a rate and run a school; they were subversive elements in the whole tradition of county politics. Their institutional significance has often been overshadowed by their importance in the history of religious controversy. The National (Church of England) School represented the rule of the parson and the squire. For instance, the disputes between the Bishop of Chester and Sir John Brunner in 1896 over the future management of Barnton School involved the ranging on opposite sides of two different conceptions of county politics. Sir John declared: 'The Bishop proposes a clergyman's school; I propose a people's school.'[1] In Cheshire the Church of England retained its strength in rural areas, and the majority of school boards were confined to the boroughs. Chester avoided the formation of a board because voluntary schools provided sufficient places, and the 'church party' in Birkenhead was able to stave off the formation of a board until 1893.[2] Rural school boards in Cheshire were confined to areas where Protestant Nonconformity was strong: in the south between Burwardsley and Wrenbury, and in the north between Daresbury and Weaverham. Liberal annoyance with the Conservative government which abolished school boards in 1902 and handed over educational administration to county councils was not limited to religious questions. The county councils did not enjoy the *ex officio* principle, but they embodied the 'aldermanic principle' which was equally deplored.

Although the County Councils Act of 1888 may have satisfied Conservative opinion that the tradition of county government could be preserved, there was one real and important change introduced by the Act which provided the greatest blow to county prestige. County boroughs were created. In 1889 Cheshire lost Chester, Birkenhead, and Stockport, and in 1913, Wallasey. This was a revolutionary step

---

[1] *Chester Chronicle*, 15 Aug. 1896, p. 6.
[2] *Return of School Districts* (C. 5963), H.C. (1890), lvi; *The Nonconformist*, 6 Nov. 1872 (Supplement).

in the history of Cheshire, because Quarter Sessions until 1888 had levied a county rate on all boroughs in the county except Chester, which was an old county with its own Quarter Sessions, and Birkenhead which had not secured its own Quarter Sessions until 1882. The adjustment of financial arrangements under the 1888 Act before the Local Government Commission represented the emancipation of these boroughs from the government of the county.[1] They became counties in their own right and were no longer part of the system of county politics into which the *ex officio* element had the right to interfere if its interests were involved. They became rivals with the county itself for political prestige.

Candidates from the business classes

The most ambitious boroughs were usually led by those who had made considerable private wealth within their boundaries. A local authority was not only a body which provided a whole series of services for the welfare of the community, but also a body which acted as the trustee of local patriotism and prestige. It attracted the wealthiest men in the society which it governed, just as a private charity depended for its survival upon the guarantees given by the men of substance who administered it. One of the most instructive actions which the stranger to a town or district council can perform is to examine the portraits of its chairmen. These faces will usually tell a story of declining private opulence when taken in succession, but they should give some indication of the wealth which used to be required before the First World War for carrying out the function of serving the community. Candidates from the business classes were for a long time regarded as the ideal public servants. E. D. Simon,[2] speaking in 1927 only two years after he had himself resigned from the town council of Manchester where he typified the businessman candidate, regretted that its affairs were no longer under the charge of 'men of first-rate ability and experience who had made good in private enterprise'.[3] Before the First World War social conditions were such that the political parties did not find great difficulty in securing the services of able men. Social leaders presented themselves to the electorate, and then asked their party organizations to help in their campaign.

---

[1] *Report of Local Government Act Commission* (C. 6839), H.C. (1892), xxxvii.
[2] Later Lord Simon of Wythenshawe.
[3] *Manchester Guardian,* 30 Sept. 1927.

Candidates from the business classes were more likely to be elected in conditions where a little judicious spending of private wealth could influence the electorate—if not by direct bribery at least by the moral blackmail of generous benefactions. There existed a number of opportunities by which a man could leave a mark on his native town or adopted home through some generous benefaction to a school, hospital, or library. When two men regardless of party were contending for a seat on the local council, it was not unnatural to ask which brought the more financial benefit to the place through his business, and which paid the more rates. At the county council election in Dukinfield in 1904, G. H. Kenyon, a rope manufacturer and one of the leading Liberals of the district, based one of his appeals to the electorate on the fact that he brought more employment to the town than his opponent, Joseph Cooke, a Conservative grocer.[1] Political activity was closely associated with economic influence. The names of institutions testify to the generosity of many local worthies. The clerk of the Macclesfield Union, John May, organized subscription lists in Macclesfield for the building of a hospital, baths, and wash-houses, and the opening of a public park between 1850 and 1870, and the town also received a library and another park, in 1876 and 1894 respectively, from private patrons.[2] The social leader naturally flourished in urban areas where he could leave a lasting monument to his own activities and interests. The gentry might have been free from this vulgar ambition, but the great political patrons were free to distribute *largesse* throughout the county. The Marquess of Westminster was one of the leading subscribers to institutions in Macclesfield.[3] The establishment of various benefactions was another subject in which the great county patrons and the new merchants and manufacturers shared common ground.

The conventions of both national and local politics demanded that in each constituency, division, or ward there should be a group of leaders whose chief function was to spend money in such a way that the political party which they supported might extend its patronage and influence. Successive Acts of Parliament which were required by the changing conditions of national politics gradually undermined this situation. The Secret Ballot Act of 1872 introduced the secret ballot into the conduct of elections in municipal boroughs as well as

---

[1] Handbill in the possession of Mr. Arnold Kenyon, Ashton-under-Lyne.
[2] Ed. C. Stella Davies, *History of Macclesfield* (1961), pp. 256–8, 277–8, 280–4.
[3] Davies, op. cit., pp. 257, 277–8.

parliamentary constituencies. The Corrupt Practices Act of 1883 which limited local expenditure at parliamentary elections forced each party to bear a large proportion of the cost of a General Election from central funds, but local government elections still depended to a large extent on private patronage. The Local Government Act of 1894[1] which introduced the secret ballot for the first time into the conduct of elections for district councils and boards of guardians made it more difficult to estimate the effectiveness of petty corruption. But the atmosphere of local politics was not radically altered until the Representation of the People Act of 1918 came into force. This Act abolished one of the procedures by which the process of political expenditure had been encouraged; it removed the courts of the revising barristers who were annually called upon to check the lists of qualified electors. The 1918 Act placed an effective brake upon the activities of social leaders by adding uncertainty to political calculation. Although the secret ballot had been introduced for parliamentary and municipal elections in 1872, the maintenance of the revising barristers' courts, which owed their origin to the great Reform Act of 1832, perpetuated political conditions in which each party, when called upon to fight an election, could count on the services of committed supporters. Because the agent of each political party who appeared before the revising barrister defended the names of the supporters he wished to place on the voters' list, and tried to disqualify as many names as he could on his opponents' list, the fate of many a parliamentary election was decided in the revising barrister's court which preceded it. This state of affairs influenced local government elections because the party political agents who dealt with parliamentary elections dealt with them also.

The extent to which the parties were dealing with lists of committed voters before the 1918 Act is reflected in the high poll at local government elections, both urban and rural. The average poll in all the divisions contested at the first two county council elections was over seventy per cent. of the electorate. In the division of Mottram in 1889 and in Nantwich in 1892, a poll of eighty-nine per cent. was recorded. Before 1914 polls of under fifty per cent. were almost unknown in county elections. Participation in politics as a voter was a function of living in a community which still depended to a large extent upon private patronage.

It is significant in itself that there are no published lists before 1920

[1] See Section 48 (3).

of local government electors in borough or county divisions.[1] The number of electors in each place remained a private matter of adjustment between the local party associations and patronage empires. These statistics were not collected by a central authority for the whole nation. The social leader could best survive an election in the days of small electorates. The County Electors Act of 1888 defined the franchise for electors to county councils as the burgess qualifications in boroughs, a year's occupation of a house and payment of rates, and the £10 occupation qualification in counties, a year's occupation of land worth £10 a year and the payment of rates. While the franchise remained limited to the property owner and the ratepayer, there was little likelihood of a large unmanageable electorate. At the first county council election in Cheshire (January, 1889) there were 57,381 qualified voters in the thirty-five divisions where contests were fought, and the total qualified electorate was 89,566.[2] In 1921, in contrast, there were almost 250,000 voters on the electoral register of the administrative county. Before the First World War a typical division electing one county councillor was likely to contain between 1,500 and 2,000 voters. There is some evidence that in such conditions various forms of bribery were used, in spite of the legal prohibitions against it. For instance, in that part of Cheshire which borders Ashton-under-Lyne, both political parties recognized the distribution of half-crowns and of free drinks in the public houses as legitimate weapons in the game of politics until the advent of the Labour party, which could not compete in this rivalry of patronage and might therefore claim that the laws against corruption should be enforced.[3] The electoral conditions before 1918 encouraged illegitimate expenditure and naturally tended to attract those candidates who could afford to spend their money in this way, if called upon to do so.

All the evidence therefore shows that the end of the First World War marked a more significant stage in the development of local politics than the Local Government Act of 1888 which created county councils. It is not surprising that a fundamental alteration in the method of appointing magistrates was made during the same period. From 1910 onwards, the lords-lieutenant were deprived of their right to nominate justices of the peace for the county bench, and were replaced by an advisory committee, appointed by the Lord

---

[1] B. Keith-Lucas, *English Local Government Franchise*, p. 237.
[2] *Return of County Council. Election*, H.C. 247 (1889), lxv.
[3] Personal information of Mr. Arnold Kenyon.

Chancellor for each area, which included the representatives of the principal political parties.[1] Before 1910 candidates from the business classes were willing to submit themselves for election; after 1920 they gradually became fewer and fewer. The first county council elections should be set against this background. By 1889 there were sufficient businessmen available to establish themselves in county politics. The more urbanized a county had become, the more likely it was to elect the social leaders of the towns to its first county council.

The background of the new councillors

The first county council elections in 1889 contrasted greatly with the first elections for urban and district councils held in 1894. The latter were to some extent characterized by the large number of candidates in the field (45 for 15 seats in Knutsford, 46 for 18 seats in Altrincham, and similarly for many rural districts);[2] but chiefly by their predictability. In several instances, many former members of the local board were returned (e.g. Bowdon, Marple, and Wilmslow). In some cases, a compromise arrangement between the parties limited the number of contests (as at Cheadle and Gatley); in others, one party succeeded in increasing its power (e.g. the Conservatives at Sandbach and Dukinfield). But in general, the new district councils were merely the local boards of health and boards of guardians under different names, with a tradition of election going back more than forty years. They were completely accustomed to the social leaders of each district. The first County Council in contrast was an entirely new venture. No one dared to forecast the result in 1889, and the electors were speculating on the extent to which the conventions of county government would be brought into line with those prevailing in other local authorities. By order of the Local Government Board, Quarter Sessions had supervised the division of the county into fifty-seven areas, each to return one member to the new council.[3] The principle determining the boundaries of each division was that, wherever possible, urban and rural areas should be combined to return a single member. Only fourteen of the divisions were in the municipal

---

[1] For further details see *Parliamentary Affairs*, XIII (1), 85–94; the Home Rule crisis tended to turn all the magistrates into Unionists, e.g. Dec. 1906, there were believed to be only 105 Liberal magistrates to 324 Conservatives: see *Chester Chronicle*, 15 Dec. 1906, p. 8.

[2] See, for example, the *Manchester Guardian*, 17 Dec. 1894, p. 6; *Chester Courant*, 19 Dec. 1894, p. 5.

[3] Cheshire Record Office, Quarter Sessions Minute Books; Public Record Office, M.H. 30/31, 66449/90.

boroughs (four in Macclesfield, three each in Crewe, Hyde, and Staly-bridge, and one in Congleton); the remaining forty-three divisions were scattered over the county without regard to existing administrative boundaries. At their first meeting the 57 new councillors were to elect 19 aldermen, making a full council of 76 members. By the elections of 1895 the number of councillors had been increased to 59 by the creation of new divisions at Crewe and New Brighton,[1] but the only other important alterations were made in connexion with the rise of the borough of Wallasey. For the elections of 1907, Wallasey was divided into five wards instead of three, which gave the county 61 councillors and the right to increase the number of aldermen from 19 to 20. The Wallasey members and one extra alderman were excluded after the town became a county borough in 1913. Therefore from 1913 until the reorganization of 1937 the County Council contained 75 members (56 councillors and 19 aldermen).

The landowning families who had traditionally run the politics of the shire, did not enter the county council elections in any force. The group who entered most strongly were the manufacturing and mercantile families who by 1888 had secured a place among the country gentry and magistracy. Except for Lord Egerton of Tatton, who was elected for the Knutsford division in 1889, the landed interest preferred to remain apart from the contest. The Duke of Westminster was later elected an alderman in virtue of the fact that he was lord-lieutenant, but on the whole the great landed families remained aloof from these affairs. After fighting a losing battle for various causes, Lord Egerton resigned his seat in 1892. By then it was clear that the leading members of the County Council with previous experience on the bench were to be the wealthy merchants and *entrepreneurs* rather than the landowners.

In 1889 only 34 county magistrates offered themselves for election; 28 were elected. Four of the six defeated magistrates were later chosen as aldermen to represent the Conservative interest. Only 5 of the 14 chairmen of petty sessional divisions stood for election; all except one were successful. When later elections are taken into account, it is significant that of the 34 magistrates who offered their services to the County Council, J. H. Leche of Carden Park, who stuck so strongly to his Protectionist principles, was the only one whose

---

[1] Local Government Board Orders, 17 Feb. 1891; 16 Nov. 1893; the New Brighton division was created after the Wallasey local board had petitioned the Local Government Board: see Public Record Office, M.H. 30/31, 97854/88.

services were not accepted.[1] To be elected a councillor, it was clearly an advantage to be a magistrate.

The magistrates who were elected councillors were predominantly elderly and predominantly Conservative. The average age of the twenty-four elected magistrates whose ages can be easily discovered was 54 years. They included General Sir Richard Wilbraham (78), who had served in the Crimean War, and William Armitage (74), the head of Armitage & Rigby Ltd., cotton spinners. The Duke of Westminster's appeal to the younger generation of magistrates for public service had obviously not been heeded. Only nine Liberal magistrates were elected, of whom four had been placed in the commission by the Duke of Westminster himself. The only magistrates under 40 who offered themselves and were elected were three young Liberals, E. H. Moss, W. B. Brocklehurst, and J. E. Barlow. The latter was parliamentary Liberal candidate for Salford.

Of the twenty-eight elected magistrates, only nine were from strictly landowning families who had sent their sons to Public School and University. Fifteen were manufacturers and merchants, of whom seven were in the cotton trade of Manchester and district. The remaining four consisted of a Chester mining engineer, a Crewe doctor, a Warrington banker, and the Registrar of Manchester County Court.

The twenty-nine new members of the council, who were *not* magistrates and had no previous experience of county administration, were also largely in commerce. Ten of them were connected in various ways with heavy industry or the warehouse trade, and only one of them, Albert Neilson Hornby, the captain of Lancashire County Cricket, who was elected for the Nantwich division, could in any way be described as a country gentleman; even he was only one generation removed from the famous Brookhouse Mills at Blackburn which gave him the right to play for Lancashire.[2] The most important result of the elections was the introduction for the first time into county government of six working farmers and eight tradesmen or small *entrepreneurs*, who were largely members of the Liberal party. A considerable number of the twenty-nine non-magistrate councillors had administrative experience in other fields. At least two of them were magistrates in their own boroughs, and at least eight were sitting on

---

[1] The following account of the elections is based on reports in the *Manchester Guardian*, *Warrington Guardian*, *Chester Chronicle*, and *Chester Courant*.
[2] W. Abram, *History of Blackburn*, pp. 398-9.

the councils of smaller authorities. Dr. Robert Hopwood, for instance, aged 75, had served on Stalybridge Town Council since 1857, been mayor twice and chairman of the local school board.[1] One of the indications of the merits of the new councillors is that ten of them were chosen as county magistrates during the first ten years of the council's life. It became quite customary for an experienced councillor to be placed on the bench.

The first county council election therefore confirmed the supremacy of the great merchants and industrialists in county administration, and introduced for the first time a group of farmers, tradesmen, and small *entrepreneurs* to work alongside them. It established the pattern of county politics before 1914. The few county squires who offered themselves as candidates for election either retired after a few years of office, like Sir Arthur Goodson or Col. Cornwall-Legh, or were so old that they died soon after being elected, like Col. John Kennedy. The majority of the active councillors were prosperous businessmen who could afford the time and the money to devote themselves to the county. In 1913 the *North Cheshire Herald* in congratulating G. F. Drinkwater, one of the county councillors for Hyde, who was a local solicitor and prominent freemason, pointed out that he was expected to spend about £25 a year in travelling expenses if he were to carry out his duties as a councillor conscientiously.[2] Some councillors made considerable efforts to attend meetings. Dr. J. W. Smith, the representative for Weaverham from 1889 until 1913, used to ride his bicycle all the way from Weaverham to Chester when he was over 60; John Norcross, a farmer representing Frodsham, who was first elected in 1910, used to walk from Kingsley to Acton Bridge Station in order to catch the train to Crewe for a committee meeting.[3] In general the most conscientious councillor was the man with a business which could run itself and the man who could afford to travel. Travelling arrangements might occasionally assume tremendous importance. The Liberals lost an important division on the election of aldermen in 1889 because W. S. Rhodes, the representative of Mottram, had to leave the meeting early in order to catch a train for Stalybridge.[4]

The rate of change in the composition of the council was not very rapid. (See Appendix A for county council election returns.) Except

[1] S. Hill, *Bygone Stalybridge*, pp. 285–7.
[2] *North Cheshire Herald*, 8 Mar. 1913, p. 6.
[3] Personal information of Alderman W. A. Gibson.
[4] *Chester Chronicle*, 16 Feb. 1889, p. 8.

in the first election of 1889, it was customary at each of the triennial elections for at least three-quarters of the retiring council to be re-elected. Once selected, a councillor had a very good chance of representing his division, frequently unopposed, until either his retirement or death. The six magistrates who were not elected in 1889 were the largest number of sitting members ever to be defeated at any election before 1946. No more than four retiring councillors in any year had to suffer the indignity of being defeated in their own divisions. Unopposed returns were almost the normal procedure. There was no contest in the Witton division near Northwich until 1922. Henry Bratt, a staunch Liberal with a drapery business in Northwich, who was unopposed in 1889, was succeeded in his retirement in 1919 by his son, W. M. Bratt, also unopposed. It is strange that two Liberals in Witton should be returned unopposed when the former chairman of the Witton Local Board and leading man in local politics was a Conservative, Thomas Ward, who was a parliamentary candidate in 1895.[1] In more rural divisions, unopposed returns might reflect the existence of one of the landed gentry who was willing to stand. The Astbury division near Congleton returned without a contest General Sir Richard Wilbraham in 1889 and his son-in-law, Sir G. B. Baker-Wilbraham, in 1892. The by-elections caused by death, resignation, or promotion to the aldermanic bench sometimes appeared to be as important as the triennial elections themselves in changing the composition of the council, particularly when the elections brought barely ten new men on to the council.

The predominance of unopposed returns depended upon the assumption that it was unnecessary to put the county to the expense of a contest if gentlemen's agreements could be reached. Before each election there was a great deal of preliminary sparring between potential candidates, particularly in those divisions where no obviously well-qualified 'social leader' came forward. Many times local newspapers would announce probable contests in certain divisions, only to follow a week later with the news that compromises had been made. The nature of county council elections before 1914 shows extremely well how successfully the landed and the business interests, described in the last chapter, had been merged to provide a common governing class for the county. The gentlemen's agreements which avoided a contest were made by 'gentlemen' who represented the successful business people setting up home in the countryside.

[1] *Cheshire Leaders: Social and Political* (1896), pp. 63–65.

The influence of party politics

The elections were fought largely on party issues and the number of contests was governed by truces arranged with the party leaders. The candidates fought their campaigns on questions of national importance. How could one choose between two social leaders of equivalent status except by their attitudes to the great political issues of the day? A Conservative, Christopher Kay, a retired salt manufacturer, was opposed in the Northwich division by a Liberal, Edward Milner, a director of the Brunner, Mond alkali works at Winnington. The electors could only choose according to party considerations. Yet it was still considered 'ungentlemanly' for the candidate to rely too heavily on the local party organization. In 1892 Dr. E. J. Sidebotham was thought to have won at Bowdon because he made use of the Conservative party machinery for the first time.[1] When purely local issues were raised they were usually on behalf of some neglected class or group interest. George Slater in 1889 opposed Col. France-Hayhurst at Davenham in order to secure some representation for the Nonconformists, and held his political meetings in the Wesleyan chapel. The Nonconformists were particularly incensed by the Anglican privilege embodied in the powers of the Weaver Navigation, a body which was largely in the hands of the magistrates and which provided subsidies for county rates. The Weaver Navigation Act of 1840 permitted the trustees to build and endow churches and schools for the Church of England. Many Anglican schools benefited from the generosity of the magistrates, and three churches were built, at Winsford, Castle Northwich, and Weston Point.

The bitterest election controversy concerning class privilege was started by Joseph Slater Lewis, the first county councillor for the Frodsham division, who fought his campaign as a Liberal candidate by launching an attack upon the Chief Constable for allowing the county police force to be used as extra gamekeepers on the estates of local landowners.[2] This developed into an onslaught upon the influence of the 'landed interest' in local government, and raised the issue—which had been seriously debated in Parliament at the time of the passing of the 1888 Act—whether or not the non-elected and unrepresentative body of magistrates should be allowed to continue

---

[1] *Warrington Guardian*, 9 Mar. 1892, p. 6.
[2] R. W. James, *History of Cheshire Constabulary: 1857–1957*, pp. 51–52, misinterprets this incident.

to have a share in the management of the police. The County Council, as a result of this controversy, even petitioned for the control to be transferred from the Standing Joint Committee to one of its own committees. The Standing Joint Committee appointed a special sub-committee of inquiry which reported in October 1890. It had eight public sittings and examined sixty-seven witnesses, and agreed that several of Slater Lewis's allegations were proved correct.[1] The 'landed interest' recovered its equanimity when Lewis, who had been secretary of the Birkenhead and District Agricultural Society, was defeated in the county council election of 1892 by Thomas Baxter of Dutton Hall,[2] the chairman of the Chester Farmers' Club and one of the most reliable Unionists. Lewis's subsequent bankruptcy in 1893 sealed his political fate.[3]

It is a great mistake to believe that the decrease in the number of contested elections for the County Council in 1889 showed a decline in the influence of party on local elections. On the contrary, it is clear that two parties in the council chamber believed that they could limit the number of contests by mutual agreement. For the party managers the ideal situation was a state of permanent electoral truce. The county council election of 1901 came closest to this ideal: the only contest was fought by mistake. Wilson Rae, who had offered himself as a Conservative candidate against George Wall, a Liberal but the nominee of both parties in West Kirby, tried to withdraw when he realized that he was causing the only contest in the county. But it was too late to withdraw and the farce of electing Wall by 203 votes to 6 had to be completed.[4] In 1913 the parties in the Wirral agreed to exchange two seats without a contest: Peter Jones, a Liberal, was allowed to replace Eric Brocklebank, a Conservative, in Neston, if Charles McIver, a Conservative, followed Fergus Smith, a Liberal, in West Kirby.[5] Occasionally independent constituency organizations would not accept these agreements. The Conservatives of the Liscard division of Wallasey in 1904 had adopted Dr. Macdonald as their candidate before they were informed that the Conservatives on the County Council had agreed that the sitting member for that division, T. R. Bulley, a Liverpool cotton merchant who had just left the Unionists and joined the Liberals, should not be opposed. The Liberals

---

[1] Public Record Office, M.H. 30/31, 96318/90.
[2] The father of Sir Thomas Baxter (d. 1951), chairman of the Milk Marketing Board. [3] *Chester Chronicle.* 22 July 1893, p. 8.
[4] *Chester Courant*, 27 Feb. 1901, p. 5; 6 Mar. 1901, p. 8.
[5] Ibid., 5 Mar. 1913, p. 5.

on the County Council in return had agreed not to oppose R. T. Richardson, a Conservative barrister, in the Chester Castle division. In spite of this agreement Dr. Macdonald's supporters retained him as their candidate and defeated Bulley by a majority of 419 votes.[1] The County Council, however, having made the informal agreement, retained Bulley's services by electing him an alderman.

The first elections in 1889 produced almost an equal balance between the parties. Local newspapers disagreed about the precise party allegiance of a few councillors. The *Manchester Guardian* announced the composition of the council in the following terms: 27 Conservatives, 25 Liberals, 1 Liberal Unionist, and 4 unknown = 57 councillors.[2] The *Chester Chronicle*, another Liberal paper, laid stress on the fact that the tie between the two main parties might be even closer on any crucial issue which brought the unknown councillors chiefly on the side of the Liberals: 28 Conservatives, 28 Liberals, and 1 Liberal Unionist.[3] Conservative newspapers, like the *Chester Courant* and *Cheshire Observer* which regretted the introduction of party discipline into the council chamber, were reluctant to speculate upon its possible outcome. But after the aldermen had been elected, it was clear that neither party had secured an over-all majority. In a total council of 76 members, the 35 Conservatives depended upon the votes of 5 Liberal Unionists and 4 Independents for a working majority over the 32 Gladstonian Liberals. The encouragement of an electoral truce between the parties tended to perpetuate this situation and give only a slight preponderance to the Conservatives.

Until the first election to be held after the First World War, when there was a considerable increase in the number of Independent members, the composition of the council remained a fairly even balance between the two main parties. The Liberal party did not begin to lose ground until after 1928, but it never won a majority of the seats. The Conservative party secured an over-all majority between 1895 and 1904 and again between 1907 and 1922, but the numbers concerned were so small that the Liberals could still provide an effective challenge to the decisions of the Conservative 'caucus' (see Appendix B). The Conservatives did not win a large working majority until 1949.

County council elections before the First World War had therefore

[1] *Cheshire Observer*, 27 Feb. 1904, p. 8.
[2] *Manchester Guardian*, 31 Jan. 1889, p. 8.
[3] *Chester Chronicle*, 9 Feb. 1889, p. 8.

some affinities to eighteenth-century conditions of electoral truce. A copy of the agreement signed by the Conservative and Liberal whips in January 1913 has survived. Each party agreed not to oppose sitting members, but 'if in any case this is found to be impossible we will each at once inform the other of the fact and thereupon the other party shall be at liberty to attack a similar number of opposition seats . . . '.[1] The chief danger to these arrangements came from recalcitrant members of each party or eccentric independents who insisted on causing a contest. The Labour party, which did not belong to the existing patterns of county patronage, could not abide by 'gentlemen's agreements' made informally in the council chamber, and therefore in order to secure a hearing was compelled to cause contests. But the real Labour challenge was not made until the 1920's, and the beginning of a Labour group on the council stemmed from two successes in the election of 1928. Before then, the Labour party had little chance of success, even in the boroughs. Two individual Socialists were successful, James Mort in Macclesfield in 1904,[2] the first Labour county councillor, and William Plant in Sale in 1922, but neither of them survived more than the three-year life of the council. The number of councillors who were Independents before the First World War was very small, and in the early years consisted entirely of Liberal Unionists. Two Independents were returned in 1907, and five in 1910.[3] The business of the council was therefore arranged by two main parties.

The management of policy was decided by both parties in 'caucus' meetings at Crewe. The County Council followed the precedent of Quarter Sessions by arranging to hold all its committee meetings in the Crewe Arms Hotel beside the railway station, which was the most accessible place in the county. The first party whips in the council chamber were both Crewe doctors, Dr. James Atkinson for the Conservatives and Dr. William Hodgson for the Liberals. Atkinson had married into the 'railway aristocracy' of Crewe, calling his house in Crewe after his wife's Christian name. She was the daughter of John Hill, the first railway contractor for the lines which became the property of the London and North Western Railway. Atkinson himself became medical officer to the L.N.W.R. and both his daughters married L.N.W.R. servants, that is, if the vicar of Christ

[1] Copy enrolled in the minute book of the Conservative and Unionist 'caucus' (in the possession of the Conservative whip).
[2] *Manchester Guardian*, 29 Feb. 1904, p. 11.
[3] *Chester Courant*, 9 Mar. 1910.

Church, Crewe, a L.N.W.R. living, may be classed with a carriage superintendent as a company servant. He had been the first mayor of Crewe and leader of the Crewe Conservatives.[1] Hodgson, who was only 35 and one of the youngest members of the County Council, was already leading the opposition to Conservative and L.N.W.R. control in Crewe Town Council; he was closely associated with the success of W. S. B. McLaren, Liberal M.P. for the Crewe division.[2] Atkinson had been a county magistrate for the Nantwich division since 1878; Hodgson was the only leading Liberal in the county to remain outside the county commission of the peace.[3] The railways had made Crewe the centre of Cheshire, and the organization of local politics had to recognize its supremacy.

The election of nineteen aldermen by the first council in February 1889 provided the first occasion for negotiation between the opposing parties. The council was encouraged to look outside its own members when selecting its aldermen. The leaders of each of the two principal parties, Lord Egerton of Tatton for the Conservatives and Joseph Beckett, a Chester milliner and general draper, for the Gladstonian Liberals, circularized a list of names among their friends, and at the first meeting of the council led their respective followers into separate committee rooms in order to secure party approval for their candidates. The only self-confessed Liberal Unionist to be elected a councillor, J. J. Evans, was deputed to act as an ambassador between the contending parties. A list of names was eventually approved by the whole council from the recommendations of a special informal committee chosen by the 'caucus' meetings.[4] Nine aldermen were to retire after three years and ten after six years; and thereafter half the aldermen were to retire every three years. When the time of the first retirement came round in 1892, the party whips declared a truce, and agreed that all the aldermen, whatever their party, would be re-elected. The Liberal councillors signed a paper to the effect that they would vote for the Conservative aldermen which was then lodged with Dr. Atkinson; the Conservative councillors for their part gave similar assurances to Dr. Hodgson. In spite of Lord Egerton's protest that such papers had no legal validity, this arrangement was the beginning of a series of compromises which established the

---

[1] Chaloner, *Crewe*, pp. 145–7, 152–3.
[2] '*Fasciculus Cestriensis*': *a Collection of Essays in Honour of Sir William Hodgson* (1934).
[3] Hodgson was a very zealous Baptist and advocate of non-sectarian religious instruction in schools.   [4] *Chester Chronicle*, 16 Feb. 1889, p. 8.

tradition that each party should have a number of aldermen in proportion to its number of councillors, one alderman to three councillors.[1] This tradition in 1934 gave its first alderman to the Labour party.

The election of the council's first permanent chairman was also a matter of party politics. Lord Egerton of Tatton had secured the post of temporary chairman by four votes in a division of the council on strict party lines with only two exceptions, both Liberal magistrates who voted with the Conservatives.[2] The Liberal party in the council prevented his succession to the permanent chairmanship by promoting another Conservative candidate whom they found more agreeable, Duncan Graham, the head of Graham, Rowe & Co., South American merchants in Liverpool and the chairman of the Wirral bench of magistrates.[3] On Graham's retirement in March 1893, the Liberals again supported a Conservative as chairman, Charles Lister, the former Registrar of Manchester County Court and the representative for Lymm. But a 'caucus' meeting at Crewe of Conservatives and Unionists led by the Duke of Westminster decided to back the election of George Dixon, the squire of Astle Hall near Chelford and the representative for Alderley.[4] Dixon remained chairman of the council until 1922.

The leaders and whips of each party were naturally concerned to secure the maximum number of their supporters in the appointments to the principal committees of the council. The first standing orders provided for five standing committees, two of which, General Purposes and Contagious Diseases of Animals, were committees of the whole council.[5] The three other committees, Finance, Main Roads, and Lunatic Asylums, were constructed on strict party lines. If the chairman came from one party, the deputy-chairman was chosen from the other. The Finance Committee under the chairmanship of Dr. Atkinson, the Conservative whip, contained 30 members: 14 Conservatives, 14 Liberals, and 2 Liberal Unionists. The Main Roads Committee under the chairmanship of Joseph Beckett, the Liberal leader, contained 36 members: 17 Conservatives, 18 Liberals, and 1 Liberal Unionist.[6] Party organization secured the tradition that the composition of committees should reflect the composition of the council as nearly as possible.

[1] Ibid., 19 Mar. 1892, p. 5.
[2] Ibid., 9 Feb. 1889, p. 8.
[3] Ibid., 12 Jan. 1901, p. 6.
[4] Ibid., 11 Mar. 1893, p. 8.
[5] *County Council Standing Orders* (1889).
[6] *County Council Year Book* (1891).

The refusal of Quarter Sessions to accept the traditions of party discipline was demonstrated in the discussions which preceded the establishment of the new police authority under the provisions of the 1888 Act, usually called the Standing Joint Committee. Lord Egerton of Tatton, as chairman of the bench, tried to limit the number of its members to twenty-three, but was overruled by a majority of his own party. After a private conference between groups from both parties, Conservatives and Liberals, which met at Knutsford, it was agreed that one magistrate and one county councillor should be chosen from each of the fourteen petty sessional divisions, making twenty-eight, to which would be added the chairman and vice-chairman of the County Council and Quarter Sessions, thus bringing the committee to a total membership of thirty-two. In appointing their quota, the County Council followed a strict party pattern: 8 Conservatives and 8 Liberals. In contrast, the quota appointed by Quarter Sessions lacked any recognition of party organization. Four were already aldermen (3 Conservatives and 1 Liberal) and two already county councillors (1 Conservative and 1 Liberal). Although two prominent Liberal magistrates were included, the remaining eight members were chiefly Conservatives, including Lord Egerton as chairman and Horatio Lloyd, the County Court judge, as vice-chairman.[1]

Administrative methods and local reputation

The manner of conducting county council business before the First World War made it possible for both councillor and county official to gain the same reputation for a knowledge of technical detail and a skill in public administration. The Local Government Act of 1888 did not create a new profession of county administrators within the first few years of its operation; it was put into practice by the same men and with the same methods as were used by the bench of Quarter Sessions. Just as the councillors gave freely of their spare time in public service, like the magistrates before them, so the leading officials frequently took in 'county work' with the day-to-day running of a private practice. The 'administrative revolution' in county government did not take place until after the First World War and was not consolidated and formalized until after the Second World War. In terms of administrative methods, the Local Government Act of 1929 is far more important than that of 1888.

[1] *Chester Chronicle*, 9 Mar. 1889, p. 3; 23 Mar. 1889, p. 6.

The effects of the Act of 1888 itself, the methods of appointment used by the new County Council, and the type of work with which it was concerned, all point to this conclusion.

Local interests successfully lobbied the Commons and the Local Government Board to ensure that the Act brought comparatively little harm to those in established offices and to those with established privileges. James Williams, the County Accountant, who wrote a small pamphlet on the effects of the 1888 Act for local circulation,[1] managed to lobby Parliament to alter the draft Bill in such a way that he could retain the office of accountant which he had secured from Quarter Sessions in 1886, and not be replaced by the district auditor.[2] The new County Council in fact abolished the office of County Treasurer, who was replaced by the representative of a bank, and increased the salary of the County Accountant from £250 to £400 a year.[3] The firm of solicitors belonging to the Potts family, which had occupied Northgate House in Chester since its erection in 1779, was also able to retain its hold upon the clerkship of the council, in spite of the fact that the head of the business was suffering from a mental illness brought upon by attacks of jaundice, which had incapacitated him since the early 1880's.[4] C. W. Potts, the clerk of the peace, was therefore incapable of performing the functions of his office and was too insane to authorize the appointment of a deputy. He nevertheless became the first Clerk of the County Council. His son and heir, Reginald Potts, replaced the former deputy clerk of the peace in 1890, and soon afterwards, on the death of the clerk, became both clerk of the peace and Clerk of the County Council.[5] Reginald Potts remained in these offices until his own death in 1931, a tenure lasting over forty years, during which so much new legislation added to the burdens of county administration. Yet throughout this time the clerk's department of the County Council continued to be part of the Potts family business in Northgate House, the family home. Reginald Potts, whose salary as Clerk was increased to £2,500 in 1891, was expected to recruit and pay his own staff out of the money he received from the county. He appears to have employed never more than twenty people in the administration of strictly county business, and there was a far greater affinity between his methods and those of his father, than between his methods and those of his

---

[1] No copies appear to have survived; see *Chester Chronicle*, 16 Mar. 1889, p. 8.   [2] Public Record Office, M.H. 30/30.
[3] Ibid., 30/31, file no. 69408/90.   [4] Ibid., 30/31, file no. 10963/90.
[5] *Chester Chronicle*, 15 Mar. 1890, p. 5.

successor, the first full-time Clerk.[1] The 'administrative revolution' could only take place after the Potts family interest had been liquidated.

The most determined lobbying in 1888 was that of the leading magistrates who were anxious that the provisions in the Act for transferring the property of Quarter Sessions to the new County Council should expressly include a subsidy known as 'the Weaver surplus'. Quarter Sessions had a great advantage over the County Council because it was able to subsidize the rate funds from the profits of the collection of tolls on the Weaver Navigation. The trustees of the latter, who were largely county magistrates, were authorized by a local Act of Parliament to pay their annual surplus into the hands of the county treasurer, and between 1778 and 1894 the county ratepayers benefited to the extent of receiving £1,090,610.[2] In some years the surplus was large, in some it was small, according to the number of plans which the trustees might have in hand for capital expenditure on improving the navigation. But like the theoretical advantage of financing local government from assigned revenues, it was supposed to increase in value as the trade and prosperity of the area increased. The County Council made every effort to retain the privilege of taking the Weaver surplus in order to subsidize the county rates, and in 1895 they fought the Bill which was promoted by the users of the navigation, who naturally believed that any surplus should be directed towards a lowering of the tolls rather than towards the financing of county government.[3] The principle proclaimed by the users was maintained in Parliament, and the new County Council was compelled to surrender its traditional right to the Weaver surplus. One of the chief reasons given for the unwillingness of Cheshire boroughs to petition for their own Quarter Sessions and their own right to levy rates, in the case of Macclesfield, for example,[4] was that any borough securing this independence would be compelled to forgo the benefits accruing to the county by the Acts governing the Weaver Navigation. Certainly in 1891, when the new county boroughs of Birkenhead, Chester, and Stockport were disputing with the new County Council over the division of the funds from the new Exchequer Contribution Account for assigned revenues,

---

[1] Personal information of Mr. Henry Potts.
[2] A. F. Calvert, *Salt in Cheshire* (1915), p. 480.
[3] *County Council Printed Minutes*, ii. 69–70; iii. 21–25, 34–35, 149–154; iv. 115–31, 157–8.
[4] *Report of Select Committee on Local Taxation*, H.C. 353, *Q.* 5332, 5352 (1870), viii.

the right of the county boroughs to a share in the Weaver surplus was hotly debated.[1] The latter was then estimated to be between £10,000 and £15,000 a year.

The creation of county boroughs by the 1888 Act naturally involved the county in some financial loss. Chester had for a long time been financially independent of the county, but the promotion of Birkenhead and Stockport to county borough status involved the county in a loss of rateable value of about £457,000 and £161,000 respectively. When the County Council succeeded Quarter Sessions in March 1889, the rateable value of the county was £3,139,304. Financial adjustments with the county boroughs and the Agricultural Derating Act of 1896 decreased the value to about £2,800,000, and the 1889 figure was not recovered until 1899. On the whole, the County Council started its life with considerable financial assets. It was allocated three-quarters of the funds earmarked for the county in the new Exchequer Contribution Account, the remaining quarter being divided among the three county boroughs. Its finances remained in the charge of the accountant who had served Quarter Sessions, James Williams, and he continued in his post until 1915.

The County Council inherited both the officials of Quarter Sessions and also the methods which the magistrates had developed for making their own appointments. Beside those of Clerk and County Accountant mentioned above, the posts of Surveyor, Analyst, Treasurer, and Chief Constable all remained in the same hands when power was transferred to the County Council in March 1889. The standing orders drawn up in March 1889 provided only machinery for the appointment of chief officials and left the employment of subordinates to their discretion. In the event of a vacancy at chief officer level the Finance Committee was required to discuss any proposed changes in salary, and the method of appointment was to take votes in the council chamber on the merits of a given list of candidates until one had received an over-all majority. This method was in direct imitation of Quarter Sessions. Both the County Surveyor, Stanhope Bull, and the County Analyst, J. C. Bell of Manchester, had been appointed in this manner at the Sessions of 1876 by an open vote of magistrates on a short list which had been prepared by a special committee. Mr. Bull remained with the County Council until his resignation in 1896, when he was succeeded by his son, H. F. Bull. Dr. Bell, who was also analyst to Salford,

[1] *Report of Local Government Act Com.* (C. 6839), pp. 329–46 (1892), xxxvii.

Birkenhead, Congleton, Stalybridge, and Glossop as well as consultant chemist to other authorities, remained in the post until his death in 1913.[1] The terms of Mr. Bull's appointment in 1876 as County Surveyor and Bridgemaster stated explicitly that he should be allowed to remain in private practice as a surveyor and land agent, provided the work did not hinder the progress of county business.[2] The County Council continued the custom of employing professional people with other business interests.

The local government service in the counties was not able to develop a strong professional spirit while the duties of county councils were confined to the maintenance of a few services. The 1872 Public Health Act had given the county some of its first professionals, the medical officers of health, who were employed by the urban and rural sanitary districts. Dr. J. M. Fox was supervising the whole of mid-Cheshire in 1878.[3] But the chief items in the county budget were small compared with the amounts spent by the large county boroughs, and the latter pursued such a vigorous policy of territorial expansion that their rateable value rapidly outpaced that of the counties. Taxable wealth lay in urban areas. By 1900 the rateable value of Liverpool and Manchester in each case exceeded that of Cheshire, and remained so until 1956. Until 1910 the total expenditure of Cheshire County Council in any given year did not exceed £500,000, while Manchester was spending as much as Cheshire on its highways and sewers, quite apart from all the health and cleansing services which the county did not maintain. The Technical Instruction Act of 1890 laid upon the County Council the duty of creating a new department outside the Quarter Sessions tradition, and of appointing a Director of Education. The Education Act of 1902 set this new department on its feet, and the education service rapidly became the chief item in the county budget. Before 1902 the Director of Education was primarily concerned with the administration of small subsidies for technical training, and of the Reaseheath Agricultural College and the Worleston Dairy School. The latter had been established by a private trust.[4] Each department in the council's care tended to act as an autonomous body. As its responsibilities grew, the county's offices were scattered all over Chester; the Clerk in Northgate House; the Treasurer at the Castle; the Director of Education

[1] *Manchester Red Book* (1913); *Manchester Faces and Places*, iv. 166.
[2] Cheshire Record Office, Quarter Sessions Minutes of Miscellaneous County Committees, 1870–93.   [3] Public Record Office, M.H. 30/30, file no. 110069/84.
[4] V. Cheke, *The History of Cheese-making in Britain* (1959).

in City Road; the Surveyor (after 1935) in Watergate House. It needed the impact of the Local Government Act of 1929 to force the County Council into considering the provision of central offices for all departments.

Before 1929 therefore and particularly before the First World War, both councillors and officials were almost on an equal footing in terms of local reputation for administrative ability. The conscientious councillor had as much chance as the part-time official to make himself familiar with the details of legislation. County councillors were in fact known for devotion and efficiency in county business. For instance, in the years about the turn of the century before the motor-car became common, the chairman of the Main Roads Committee, Joseph Beckett, received a great deal of praise for the excellent condition of Cheshire roads. Cyclists were particularly grateful.[1] Beckett, who kept a draper's shop in Eastgate Row, Chester, but lived in a country house on the southern borders of the county near Whitchurch, retired from the County Council in 1904. Perhaps a more striking example of the lack of a clear distinction between the elected representative and professional official was the fact that it was then possible for the clerk of a small urban or rural authority to sit on the County Council. This was a rare occurrence after 1918 and impossible after 1929. Algernon Fletcher, the clerk of the Northwich R.D.C. and also a solicitor, was elected county councillor for North-wich in 1904. The town clerk of Dukinfield, T. H. Gordon, was also chairman of Tarporley U.D.C. and county councillor for Dukinfield; he became an alderman in 1916. The clerk to the Marple U.D.C. and to the Stockport Board of Guardians, C. F. Johnson, was also county councillor for Marple from 1895 to 1898. The majority of the councillors, like the majority of the magistrates, accepted the assumption of the landed gentry who had served before them, that it was their duty as trustees for posterity to maintain the county inheritance intact. The historic boundaries of the shire continued to have a significance of their own. The County Council offered notable resistance, for example, to the idea of losing the small strip of land which lay between the Manchester Ship Canal and the River Mersey. Lancashire first broached the subject of making the county boundary follow the canal in 1897, and the matter was frequently revived, particularly in 1904[2] and 1914. But Cheshire did not reach agreement

---

[1] *Warrington Guardian*, 19 Feb. 1898, p. 4; 16 Feb. 1901, p. 4.
[2] Ibid., 13 Feb. 1904, p. 3.

about this until 1932, and then only under the threat of a parliamentary Bill promoted by Warrington. The County Council was similarly
adamant in rejecting the suggestion of the Boundary Commission
in 1888 that Tintwistle, the extreme north-eastern parish of the county
which formed a 'pan-handle' running between Derbyshire and the
West Riding of Yorkshire, should be joined to Derbyshire, in spite
of the fact that the majority of its inhabitants appear to have been in
favour of such an alteration.[1]

Government by social leaders

Only a few councillors took advantage of the opportunity for
participating in routine administration. The burden of the work fell
upon the shoulders of those who were willing to spend the time it
required. While it is true to say that the County Council inherited
the methods of Quarter Sessions in making policy decisions at
occasional meetings, like a board of directors who leave the day-to-
day administration to the managerial class, it would be wrong to
suppose that the new services which the council was required to perform did not cause certain adaptations of the traditional methods
of business. The county's welfare demanded greater devotion to duty
from the chairman, vice-chairman, the party whips, and an 'inner
ring' of councillors. Yet these changes were hardly perceptible while
the nature of 'county society' appeared to remain stable, and there
is a political unity about the period from 1893 to 1922 when Sir
George Dixon was chairman. The atmosphere of local politics before
the end of the First World War was very different, politically, socially,
and administratively, from that prevailing during the 1930's. Some
of the most fundamental changes were made before 1914, but the
survival of 'county society' satisfactorily disguised their consequences.

The higher a person stood in the hierarchy of county society, the
less likely he was to attend any meetings. Also the higher a person
stood, the less likely he was to be summoned to a large number of
committee meetings. In 1898-9 those who received the least number
of summonses to attend committees or sub-committees included the
Duke of Westminster and Lord Tollemache, who headed the great
political patrons of the shire. It is not surprising that the burden of
the administrative routine of both Quarter Sessions and County
Council should have fallen to the lot of a few people, but it is worthy

[1] Public Record Office, M.H. 30/31, file nos. 58854/89; 89358/89.

of note that the two groups did not contain the same class of person. Quarter Sessions were dominated by those families who had political connexions with the great landowners, while the petty sessions were run by many new magistrates from the business class. The County Council was dominated by a group of conscientious members, while the majority of councillors concentrated upon the leadership of their own communities. A significant feature of the early history of the County Council was that the great landowners who controlled the political representation of the shire wished to treat this new institution as they had treated the old—by attending only when they wished to be consulted. They tried to perpetuate the *ex officio* principle which gave the magistrate the right to attend a meeting of any public body and this was done most easily by securing a nomination as a county alderman. In 1898–9 ten of the nineteen aldermen were among the least active members who were summoned to less than forty committee meetings in the year, and six of these made less than half the number of possible attendances. In that year, when the party whips were putting in more than 150 appearances at committee meetings, the Duke of Westminster was seen seven times, Sir Philip Grey-Egerton nine times, and Lord Tollemache only sixteen. Only four aldermen served as the chairmen of any committees. The increased burden of administrative work therefore attached greater importance to the need for regular attendance at committee meetings. Those who performed this function constituted the model for the county councillor as a 'public person', but before the First World War each of the regular attenders remained a social leader in his own community, usually an urban area. The gradual drifting away of the great landowners from county council business, first by disinclination and second by economic changes, tended to break the tradition that public service was the privilege of those with the requisite social standing.

Two features of impending change were apparent before 1914. In the first place, the number of necessary meetings was expanding as the amount of work increased. About 1900 over 5,000 summonses were issued a year to seventy-six councillors for their attendance at committee meetings; by 1910 this figure had risen to 9,500. Before 1900 only about six or seven people had received more than 120 summonses a year, but by 1911–12 there were twenty-five in receipt of that number. This figure became the established pattern. In the second place, the idea was growing that the election of aldermen should be a reward for conscientious service as a councillor, and not a token of social standing in the county. As the first aldermen died off or resigned, the senior councillors expected promotion.

The convention had been established that the aldermen retiring after their six-year term of office should be re-elected without opposition unless they wished to resign. If death or resignation brought a vacancy, the party whips came to an agreement that the election should be decided by whichever party had the right by virtue of its strength on the council to make the next nomination. While the Conservatives and Liberals enjoyed equal success, the aldermanic bench was divided between them. Each party caucus filled its own vacancies by election among its members. William Bromley-Davenport in 1912 was the last alderman to be chosen from outside the council. Since that date all aldermen have been promoted councillors. At the party caucus meeting which made that decision, those Conservatives who thought that 'good service inside the Council should be recognised first' insisted upon an insertion in the minutes that the nomination of Bromley-Davenport was 'an entirely exceptional case under special circumstances' and that he should be asked to resign if he were re-elected to Parliament.[1] Before 1912 when it was still possible for aldermen to be selected from outside the members of the council, their nomination was always considered in relation to the representation of geographical areas. An alderman was another democratic representative. When Alderman Kay died in 1907, for instance, the Conservatives were anxious that his successor should be chosen from west Cheshire, because they had only one alderman for this region whereas the eastern and central areas of the county each had four.[2] They therefore nominated R. T. Richardson of Capenhurst, but only on condition that 'he can assure the party there is reasonable ground for believing that his seat on the council will not be lost to our party'.[3] In promoting a councillor to the aldermanic bench, good care was taken that this action would not endanger the balance of power which the parties maintained. One of the essential features of a permanent electoral truce was the need to minimize possible grounds for conflict.

The end of this system could only be brought about by the councillors' own insistence that the alderman should be chosen from the

[1] Minutes of the Conservative party caucus (in the possession of the Conservative whip).
[2] *Chester Courant*, 17 July 1907, p. 4.
[3] Minutes of the Conservative party caucus.

senior members of the council, regardless of the possible consequences to each party, or by the challenge of a new party which was not a partner to the bargain. After 1919 the Independents and the Labour party upset these neat arrangements, and the convention was established that each party should promote its members to the aldermanic bench in order of seniority. The number of vacancies allotted to each party depended upon its strength in the council. Three councillors elected gave the right to nominate one alderman. The result of this new system was of course a complete abandonment of the principle that an alderman also represented a geographical area. In 1931 there were no aldermen at all living in north central Cheshire; in 1911 this fact would not have passed unnoticed. The system created a new ambition. The pattern was established that any councillor who could survive four consecutive triennial elections or give a minimum of 10 to 15 years' service was likely to be elected an alderman and remain in that office for life. This pattern was already emerging before 1914, and this ambition was first voiced, significantly enough, at the Conservative caucus meeting.

This change in the nomination of aldermen had two important consequences. First of all, it gradually severed the County Council's personal connexions with Parliament. Secondly, it converted the office of alderman, from a position of honour in which an influential man could be placed in order to be consulted, to a possible position of power in which an experienced councillor could gain many chairmanships and other political rewards. Before the First World War there were between fifteen and twenty county councillors and aldermen with parliamentary experience, either as members for the county divisions of the shire or for places outside Cheshire. An M.P., such as W. B. Brocklehurst (from 1906 to 1918) or James Tomkinson (from 1900 to 1910), retained his seat as a county councillor during the period he served in the Commons, just as 'county members' before 1888 were automatically placed in the county commission of the peace. Furthermore, county councillors included men who were regarded as the only suitable parliamentary candidates for county divisions. Duncan Graham and Christopher Kay were several times invited to stand for Parliament by the Conservatives, and it was not unusual for Liberal county councillors before 1914 to be chosen as parliamentary candidates for leading an attack upon Conservative seats. When the leader of the Liberals, Joseph Beckett, had declined to stand, another county councillor, Roger Bate, was invited to fight the Eddisbury division in 1895. Peter Jones, the unsuccessful Liberal candidate for the Wirral division at the first General Election of 1910, became county councillor for Neston in 1913. The nomination of Thomas Peacock, the councillor for Tarvin Rural, as National Liberal candidate at the Eddisbury by-election of 1943, was a reversion to a

TABLE 3

Leading Members of the Council: 1900

		Party		Alder-men	No. of years' service	Chairmen committees	Vice-chairmen committees	Occupation	Age
		Cons.	Lib.						
(a) Chairman	(1)	×	..	×	11	(ex officio members of all committees)		Gentleman	58
Vice-chairman	(2)	..	×	..	11	..	..	Merchant	51
(b) Party whips	(3)	×	..	×	11	..	..	Mining engineer	68
	(4)	..	×	..	11	Weights and Measures	..	Doctor	46
(c) Members with best attendance record	(5)	×	..	..	11	..	Small Holdings	Farmer	c. 80
	(6)	..	×	×	8	..	Roads and Bridges	..	..
	(7)	..	×	×	11	..	..	Coal merchant	..
	(8)	×	..	×	11	..	..	Gentleman	60
	(9)	..	×	..	11	..	Tech. Instruction	Farmer	75
	(10)	×	..	..	8	..	..	Solicitor	56
	(11)	×	..	..	11	Tech. Instruction	..	Gentleman	51
	(12)	..	×	..	11	..	Weights and Measures	Farmer	..

practice which had almost been forgotten. By the 1920's the links with Parliament, which rested partly on the convention of electing social leaders and partly on the office of alderman, had been broken.[1]

There is no better indication of the new significance of the office of alderman than an analysis of the 'inner ring' of the council—those who did the bulk of its committee work. The most striking feature of such an analysis (see Tables 13, 14, and 15) is the consistency of the period after 1920 compared with the period before it. After 1920 the

---

[1] H. E. R. Peers, councillor for Bollington, elected 1959, was Conservative candidate for Carlisle in 1950—i.e. not a local division (see below, p. 177); B. L. Butcher, councillor for Wilmslow, elected 1961, was Conservative candidate for Bishop Auckland in 1951, and for Widnes in 1959 (see below, pp. 163–4).

most regular attenders at committee meetings tended to be aldermen and the leading chairmen of the council. But during the first thirty years of the council's life, 1889–1919, many councillors held the leading chairmanships, and many aldermen were among those with the poorest record of attendance at meetings. About 1900, 17 of the 21 leading chairmanships and vice-chairmanships were held by councillors; about 1920, the equivalent figure was only 5 out of 15.

TABLE 4

Leading Members of the Council: 1910

		Party			Alder-men	No. of years' service	Chairmen committees	Vice-chairmen committees	Occupation	Age
		Cons.	Lib.	Ind.						
(a) Chairman	(1)	×	..	..	×	21	(*ex officio* members of all committees)		Gentleman	68
Vice-chairman	(2)	..	×	..	×	21	..	..	Doctor	56
(b) Party whips	(3)	×	..	..	×	12	County Rate	..	Barrister	48
	(4)	..	×	..	..	12	..	..	Draper	78
(c) Members with best attendance record	(5)	..	..	..	..	9	..	Midwives	Clergy (C. of E.)	59
	(6)	..	×	..	..	21	..	..	Silk manufctr.	61
	(7)	..	×	..	..	15	Standing Orders	..	Solicitor	61
	(8)	×	..	..	..	12	..	..	Analytical chemist	42
	(9)	×	..	..	..	3	..	..	Gentleman	52
	(10)	..	..	×	..	3	..	..	Architect	c. 40
	(11)	..	×	..	×	21	Public Health	..	Director: chemical firm	c. 70
	(12)	×	..	..	..	1	..	..	Farmer	..

The nature of the change can be seen by comparing the 'inner ring' of 1900 with that of 1910. The latter has noticeably more professional people and more representatives of urban areas than the former (see Tables 3 and 4). Each of these groups of twelve people (including the chairman and vice-chairman of the council) put in about a third of all the possible attendances at committee meetings.

County government by social leaders about 1910 must not be confused with the image of county government by landed gentry about 1840 or even county government by the newly recruited magistrates about 1880. A glance at the names of those who paid regular attention to the business just before the First World War shows how quickly control was passing to professional people from suburban areas. Yet the association with the landed gentry and the social leaders who made suitable parliamentary candidates for the county divisions remained in force until after the First World War. Only the social changes of the 1920's could bring about the abandonment of social leadership as a principle of local politics.

CONCLUSION

THE main thesis of Part II is that the government of the countryside was transformed between 1840 and 1880 by the building of railways and the availability of land for residential and industrial development. Land commanded a new price. By altering the composition of that body of persons who considered themselves to be the *élite* of the county, this social revolution destroyed the rule of the magistrates and landowners who had expected to be consulted on all public affairs as *ex officio* members of various local authorities. It broke down the traditional division between the institutions and conventions of town and country, and raised up in their stead new social distinctions and the opportunity for new local authorities. But it did not remove immediately the need for considerable social standing as a qualification for public service. The landed gentry were displaced from their monopoly of local politics by new social leaders.

The impetus for social and political change came from the expanding urban areas. They were the first to develop suitable conditions for the growth of a full-time professional service in the pay of local authorities. Every borough and urban district council was anxious to break away from the tutelage of the county magistrates. The politicians who led this movement were usually social leaders of each town who gave generous contributions for the maintenance of its welfare. The upper middle classes who had made their wealth out of the expansion of urban industry settled in the countryside as neighbours of the landed gentry and brought new principles of politics into the county. Common interests and activities soon encouraged the merger of the landed and the business interests. The few landed families who had control of the politics of the shire quickly found a great deal of common ground between themselves and new industrialists and merchants. The squires who depended for their income on small country estates were the chief members of the governing class to suffer. The aristocratic patrons only extended the scope of their activities to places outside the county to such an extent that they began to place the whole conception of social leadership in considerable danger. The new county society could only retain its importance while those with the requisite social standing continued to perform their local government duties conscientiously.

In terms of electioneering and the arrangement of administrative business, the new situation brought a greater importance to the organizations of political parties. The methods of party warfare developed in the boroughs were also extended to the county. The first County Council was strongly influenced by the parties in making its first standing orders and conventions of debate; its composition was a mirror reflecting the social change of the previous forty years. It was not socially homogeneous like Quarter Sessions before the 1840's but an aggregate made up from the social leaders of all urban areas and the members of the new county society. They were all linked together by their ability and their stake in the community.

Before the First World War the only sign that the principle of social standing as the sole criterion for public service might not be able to survive was a change in the business of the County Council itself. After the 1902 Education Act it became apparent that more frequent meetings were necessary and that the council would have to rely more and more on professional experts. In particular, the education services required some form of planning which introduced a new element of professionalism. Professional people in private practice could not take on this aspect of county council business as part of their normal routine. These new functions required some adjustments in the habits of county councillors. It gradually became necessary for the efficient dispatch of business that the burden of the committee work should fall on the shoulders of a few dependable councillors who appreciated the needs of the situation. This tendency led to the beginning of a divergence between those who ran the County Council and those who considered themselves 'county society'. The conception of a public person rests upon a knowledge of the reliable 'committee man' who has the confidence of the professional officers, and not of the gentleman performing a social duty. The social changes of the 1920's and 1930's, which are the chief concern of Part III, brought the next phase in the transformation of county government.

PART III

PUBLIC PERSONS

INTRODUCTION

BOTH councillors and officials have for a long time been aware of great changes in the practice of county government which have taken place since the period between the First and Second World Wars, particularly since the Local Government Act of 1929, but they have always found it difficult to isolate any specific reason for this development which has only a local origin from all the causes which were responsible for the transformation of the British State during the same period—the redistribution of incomes, the increase in educational opportunities, the amalgamation of large industries, the growth of the public sector, and the extension of governmental activity in personal, health, and welfare services. The change in local government is correctly attributed to forces at work throughout the whole political process. Local authorities are now more conscious of their role as agents of the central administration than of their power to initiate legislative action, and this feeling of subordination discourages any self-examination which might throw light upon the impact which 'mass society' has made on local conditions of work, or upon the apparent loss of prestige which local authorities have suffered.

Explanations tendered for this state of affairs are frequently concerned only with the need to improve the quality of elected councillors, as if a solution to this problem would automatically restore local authorities to their former independence. Political parties try to find the 'right candidate', often with great difficulty, and local government officials try to educate new councillors in the technical details of modern administrative methods. Some people tend to regret the passing of the social leader and to regard the years before the First World War as a kind of 'golden age' in which 'local government was really local'. The former autonomy of local authorities is largely a myth associated with the superior social standing and political influence of social leaders. Those who believe in the benefits of government by the gentry dislike the prospect of government by trade unionists or councillors drawn from the working classes. But even the Conservative party can no longer rely on the public services of persons with considerable social standing. There is clearly no longer a 'governing class' with its own social *mores*. How then does the local government system of part-time and unpaid politicians continue to operate? In the absence of a 'governing class', what is it that brings people into public life and the work of local authorities?

It would be wrong to suggest that the modern councillor only gives of his services in the hope that he might be rewarded by being elected an alderman, or appointed a magistrate, or even awarded a place in the Honours List. The motives of a public person are hard to determine. The councillor who is elected because of his drive and ability, and not because of his social station, may perform his duties in order to enjoy the thrills of office. This part of the book describes the evolution of the conditions in county government which have made it possible for a councillor who becomes a chairman, or a leading member of one of the committees, to perform the functions of a 'minister' in charge of a particular service. There are three aspects of this development. First, the economic and social changes of the inter-war years, described in Chapter 4, presented new problems of administration. Second, the full-time officials, described in Chapter 5, acquired greater technical skills for the guidance of councillors and placed themselves as important persons in public life. Third, the electoral process, described in Chapter 6, had to provide the councillors from which leaders were selected. There was some possibility that the political parties would find it hard to select candidates who were capable of dealing with the new administrative methods. All these changes make it clear that the responsibility for county government rested upon a combination of the chief officers with the leading councillors, which formed a kind of ministerialist party or 'inner ring'. The vitality of the administration depended upon the vigour of the few.

4

THE GOVERNMENT OF A CHANGING SOCIETY

THE effects of economic and social change on the national level are best seen in the transformation of local leadership. Before the economic catastrophes of 1929–31 the government of the countryside still appeared to rest upon the shoulders of social leaders and upon their sense of identification with the local community. The forces of change were those which destroyed the sense of 'community interest'. The period after 1929–31 witnessed the final stages in the process which made it difficult to equate the personal interests of political leaders with those of the areas which they represented. The electioneering methods of candidates in local elections before 1929 encouraged a high poll from a small electorate. The decline after 1929 in the proportion of those going to the poll, when at the same time the size of the electorate was in fact increasing, gave some indication of the growing disparity between the elector and his chosen representative.

If a 'governing class' no longer exists, what is it that brings unpaid councillors into the public service? It is hard to date exactly the arrival of a new type of councillor. Because a whole generation of young men died in the First World War, and because those then in local government frequently enjoyed a very long life, it sometimes seems as if county government in England remained in the hands of social leaders until the outbreak of the Second World War. The chairman and vice-chairman of Cheshire County Council in 1939 had originally been elected in 1907 and 1913 respectively. Even after 1945 several members of well-established gentry families continued to serve on local authorities and to perform various 'decorative functions' by lending their names to local organizations, thus creating the illusion that social leaders were still important. Both Altrincham and Bebington, for instance, chose a peer to be mayor in the year during which a borough charter had been secured, the Earl of Stamford and Viscount Leverhulme.

There were two important changes in the 1920's and 1930's which had far-reaching effects on local leadership. The first was a change in the manner in which local industries were organized; and the second, a change in the volume of both public and private transport which extended the distance between work-place and home for a large number of people in the 'great towns'. The former was part of the process by which the management of industry became more and more a professional occupation and less and less a business confined to those owning the capital. The latter belonged to the process of urbanization which covered large areas of the countryside with semi-detached or detached houses, each standing in its own garden. Local politics in which public persons played a part must always be associated with the building of new suburbs.

From the point of view of a county council, particularly in a county such as Cheshire where the 'overspill' of population from Liverpool and Manchester was already apparent, the chief problem of local government since the Act of 1929 has been the provision of services in those areas which are developing more rapidly than others. What kind of authority shall govern the new suburbs? This central question runs through all the disputes of the period. The contrast between social leaders and public persons can best be seen in the provisions which were made for administering suburbs built before 1914 and those made after 1929. Urban district councils were created for new urban areas before the First World War, just as local boards of health under the Act of 1858 were established in the late-nineteenth century by those businessmen from the 'great towns' who had migrated into the country. Any place which could show sufficient degree of social leadership was likely to set up its own local authority. In Cheshire the last authorities to be founded in this manner were the Urban District Councils of Ellesmere Port[1] and Hale. The latter, which dates from 1900, was almost entirely the creation of Alfred Tarbolton, its first chairman.[2] But after 1929, to petition for making a new authority was a rare occurrence because there were no social leaders to organize such an action. What kind of authority shall govern the new suburbs? After 1929 the central government answered this question only by allowing existing authorities to fight for the privilege. The boundary disputes between county councils and county boroughs which are predominant during the decade 1926–36, were in a large measure a reflection of the fact that the new suburbs did not accept the principles of social leadership or produce the kind of people who, in the prevailing opinion of the day, could be entrusted

[1] Established 1902.   [2] *Sale and Stretford Guardian*, 13 May 1935.

with the creation of a new authority. The new suburbs could only be administered by an adaptation of existing authorities, which was likely to alter radically the relationships between the County Council and its district councils. They also brought forth a new kind of person for the work of local government.

Forces of economic and social change

From all the complex changes of local society in Cheshire during the 1920's and 1930's, it is difficult to select those which had an immediate bearing upon the conduct of local government. An exhaustive description of such developments always runs the risk of sounding commonplace, because local evidence merely provides a commentary upon far wider changes which are taking place over the country as a whole. But the two changes already mentioned which were most important in connexion with the evolution of local government —the change by which local industries were organized and the change in the volume of transport—fortunately shared one common feature, as far as Cheshire was concerned, which makes it possible to isolate them from all other contemporary phenomena. The changes in Cheshire industry and transport both involved an intensification of the existing pattern of development rather than a creation of new patterns. Industry remained concentrated in those areas where it had been developed in the nineteenth century, the Wirral peninsula, the Weaver valley, and the Manchester region, and the system of transport generation by rail and by road continued to follow the lines which Victorian requirements had laid down. The county continued to be dominated by its northern neighbours. The new suburbs which proved to be such a strain on existing forms of local administration were primarily extensions of the great towns. The chief political problem stemmed from migration. Industrial firms stayed where they had begun and expanded on the same site, while they attracted more workers from a wider area because of the improved system of transport.

The industrial estate at Trafford Park near Manchester, for instance, on which development did not begin until 1896, provided a centre to which workers living in north and north-east Cheshire might be attracted. The existing firms of Lever Brothers at Bebington and Brunner, Mond Co. at Northwich expanded their manufacturing plant on the same site and were able to draw on a much larger labour force. Both attracted large numbers of migrants into the county and both provided classic examples of family firms developing into large international combines. In 1926 Alfred Mond of Brunner, Mond combined with H. C. McGowan of Nobel Explosives and other chemical companies to form the massive industrial concern of Imperial Chemical Industries. The Winnington works near Northwich have remained the headquarters of the I.C.I. Alkali Division. In 1929 Lever Brothers at Bebington was merged into the vast organization known as Unilever.

The real significance of such industrial developments for local politics is the gradual disappearance of the resident *entrepreneur* with strong local ties. The managers of large combines are far less likely to participate directly in the social and political activities of the district in which they live because they develop loyalties to a firm which possesses interests in places very remote from their homes. This was an important factor in the disappearance of 'social leadership'. The resident *entrepreneur*, the owner who lived in a large house beside his factory, became a rare figure after 1929, and his social leadership could not be relied upon to solve economic difficulties.

The depression of 1929 and the years of unemployment during the early 1930's proved finally the inadequacy of the methods of social leadership to cope with vast economic problems of the kind produced by industrial society in the twentieth century. Over 15 per cent. of the total number of insured persons in the county were still unemployed in March 1933. The highest rate of unemployment in Cheshire was in Birkenhead and Wallasey; any improvement there depended upon a return of prosperity to Merseyside as a whole. It did not really make sense to think of the problem of unemployment in terms of the geographical county. Yet the Clerk of the County Council, falling back upon the principles of social leadership, in February 1932 called a meeting of representatives of all local authorities at which the establishment of a development council was proposed.[1] Although this conference decided to elect a committee of ten representatives from urban authorities, the first members of the Cheshire Publicity and Industrial Development Council, which met in Chester on 9 May 1933, included six representatives of local industry and four who served in virtue of their position as local leaders, the Mayor and Bishop of Chester, the lord-lieutenant, and the M.P. for Northwich.[2] The failure of the development council to produce any effective action illustrates how different were the

[1] *Manchester Guardian*, 13 Feb. 1932, p. 13.
[2] *Cheshire Life* (Nov. 1934), p. 169.

conditions in industry during the 1930's from those in the period before 1914. Depression could not be solved by local leadership alone; it had to be tackled through the policy of the central government.

The improvements in transport provided one solution to local problems of unemployment. The changes in transport of the 1920's and 1930's gave greater flexibility for the management of industry in recruiting a labour force. For instance, in 1896 when John Summers moved his steel works from Stalybridge to the banks of the Dee near Hawarden Bridge, he found it impossible to recruit enough skilled men from the surrounding countryside and was therefore compelled to scatter his Stalybridge employees in lodgings all over the district near Chester until such time as the firm could afford to build a new model village for them, close to the factory, which it did in 1910–13.[1] Other firms also provided accommodation. Lever Brothers built a model village at Port Sunlight and Brunner, Mond Co. bought Owley Woods near Weaverham for a housing estate which was completed in 1922.[2] But after 1930 improved public transport allowed more rapid adjustments of the employment pattern. The map of the 'journey to work' based upon the 1921 Census gives the same general outline as the map of 1951, movements in and out of the centres around Liverpool and Manchester.[3] By 1951 the increased use of private transport had introduced many cross currents, but these were chiefly confined to conurbation areas.[4] After 1929 the managers of industry could afford to be less concerned where their workpeople had decided to settle.

New means of transport, particularly road transport, were primarily responsible for the building of the new suburbs. The motor bus and later the private car extended the distances which people were prepared to travel to work. The County Council was itself required by the Local Government Act of 1929 to take over from the district councils the responsibility for maintaining the surfaces of the majority of main roads because of the increased wear which they were receiving. The late-nineteenth-century tram routes on the Wirral and around Manchester were naturally confined to certain rails, but the new motor buses ranged far and wide over the countryside. The motor bus came into its own in the 1920's. The Stalybridge,

---

[1] W. H. Scott, *Technical Change and Industrial Relations* (1956), p. 41.
[2] See Map 2, facing p. 119.
[3] W. Dobson Chapman, *A Survey and Plan for Cheshire* (1948), opposite p. 74.
[4] e.g. H. B. Rodgers, 'Employment and the Journey to Work in an Overspill Community,' *Sociological Review* (VII (2), Dec. 1959), pp. 213–29.

Hyde, Dukinfield, and Mossley Electricity Board, which ran its first electric tram-car in 1904, turned to petrol buses for the first time in 1925.[1] It was a period of open warfare between 'one-man' bus services on the roads of the county, of 'buccaneering' and fighting in the streets for custom. The Crosville Company, which established almost a monopoly of the country bus services in the western half of the county and North Wales, did so by buying out its small competitors. Between 1919 and 1939 this company purchased 91 businesses, the majority of which were acquired after the L.M.S. Railway had secured a controlling interest in 1929–30. It began in 1911 by running two buses between Chester and Ellesmere Port, carrying some 80,000 passengers a year. By 1921, 45 buses were carrying 4 million people; by 1931, 580 buses carrying 49 million, and by 1941, 1,101 buses, 100 million.[2] The number of passengers carried is some indication of the degree of mobility which public transport offered.

The railways into Liverpool and Manchester, which continued to play an important part in carrying the workers of those cities, were supplemented after 1920 by many different bus companies and a whole series of running agreements between the transport departments of neighbouring boroughs.[3] There was no success in attempting to co-ordinate public transport by rail and public transport by road, and the Road Traffic Act of 1930 only made some semblance of order out of the chaos of free competition. Although the Manchester firm of Mather and Platt was responsible for the first electric 'tube' in London in 1890, the proposal to build an underground railway for Manchester, first made in 1902, was still being ineffectively discussed in 1936.[4] The only important improvement of public transport in Manchester was the electrification of the railway line to Altrincham and Bowdon in Cheshire in 1931.[5] Where the railways were in use, the new pattern of settlement was to a large extent dictated by the choice made in the more exclusive suburban developments of the late-nineteenth century.

The use of the private motor-car was not a predominant feature of the development of the new suburbs until after the Second World

[1] *Stalybridge Year Book* (1937), p. 59.
[2] W. J. Crosland Taylor, *Crosville: the Sowing and the Harvest* (1948), Appendix.
[3] W. J. M. Mackenzie and C. M. Higgins, 'The Co-ordination of Public Passenger Transport in S.E. Lancs.', *The Manchester School*, xxii (1954), pp. 276 ff.
[4] *Manchester Guardian*, 10 Jan. 1936, p. 11; 6 Feb. 1936, p. 13.
[5] Ibid., 11 May 1931; the electric train service from Bury to Manchester was opened in April 1916.

War, when it became increasingly common for the cost and running expenses to be paid for by the firm which employed the user. Although a Manchester councillor was denouncing the menace to traffic of the 'one-person motor' as early as 1936,[1] it was not until the 1950's when several new roads had been completed that such vehicles caused serious congestion. The outbreak of war in 1939 prevented the rapid development of motorway construction by local authorities, and after the war the Ministry of Transport took charge of planning a national system.

The total number of motor vehicles licensed in the county was some guide to the revolution in transport, but the returns made by traffic census were a more reliable source of information on the extent to which the greatest volume of traffic was confined to movement in and out of the conurbation areas. The number of vehicles licensed in Cheshire increased from 214 in 1907 to 244,548 in 1957. The most rapid increases took place in the 1930's and 1950's.[2] The greatest traffic problems arose on the principal routes in and out of Liverpool and Manchester and on the principal crossing-points of the Mersey. The projected building of a tunnel under the Mersey between Liverpool and Birkenhead prompted Lord Montagu in 1925 to make one of the first abortive suggestions for a motorway or toll road through the county from Birmingham to Birkenhead on one side, where the tunnel would connect it with Liverpool, and to Manchester on the other. This proposal was still being discussed in 1929,[3] but it required the co-operation of the many local authorities to make it possible. The tunnel under the Mersey, which was in fact completed and opened in 1934, did a great deal to encourage the use of the private motor-car and the building of residential areas on the Wirral. By 1959 the daily average number of vehicles using the tunnel was between 33,000 and 43,000.[4] Whenever an accident blocked the tunnel, traffic chaos in both Liverpool and Birkenhead ensued. Talks began in 1961 on the alternatives of building another tunnel or a new bridge. Further up the river, in the gap between Runcorn and Widnes, a transporter bridge opened in 1905, which was both slow and dangerous, provided the only means of crossing until a new bridge was opened in 1961.[5] This magnificent single-span construction was

[1] *Manchester Guardian*, 6 Feb. 1936, p. 13.
[2] There was a 40 per cent. increase each year during the 1950's.
[3] *Manchester Guardian*, 23 Oct. 1929, p. 4.
[4] *The Guardian*, 23 Dec. 1959, p. 12.
[5] *County Councils Gazette*, Nov. 1961, p. 258.

a monument to the co-operation between the County Councils of Lancashire and Cheshire, authorized by an Act of 1947, and opened new opportunities for swifter transport. The building of the principal roads out of Manchester was delayed by the Second World War. Kingsway, planned as early as 1908, was not laid down until 1921–3.[1] It did not provide a really effective entrance into the city until a new bridge over the Mersey had been opened in 1959.[2] Princess Parkway, completed in 1932, was going to be extended into Cheshire. The first talks on this extension were held in 1936,[3] but the probable route which it might take was not finally announced until 1960.[4] By then, the Ministry of Transport had announced its plans for the Birming-ham–Preston motorway (M. 6) which crossed the eastern half of the county.[5] The history of the Northwich by-pass typified this piecemeal development. The middle section, planned in the early thirties, was completed in 1939, but could not be properly used until the western and eastern sections had been added in 1958 and 1960 respectively.[6] The demand for new roads which the new suburbs created was met only in fits and starts, as the local authorities could find the neces-sary capital.

The irregular pulse of the process of urbanization in the 1930's and 1950's made a considerable contrast with the smoother developments in the building of suburbs before the First World War. The later expansion of the towns produced greater political tensions, partly because of sheer numbers, and partly because of the social ambitions of the class of persons making this migration which produced the psychology of the new suburbs. The tram suburbs were much more attached to their native city than the motor-bus suburbs and private-car suburbs. A leading article in the *Manchester Guardian* for New Year's Day, 1904, stressed that the decentralization of residence had nevertheless driven the diverse factors of 'Greater Manchester' 'towards a greater unification, a closer and more organic relation'. Such sentiments would not have made sense in the 1930's or 1950's. By that time the new suburbs were beginning to develop centres of their own. (The shopping centre at Wilmslow, for instance, was opened in 1956.) The migration from the 'great towns' had changed

[1] *Manchester Official Handbook* (1924), pp. 429–30.
[2] *The Guardian*, 13 Oct. 1959.
[3] *Manchester Evening Chronicle*, 17 Sept. 1936.
[4] *The Guardian*, 11 Jan. 1960.
[5] Ibid., 10 Dec. 1960.
[6] Ibid., 26 Nov. 1960.

the traditional political loyalties upon which the functioning of local authorities had depended.

The disappearance of social leaders

The changes in industry and transport removed the social leader from the local political scene. The politics of social leadership depended not only upon the existence of a resident gentry or squire-archy but also upon the owners and managers of industrial firms who found themselves drawn into local affairs by the nature of their work. All the developments of the 1920's and 1930's were against the survival of social leadership and the atmosphere of respect and confidence in which it had flourished.

The owners and managers of industrial concerns before the First World War participated in local politics almost as part of their commercial activities. W. H. Lever was county councillor for Bebington from 1903 to 1904, and a leading supporter of the Wirral Liberal party; he was M.P. for the Wirral division from 1906 to 1910. Sir John Brunner was M.P. for the Northwich division from 1887 to 1910 and he was succeeded by his son, John F. L. Brunner, who was not defeated until the General Election of 1918. Although an active member of the bench in Quarter Sessions, Sir John Brunner did not stand for election to the County Council, but both his sons served short terms as councillors, John for the Sandbach division from 1894 to 1895 and Roscoe for the Northwich division from 1907 until he succeeded as managing director of the firm in 1918. A. T. Smith, the founder of Castner, Kellner Co., alkali manufacturers, who served as councillor for the Runcorn division (1913–26), was perhaps the last important *entrepreneur* to enter county politics as a natural extension of his managerial activities.[1] Other directors of Brunner, Mond Co. were active participants in the affairs of the County Council. Edward Milner, who had been primarily responsible for siting the works at Winnington, represented the Northwich division from 1889 to 1902; and Dr. D. B. Hewitt, an Irishman with a curious passion for gipsy music, who had married the daughter of his former partner, the owner of bleaching works near Manchester, was an alderman from 1889 until 1913 when he retired to live in London.[2] But none of the later managers of I.C.I. were as active in local affairs while they were employed by the company. T. Arthur Johnson,

[1] *Chester Chronicle*, 10 Apr. 1926, p. 11.
[2] Ibid., 22 Mar. 1913, p. 3.

who retired from the engineering side of Brunner, Mond Co. in 1919, became chairman of Northwich Rural District Council in 1925–6 and county councillor from 1925 until his death in January 1927.[1] He represents an early example of the 'public person'—one who enters 'public life' on his retirement.

Even where the business has remained in the hands of the same family, the owners have rarely stayed alongside their factory and continued to participate in local affairs. The industrialized area of north-east Cheshire between Stockport and Ashton-under-Lyne contains a large number of the houses which used to be the homes of the mill owners who lived beside their factories. Some were abandoned through bankruptcy or misfortune. Gorse Hall near Stalybridge was deliberately demolished after the mysterious murder of its owner in 1909.[2] But the majority have been abandoned for social reasons. Daniel Adamson, the original promoter of the Manchester Ship Canal, established boiler works at Dukinfield in 1851, and his family was brought up in Oakfield Hall near by. Although the business has remained in the possession of his heirs they have gradually lengthened the distance between themselves and the factory. Daniel Adamson himself died in Didsbury, Manchester; his son-in-law and heir died at Buxton; his grandson died at Alderley Edge; and his great-grandson, the present owner, lives at the Manor House, North Rode.

Merseyside and the 'great towns' of the north-west have suffered another social change which is perhaps peculiar to this region. The whole area is no longer as acceptable for a place of residence as the Home Counties or the south of England. Not only have the industrialists abandoned their houses which were built alongside their factories, but many have also abandoned the region entirely. It is one of the political features of modern Cheshire that many of the natural social leaders have either moved southwards or emigrated abroad. Some of the landed families were prepared to leave England in the hope of continuing to enjoy the pleasures of a country estate. In the early 1900's Lord Delamere of Vale Royal was largely responsible for starting the first white settlements in Kenya.[3] Lord Egerton of Tatton, and in the 1930's, Sir Henry Delves Broughton, followed his example. Here the county lost two of the old 'country party' families. Similarly, the wealth made in Liverpool shipping or Manchester

[1] I.C.I. Information Service.
[2] *Ashton Reporter*, 5 Nov. 1910, p. 10.
[3] Elspeth Huxley, *White Man's Country: Lord Delamere and the Making of Kenya* (2nd ed., 1953, 2 vols.).

cotton, which in the late-nineteenth century had been invested in the country houses of Cheshire, was by 1920 finding outlets elsewhere in England or abroad. There is some truth in the statement that the monuments of Manchester cotton are to be found among the tombstones of Bournemouth. Before the First World War Liverpool and Manchester provided cultural and social life of a metropolitan character for the wealthy merchants and manufacturers who might own a country house or shooting-box in Cheshire as well as an elegant mansion in Prince's Park (Liverpool) or Victoria Park (Manchester). But during the 1920's the social life of the middle classes in these 'great towns' began to decline. Sir Gerald Hurst, who moved from Manchester to London about 1920, was conscious of the fact that the intellectual contacts which he had enjoyed in the Manchester area were going to be increasingly difficult to make.[1] Henceforward the social ideals of London, the great metropolis, were to play a greater part in the lives of professional men from the north-west. The Cheshire Society in London was founded in 1914 under the chairmanship of Major Louis Newton.[2] The latter, who became Lord Mayor of London in 1924, was acting in the old tradition of a merchant remembering his native home, a Macclesfield boy who had prospered in the City, but several of the founder members of the society were Cheshire gentry who maintained both a country house in Cheshire and a town house in London. A study of the address list of the society reveals that when it became no longer possible to maintain two homes, a Cheshire family frequently preferred to abandon its native county and buy a house in the Home Counties within a short distance of the capital. Lord Crewe did not sell Crewe House in London and Crewe Hall in Cheshire until the early 1930's, but when he did, he acquired a new home near Leatherhead in Surrey.[3] The attraction of the metropolis was so great.

The movements of the 'managerial classes' have had profound effects upon local society in terms of leadership and participation in local government. The most important single factor in this development was that the economic changes of the 1920's and 1930's destroyed the 'country house ideal'. The landowners in their ancient family seats and the mill owners in their houses close to the factories

[1] Gerald Hurst, *Closed Chapter* (1942), p. 53.
[2] Information from the secretary.
[3] J. Pope-Hennessy, *Lord Crewe* (1955), p. 176; in 1931 only six of the descendants of the eighteen resident landowners listed in 1872–3 (see above, p. 19) had retained a London house.

had several ideals in common. They recognized a society in which certain families secured the position of natural leaders in their own immediate vicinity and other families were regarded as the natural leaders for the whole region. They cherished the large household and the function of hospitality. The trade depressions in agriculture and in Manchester and Merseyside undermined these ideals. The 'old order' never recovered from the 'great slump'. In 1929 the great country houses and the prosperous merchants' houses in Bowdon and Hale were in a similar plight: both lacked tenants and the means of support.

It is difficult to get an accurate picture of the decline of the great country houses. The commercial directories are not a wholly reliable source because they do not always state when a house is 'unoccupied' or when the owners have leased it to a series of tenants. But all the indications are that a large number of the great houses were abandoned by their owners or changed hands during the 1920's. Kelly's Directory for Cheshire in 1914 listed 137 'principal seats' belonging to the gentry. It is no use merely counting the changes made to this list in succeeding years because houses were added or taken out according to the opinion of the editor about the social status of the owner or tenant. For instance, in the directory for 1923, 15 houses were added and 9 omitted which had been in the 1914 list; and in the directory for 1928, 6 were added and 28 omitted which had been in the 1923 list. The increasing number of omissions may be some evidence for the changing property market. Furthermore, it appears that as many country houses changed hands during the five years 1923–8 as during the nine years 1914–23, about 30 in each case, if one confines the count to those houses which were included in Kelly's list of 'principal seats'. There is another historical landmark which sets a limit to the study of life in the country houses of Cheshire. It appears that the last dance to be held under the auspices of the Knutsford County Assembly was given at Arley Hall in December 1930.[1] These traditional assemblies of Cheshire gentry had always been divided on the basis of small house parties. The invitations were sent to the head of the household who made up his own group of guests, and the programmes referred to the number of houses which were represented. At Tabley House in 1925 there were 230 guests from about 30 houses ranging from Arley, Capesthorne, and Alderley Park to smaller places like Nunsmere at Sandiway and

---

[1] *Chester Chronicle*, 20 Dec. 1930, p. 12.

Rangemore at Rostherne.[1] The end of these assemblies shows how little of the traditional life of Edwardian Cheshire survived into the 1930's.

In 1926 at the annual dinner of the Cheshire Society in London, Sir William Bromley-Davenport referred, without mentioning any names, to the number of Cheshire homes which were no longer occupied by their owners, and welcomed the guest of honour, Lord Stanley of Alderley, as one of the few remaining resident aristocrats.[2] He could have named, for instance, Oulton Park, the seat of Sir Philip Grey-Egerton which in June 1923 was leased to F. W. Cooper, the managing director of Partington Steel and Iron Company of Irlam near Manchester, while Sir Philip moved to live in London. Mr. Cooper was still in residence in February 1926 when a great and uncontrollable fire gutted the house completely. Similarly, soon after the First World War, Sir W. G. Shakerley retired to Bournemouth leaving unoccupied his house in Somerford Park, which was eventually bought by a nephew of Lord Grenfell.[3] All the Shakerley estates in Cheshire were then sold. The most distinctive changes in country-house geography perhaps took place in the Weaver valley. The riverside estates which had enjoyed such landlords as Sir Richard Brooke, General Talbot, and Lord Barrymore came into the hands of the owners of salt and chemical industries, and the great houses into the hands of bankers and industrialists. The Weaver valley suffered its own peculiar loss which was considered by the more patriotic of Cheshire men to have been caused by a betrayal of the paid officials employed by the County Council.[4] Dutton Hall, an early-sixteenth-century half-timbered manor house which had been acquired by the County Council from General Talbot's estate when the land was converted into smallholdings, was sold in 1926 to a Warrington con-tractor.[5] The latter was glad to dismantle the house, cart away its carvings and panelling and sell them to J. A. Dewar, a millionaire whisky manufacturer, who re-erected parts of this Cheshire mansion to make a house for himself near East Grinstead in Sussex. The destruction of Dutton Hall and its partial reappearance in Sussex were symbolic both of the decline of the country houses and of the decline of Cheshire as a county in which wealthy people might live. The 'country house' ideal never recovered properly after the

[1] Ibid., 2 Jan. 1926, p. 9.   [2] Ibid., 6 Mar. 1926, pp. 4, 12.
[3] Ibid., 20 Feb. 1926, pp. 2, 8.
[4] F. H. Crossley, *Cheshire* (Robert Hale Regional Books), 1949, pp. 342-3.
[5] *Manchester Guardian*, 24 Feb. 1926.

agricultural depression of the 1920's. Outbreaks of foot-and-mouth disease caused very severe losses of cattle, sheep, and pigs in Cheshire, a great blow to the county's pastoral farming. In 1923 there were as many as 1,066 separate outbreaks of the disease in the county, and 311 in 1924.[1] Recoveries from this pest were not made until after 1925. The Royal Show, which was held in Chester in 1925, with a committee headed by Sir Gilbert Greenall, the brewer, marked the end of a period in Cheshire agriculture, the end of the great landed estates and the willing tenant farmers. The previous Royal Show to be held in Chester had been in 1893 when the Prince of Wales had stayed with the first Duke of Westminster at Eaton Hall in the house party which he had arranged for its duration. It was a sign of the new situation in Cheshire politics that in 1925, the King, who visited the Show for only a few hours, should have stayed with his friend, the Earl of Derby, at Knowsley in Lancashire, and not in Cheshire. Since the scandal of the second Duke of Westminster's first divorce in 1919, Cheshire could not provide a magnate of Lord Derby's standing. The latter's great power in Lancashire was already an exceptional phenomenon.

The most obvious change in the function of social leaders was that the landed gentleman ceased to be the articulate representative of the agricultural interest. The tenant farmers fought their own battles in order to market their own produce, and in consequence produced their own leaders. The Cheshire branch of the National Farmers' Union developed its own tactics as a pressure group. Its ideas found expression in the formation of an Independent party on the County Council at the end of the First World War and in various methods of abolishing the middleman between the farmer and the consumer by new marketing techniques. The Independent party was organized by J. O. Garner, the local secretary of the N.F.U. The Cheshire farmers, working through the local branch of the N.F.U. with its headquarters at Crewe, organized their own service for supplying milk in Manchester and Salford from a cold-storage plant at Trafford Park, which they acquired for the purpose, in order to compel the ordinary distributors to accept a nationally negotiated agreement on prices. For two months, October and November 1928, the Cheshire N.F.U. ran this distribution service single-handed and as a result greatly extended its membership among local farmers.[2] T. C. Goodwin, chairman of

---

[1] Cheshire County Council Chairman's Triennial Speech (1928), p. 22.
[2] *Manchester Guardian*, 5 Nov. 1928, p. 2.

the County Milk Committee, who was elected county councillor for
the Church Coppenhall division in 1919, and John Done, elected
for the Malpas division in 1925, were important leaders of the local
branch of the N.F.U., which had passed a resolution in 1926 that it
would only achieve success in establishing a Milk Marketing Board
if a county organizer were appointed to co-ordinate the efforts of
all farmers. Thomas Peacock, who became chairman of the Milk
Marketing Board, was a typical local leader thrown up by this movement, the pressure group politics of farmers. He was elected a county
councillor for the Tattenhall division in 1931, and was an unsuccessful National Liberal candidate for Parliament in the Eddisbury by-
election of 1943.

The destruction of the 'country house' ideal and the gradual disappearance of gentry, *entrepreneurs*, and managers from leadership
in local affairs had immediate effects upon the nature of 'county
society' and upon the manner in which parliamentary candidates
were selected to carry out existing political duties. The constituency
party organizations continued to look for a suitable social leader from
their own districts whom they could nominate to contest the next
parliamentary election. Such men were rare. The Conservatives of
the Knutsford division found themselves obliged to choose Brigadier-
General Makins in 1922 although his only local connexions were
those of friendship with the gentlemen of the hunting field! The
Liberals of the Northwich division, which had for many years
returned a Brunner of Brunner, Mond Co., found themselves
manœuvred by the Conservatives in 1922 into nominating the son
of a Conservative peer, Lord Colum Crichton-Stuart, who had no
local connexions whatsoever.

A list of Cheshire M.P.s since the First World War therefore provides an excellent illustration of the disappearance of social leaders
from local politics. The member for a county division had been, by
the principles of social leadership, one of the leading men in local
affairs. The predominance of Conservatives and the weakening of
local ties after the Second World War demonstrated both the nature
of economic and social change in Cheshire and the corresponding
dearth of local gentry who might put themselves forward for election. By the General Election of 1959, only the county borough of
Birkenhead and the two most industrialized county divisions, Stalybridge and Hyde, and Crewe, returned Labour members. The county
was largely made up of 'safe Conservative seats', particularly in those

areas where the new suburbs were being built. Those constituencies which received the largest number of migrants from other areas as new voters were strengthened rather than weakened in their devotion to the Conservative party. Between the General Election of 1929 and that of 1945, a period during which there were few boundary changes, almost 60 per cent. of all the new voters added to the register in the nine county divisions resided in the Wirral constituency or in the Altrincham constituency (which was split into two parts for the 1945 Election). These two divisions after 1945 elected two future Conservative ministers, Selwyn Lloyd, Chancellor of the Exchequer, and F. J. Erroll, Minister of State at the Board of Trade. Similarly, between the General Election of 1950 and that of 1959, the parliamentary divisions of the Wirral and Cheadle were the only constituencies in the whole county with a rapidly increasing number of electors. Indeed, it was almost a function of increasing suburbanization to strengthen the power of the Conservative party. The Knutsford and Chester divisions which also increased the size of their electorate between 1929 and 1945 returned Conservative members. The most noteworthy feature of the history of the county divisions was that, with the exception of Chester, all returned new members in 1945. The break in the continuity of constituency tradition came *before* the complete reorganization of boundaries in 1948, and not *after* it. (See Diagram II.) Members for county divisions after the Second World War were distinguished in Parliament, but not notable members of any recognizable 'county society'. Selwyn Lloyd served on Hoylake U.D.C. and Dennis Vosper, with Liverpool connexions, was Conservative agent for Knutsford before taking the seat for Runcorn. But the other members were either chosen from Central Office lists or were acceptable barristers with local professional ties.

The most notable exception to the decline in importance of local gentry connexions in selecting candidates for Parliament was the position in the Knutsford division of the Bromley-Davenport family at Capesthorne Hall. Walter Bromley-Davenport, who benefited from his mother's experience in county affairs, was elected for the Knutsford division in 1945. Scandal and apathy amongst the local peerage brought his family into prominence. The second Duke of Westminster was compelled to resign from the lord-lieutenancy in 1919 because of the circumstances of his first divorce;[1] the fourth

[1] Compare the resignation of the Marquess of Winchester from Hampshire in 1917, see R. Blake, *The Unknown Prime Minister* (1955), pp. 510–11.

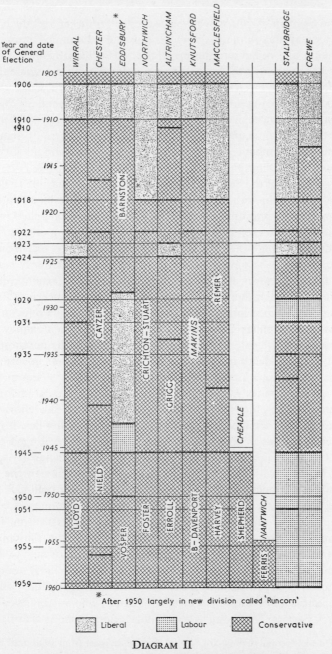

DIAGRAM II
Cheshire County Members of Parliament: 1906–59

Baron Egerton of Tatton who succeeded to his father's estate in 1920, was uninterested in maintaining his political inheritance, remained a bachelor, and became rather a recluse. Sir William Bromley-Davenport was appointed to the lieutenancy after the divorce scandal, and found himself a leading member of the Knutsford Conservative Association because of Lord Egerton's apathy. Although Sir William was also a bachelor, his relations took advantage of his good fortune, and his own immediate family and their connexions by marriage formed the remnant of a 'country party' connexion in Cheshire politics. (See Diagram III.)

By the end of the Second World War it was not sensible to equate social leadership with existing 'county society'. The lord-lieutenant was no longer presiding over a group of families established in land or business who exercised political functions by reason of their social standing. The high sheriff was no longer chosen every year from this same group to be present at the County Assizes. 'County society' had become a term used to describe families with certain common habits of leisure rather than families with political concerns. 'County society' developed independently of local politics. The reluctance of Sir William Bromley-Davenport to resign from the lieutenancy when he became too feeble to exercise its duties placed the next appointment after his death in 1949 in the hands of a Labour government. Attlee chose Lord Leverhulme, the grandson of W. H. Lever whose industrial activities had been largely responsible for transforming Bebington and other parts of the Wirral. Although this choice may have offended some of the well-established gentry families, it represented the needs of the new situation. Leverhulme belonged by his wealth and habits of leisure to 'county society' in its new sense, but also by his ease of manner and conscientious bearing to the community of 'public persons' who participated in local politics.[1] There were two 'county societies', those who spent their money in certain accepted ways and those who helped in local administration. It had become rare for one man to belong to both groups. This may be illustrated by examining the list of high sheriffs. Since 1890 the sheriffs of Cheshire have been drawn largely from the fairly numerous group of Liverpool and Manchester businessmen, military officers, or directors and chairmen of local companies, who inhabit its country houses. Before 1920 county councillors often acted as sheriff; after

---

[1] He was a county councillor for the Neston division from 1946 until he succeeded to his title and the lieutenancy.

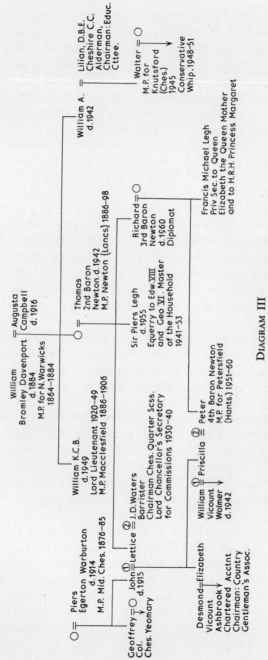

DIAGRAM III

County Families: The Bromley-Davenport and Legh Connexion

1920 and particularly after 1930 they rarely did so. Charles Cornwall-Legh, high sheriff in 1939, was an exception: he was not elected a county councillor until 1949, as a landowner concerned about Manchester 'overspill' at Lymm. There was in general a growing divergence between the men who qualified for the office of sheriff and those who were willing to stand for election to the County Council. Similarly, the Tarporley Hunt Club could no longer be equated with the political *élite* of the county. As a club of forty members qualified by 'Property, Family or Residence in the County', it used to be the epitome of social leadership. The Tarporley Races have not been run since 1939, and the club's annual meeting was shortened after the Second World War. The composition of the club, which in the 1950's included men whose families had made their entry into county society through brewing, the cotton trade, or the shipping of Merseyside, reflected the complete merging of the landed and business classes in the new county society rather than an expression of any political significance in county administration.

Members of the new county society lived in the country houses and villages of Cheshire, but did not find that residence involved them necessarily in local political affairs. 'Smart society' was becoming divorced from political responsibility at the local level, and more and more concerned with its own self-advertisement and the manners of metropolitan interests. There was no difference in principle between James Summers, the steel manufacturer, moving from Stalybridge to Emral Hall near Whitchurch in the 1890's and Lawrence Hargreaves, the founder of the Stalybridge firm of Aerialite, moving from his suburban home at Bramhall to Swettenham Hall near Congleton in the 1940's, but there was a great difference in the practice of political leadership. Summers served on Flintshire County Council and was M.P. for the Flintshire boroughs; Hargreaves did not succeed to any public office, although he had purchased the home of the former chairman of the County Council, Major T. C. Toler, one of the last country gentlemen. The latter, an Etonian and formerly a fine athlete who had been Master of the Christ Church Beagles during his undergraduate days in Oxford, practised in business as a land agent. There could be no greater contrast between such a person in the 1920's and wealthy sportsmen of the new county society such as the members of the Cheshire Polo Club in the 1960's.[1] The latter were of no importance in local affairs, and did not wish to be. The divorce between the

[1] *The Guardian*, 7 July 1960.

new county society and the community of 'public persons' who operated the institutions of government was well illustrated in the pages of *Cheshire Life*. This magazine, begun by the development council for publicity purposes, by 1936 had become a gossip journal for the 'smart set' who considered themselves above the normal level of suburban manners. After the magazine had been acquired by the Philips Park Press in Manchester, it became the symbol of the extent to which the culture of the 'great towns' had conquered the countryside. The issue for June 1935 published the first 'debs' page', photographs of marriageable young ladies from Wilmslow and Altrincham, and reports of weddings written in a spirit of self-advertisement wholly alien to the social leaders who had constituted the old 'county society'. The pages of later issues mirrored the use of the private motor-car for pleasure, and the building of country clubs and road-houses which could only be reached by car. For instance, the Golf and Country Club at Mere Hall was opened in 1934.[1] It was the scene in 1961 of a 'Swim-and-Swing Summer Ball' given by the Twenty-one Club, described by the *Daily Mail* as 'eighteen of Cheshire's prettiest girls who all love fast cars, swimming and dancing'.[2] Such events and the sports matches of various kinds received sufficient publicity for local people to be aware of their existence. The community of 'public persons' in general worked with the minimum of publicity, except perhaps for the reports of occasional disputes in municipal council chambers, in the tradition of the county society of social leaders.

The last generation of social leaders have their monument in the windows of Chester Cathedral cloisters, restored in 1913, which carry armorial glass inserted in the 1920's to the memory of various local worthies. The Church of England until the First World War in some fashion held together the old county society, giving it a loyalty and sense of belonging which was unknown to the new. The Cathedral was also a reminder of another force which transformed county society. On the west wall of the south transept in Chester Cathedral there is a plaque commemorating the thirteen members of the family of Grey-Egerton of Oulton Park who were killed in the First World War. They included the twin sons of the twelfth baronet whose title has therefore passed to a junior branch of that family. This is a classic case of the effect upon local society of the catastrophe suffered by the generation born in the 1890's who should have provided the leaders of the 1930's.

[1] *Cheshire Life* (June 1935), pp. 12–13.   [2] *Daily Mail*, 21 July 1961.

New suburbs

The building of the new suburbs rendered obsolete the politics of social leadership because, in the first place, the massive development of house building called for some measure of planning, and in the second place, the demand for local government services could only be met by full-time professional officers. The inhabitants of the new suburbs were usually congregated in groups of a single social class which therefore produced no 'social leaders' in the old-fashioned manner, and usually possessed rather ambivalent attitudes about the loyalty which they owed to the place from which they had moved and to the place in which they had chosen to live.

The whole question of local allegiance became complicated by the cross-currents of party and class loyalties which are difficult to disentangle from each other. The rise of the Labour party in the boroughs was closely associated with the problem of re-housing the poorer sections of the community in a more spacious manner. The improvement of public transport services permitted the working classes to follow the wealthy in extending their 'journey to work'. The building of the new suburbs, whether they were council houses for the poorer people or private houses for those who could afford the higher rents of a more select district, provided the setting for the theme of social historians which is usually referred to by the phrase, 'loss of community'. The predominant ideal was different from that held by the first middle-class suburbs in the 1880's and 1890's, because it involved a division of life between work-place and home which divorced the sense of community from the sense of political responsibility. Several sentences written in 1935 by E. D. Simon, one of Manchester's leading Liberal councillors from 1911 to 1925, illustrate the reaction of the radicals to this new situation: 'Manchester . . . ought to control a large area on its southern borders. That is where the richer citizens of Manchester live. . . . the successful business men . . . ought . . . to contribute their share in the rates . . . and to regard themselves as citizens of Manchester. . . . In fact, with very few exceptions, they do neither; most of them get out of Manchester as soon as they can in the evening and have no feeling of responsibility for its welfare.'[1]

The new suburbs were therefore built with all the psychological tensions in local leadership caused by the county boroughs losing large numbers of their inhabitants to the country districts around

[1] E. D. Simon and J. Inman, *The Rebuilding of Manchester* (1935), pp. 148–9.

them. In Cheshire the majority of the migrants entered three areas, the Wirral peninsula and two areas close to Manchester, the Altrincham region and the Cheadle region. These three areas, which were designated economic sub-regions 1, 7, and 8 in the County Development Plan (1952), dominate the whole of recent history in local politics (see map at end). Even in 1921 they contained over 34 per cent. of the total population of the administrative county; by 1961 this proportion had been increased to 48 per cent. This concentration merely intensified the pattern of settlement already established by Victorian industry and transport. It was the speed of development in the 1920's and 1930's and again after the Second World War, and not its distribution, which wrought such effects upon the system of local government.

In the Wirral (Region 1) the country districts around the county boroughs of Birkenhead and Wallasey, particularly the urban district of Bebington, between 1921 and 1931 received almost 40 per cent. of all the immigrants entering Cheshire. Ellesmere Port presented the only clear example of population increasing as a result of industrial development. The first oil dock there was opened in July 1922 and the second in May 1933. Its population increased from 16,432 in 1921 to 23,057 in 1931; and after the Second World War, from 32,653 in 1951 to 44,714 in 1961. Elsewhere in the Wirral a large proportion of the development took the form of purely residential housing, particularly in the Hoylake and Wirral urban districts. After the Second World War the population of the Wirral region increased by about 18 per cent. between 1951 and 1961.

But the most fantastically swift developments took place around Manchester in the regions of Altrincham and Cheadle (Regions 7 and 8). The municipal borough of Sale and the urban district of Cheadle and Gatley between 1931 and 1939 were each absorbing more than 1,000 immigrants a year. The Cheadle region almost doubled its population between 1921 and 1949 (41,136 to 81,730) and 87 per cent. of the increase was accounted for by immigration. This rate of development continued in the Cheadle region after the Second World War. Between 1951 and 1961, in this single decade, the population of the Cheadle region increased by over 39 per cent. (81,925 to 114,423), largely because of voluntary migration from the Manchester region. Similarly, the net immigration of 7,000 into the Cheshire parishes of Stockton Heath, Grappenhall, Appleton, and Walton between 1921 and 1939 represented largely the suburban expansion of

Warrington. The total population of the administrative county increased by 187,764 between 1921 and 1948; of this number, 117,424 represented the net immigration of outsiders into the county, of whom as many as 111,594 settled in the three regions of the Wirral,

TABLE 5

Growth of Population, 1951–61, and Increase in the Number of Houses, 1945–60

Economic sub-region	Population as percentage of regional total		Decennial increase as percentage of total increase	Houses completed 1945–60 as percentages of total		
	1951	1961		Local authority	Private	Total
1. Wirral .	17·0	17·7	23·1	20·2	21·4	20·7
7. Altrincham	17·9	18·5	23·4	12·5	21·8	16·9
8. Cheadle .	10·0	12·4	30·9	7·8	27·1	16·8
Sub-total	44·9	48·6	77·4	40·5	70·3	54·4
2. Chester .	4·9	4·7	2·5	3·8	4·4	4·1
3. Runcorn .	7·3	7·2	6·2	7·6	6·4	7·1
4. Northwich.	9·2	8·5	3·7	14·9	3·2	9·3
5. Crewe .	12·7	11·9	5·2	12·4	6·7	9·7
6. Macclesfield	11·4	10·8	6·3	11·9	7·5	9·9
9. Hyde .	9·6	8·3	−1·3	8·9	1·5	5·5
	100·0	100·0	100·0	100·0	100·0	100·0

Altrincham, and Cheadle. This fantastic rate of growth continued after the Second World War. Seventy-seven per cent. of the total increase in population of the county between 1951 and 1961 was to be found in the same three regions, the Wirral, Altrincham, and Cheadle. (See Table 5.) Such are the staggering statistics of social change in Cheshire.[1]

The most important feature of these three regions is that the houses built to accommodate the new Cheshire voters were almost entirely erected by private enterprise, and not by the local authorities. In the county as a whole the proportion of council houses being built was well below the national average, and in these regions in

[1] The most convenient summary of these statistics may be found in the County Development Plan: *Preliminary Statements: House Building Programme and Growth of Population: 1951–1971* (1950); L. P. Green, *Provincial Metropolis* (1959), pp. 74–75, gives details of emigration from the Manchester area (e.g. 22,000 into north Cheshire between 1921 and 1931).

particular, it was negligible. During the four financial years for which figures are available before the Second World War (1 April 1936–31 March 1940) the annual average number of council houses was 3·18 per cent. of the total number of houses completed in the Wirral region; 9·15 per cent. in the Altrincham region, and 4·75 per cent. in the Cheadle region. After the war the building of private houses in these three regions was again the most important feature of the county's development. Between 1945 and 1960 70 per cent. of all the private houses completed in the county were to be found in these three regions—and also 40 per cent. of all the council houses, mainly in the Wirral region. (See Table 5.)

One consequence of this highly concentrated form of private development was to make nonsense of the figures produced in the Development Plan (1950) to represent the estimated rate of growth. The estimated total for 1971 in the Altrincham and Cheadle regions had almost been reached by the time of the National Census in 1961. The failure to calculate accurately the pace of 'voluntary migration' away from the great urban centres emphasized what great political pressures were being generated by the desire to live in a private house in one of these three regions. Local government services in these areas dominated the development of county administration.

Naturally, the new suburbs, particularly those of privately built houses, provided the largest increases in the county's rateable value. The effects of development by private builders were obvious. In Timperley, for instance, there were 35 houses being built in 1926; but 274 houses in 1927. During the 1930's the rate of building there never dropped below 200 a year, and the rateable value of the district which had been £26,775 in 1896 was over £70,000 by 1935.[1] It is possible to construct a social 'profile' for any settlement, when figures are available for the groups and classes of property expressed as percentages of the total rateable value, which demonstrates how lasting were the effects of suburban development before 1914 and suburban development between 1919 and 1939. Figures published in *Cheshire County Finance* in 1953 show similar patterns for the places developed before 1910, like Alderley Edge, Bowdon, and Hale, where more than 30 per cent. of the rateable value consisted of domestic property valued at over £50; and similar patterns for the 'new boroughs' of the 1930's, Altrincham, Bebington, and Sale, where more than 45 per cent. of the rateable value consisted of domestic

[1] *Sale and Stretford Guardian*, 9 Feb. 1934; 3 May 1935.

property of between £14 and £30. Hale in 1953 may have been exceptional because of post-1946 development, but in general these figures show clearly and simply how different were the two waves of suburban expansion. They also demonstrate how different socially were the areas developed during the twentieth century from the boroughs like Hyde, Dukinfield, and Stalybridge which were produced by industrial expansion during the nineteenth, and from the old market towns like Congleton, Nantwich, and Macclesfield.

The impact of the new suburbs brought forth the first attempts at planned development. Significantly enough, town and country planning in Cheshire was divided between three separate advisory bodies, two for the three regions where houses were being built in such vast numbers, and one for almost all the remaining parts of the county. The county boroughs adjacent to the developing regions played a considerable part in the work of joint committees which gave advice on the shape of future building projects. The Altrincham and Cheadle regions came under the survey of the Manchester and District Town Planning Advisory Committee, formed in 1921, of which Manchester county borough was the leading member. The Wirral region was the responsibility of the Wirral Joint Committee, formed in 1922, which included representatives of the county boroughs of Birkenhead and Wallasey, and which later acquired statutory powers. All the remaining parts of Cheshire, except Deeside, were covered by the Mid-Cheshire Joint Town Planning Advisory Committee which was formed by the County Council in 1920. The substance of this committee's final report, published in 1929, was governed by events in the three developing regions already described. Its principal recommendation was that industrial development in Cheshire should be confined principally to its northern border, the waterfront of the Manchester Ship Canal, so that a narrow industrial region should join the Wirral to the Manchester area. The work of these planning committees did not have a great deal of effect upon the rate of development, because they were acting only in an advisory capacity. They did little to reconcile the conflicting claims of counties and county boroughs. Manchester and Cheshire, for instance, in 1936 held their first talks about the extension of Manchester's southern motorways, Princess Parkway and Kingsway, into the county, but no plans were agreed before the outbreak of war. The Town and Country Planning Act of 1947 emphasized the natural antagonism of counties and county boroughs by making them planning authorities instead of district councils. The report of the South Lancashire and North-East Cheshire Advisory Planning Committee (the new name of the Manchester and District Committee), published in the same year, issued a warning against the development of the Manchester region being controlled from the county offices of Chester and Preston.

The political significance of boundary disputes

All the factors involved in the changing social conditions between the two world wars achieved their political expression in a series of disputes between the county and those county boroughs which sought to extend their boundaries. The County Council reached its political maturity and established itself as an effective upper-tier authority in a two-tier system of government by being compelled to defend its territory against the demands of ambitious urban neighbours. The struggle lasted for almost twenty years. The Local Government (County Boroughs and Adjustments) Act of 1926, which embodied the recommendations of a Royal Commission, had established the principle that if there were any objections to an application for the extension of the boundaries of a county borough, the latter could only proceed by promoting a Local Bill. The objectors were then at liberty to secure the rejection of the Bill by Parliament. Between 1926 and the appointment of the Local Government Boundary Commission in 1945, many county councils were involved in the wearisome business of preparing briefs and memoranda to justify their retention of large tracts of land in urban areas which were claimed by county boroughs. Officials and councillors spent a great amount of time in the committee rooms of Westminster listening to leading members of the parliamentary Bar arguing their case. The substance of these arguments was drawn from different interpretations of the forces of social change which presented new problems of administration to the authorities of local government. Those present in the stuffy atmosphere of committee rooms in the House of Lords in fact heard a commentary upon the improvements in public transport, the reorganization of industry, and the expansion of the suburbs.

The county council as an instrument of government was on trial. Throughout these disputes the central problem was whether or not small urban and rural district councils should be allowed to remain the local authorities in rapidly expanding suburban districts. Who should govern the new suburbs? The county boroughs answered this question by maintaining that efficient services could only be supplied if the small authorities were absorbed by their larger neighbours. This policy had been successfully followed during the first wave of suburban expansion before the First World War. Manchester, for instance, took in Chorlton, Withington, Didsbury, and Burnage in 1904, and parts of Heaton Norris in 1913, all at the expense of Lancashire.[1] The county councils answered this question by maintaining that district councils should be given greater powers and be aided from county funds so that efficient services could be supplied without a transfer of rateable value to large urban authorities. The county borough arguments were more consistent; they implied a continuous patch-work of contiguous administrative areas, each with the same status and powers. The county council arguments suffered from a certain equivocation, because the county authority was the senior partner in a two-tier system of administration in which the junior partners were likely to nurse the ambition of escaping from its tutelage. The creation of county boroughs in 1888 had created a precedent and an example. It was easier for the County Council to defend an authority which was too small to apply for borough status than to help a municipal borough which might pursue a policy of aggression against county districts to achieve its independence. This equivocal position forced the County Council to take seriously the best defence of county government—an effective system of delegation of powers from the county to municipal boroughs and county districts. By 1947 and 1948 the Clerk of Cheshire County Council was able to take his stand before the Boundary Commission with a well-reasoned case for delegation.[2] By 1958 the chairman of the County Council was prepared to speak in terms of delegating powers even to parish councils.[3] Twenty years of dispute with county boroughs had brought into being a new kind of county authority.

The Local Government Act of 1929 made possible an effective system of county government by abolishing the last important *ad hoc* bodies, the boards of guardians, which administered the poor law. It also extended the county's responsibility by transferring from district councils the job of maintaining second-class roads. The County Council therefore became for the first time responsible for some health

---

[1] A. Redford, *Local Government in Manchester* (1940), ii. 304; cf. *City of Manchester Plan* (1945), pp. 174–5.

[2] Cheshire County Council Memoranda: (1) The Two-Tier System of Local Government (Oct. 1947); (2) The Problem of the Delegation of Powers (Feb. 1948).

[3] *Cheshire Observer*, 1 Nov. 1958.

and welfare services, as well as roads and education. The Act also recognized the council's superior status over district councils and municipal boroughs. Section 46 empowered the council to revise administrative areas and electoral divisions within its boundaries by making certain review orders. The Local Government Act Committee which was formed by the County Council in order to carry out its duties under this section, became the natural companion of the Parliamentary Committee, which fought Local Bills. The powers acquired in 1929 led naturally to a reconstitution of the council's methods.

The chief officers of the County Council were the first to benefit from its increased powers, and from the prestige to be gained in preparing the defence of its territory. Not only did the new responsibilities call for greater technical competence[1] but also the new hazards of parliamentary work required expert professional guidance. In 1927 the battle with the county boroughs was first joined in earnest when Cheshire opposed the Bills promoted by Birkenhead, Wallasey, and Manchester. The Director of Education has recorded in his memoirs that the chief officers spent the greater part of 16 or 17 weeks in London during that year in preparing the council's case before Parliament.[2] But the councillors were still reluctant to recognize their importance. The chairman, Sir William Hodgson, made a speech comparing the county to Naboth's vineyard which has been the envy of its more powerful neighbours, and praised those councillors 'who have charge of the defence of the county', hoping that they would give a good account of themselves 'in the hours of stress and difficulty in Parliamentary Committees'.[3] C. S. Pain, chairman of the County Parliamentary Committee, a councillor from Bebington and the senior partner in a firm of Liverpool surveyors, knew that his task of defending the county depended on expert legal advice which the members of the Clerk's department could best supply. It was no use submitting to cross-examination before a parliamentary committee unless one had been properly briefed.

It might not be too much of an exaggeration to say that the social leader in Cheshire politics was laid to rest by the pathetic performance of the chairman of the County Council, one of its original members, when he was examined on 2 July 1930 about Manchester's claim to Wythenshawe by Tyldesley Jones, one of the most devastating

---

[1] See below, pp. 151–6.
[2] F. F. Potter, *Educational Journey* (1949), p. 106.
[3] *Manchester Guardian*, 18 Mar. 1927, p. 4.

barristers at the parliamentary Bar. Against the advice of his officials, Sir William Hodgson, then aged 76, insisted upon going into
the witness-box in spite of the fact that he had been away on a
Mediterranean cruise during April when several important meetings
had taken place, and was not in consequence fully conversant with
the facts.[1] Tyldesley Jones, the counsel for Manchester Corporation,
deflated him completely, and the Manchester Extension Bill was
passed. This experience left a lasting impression upon the minds of
the county officials, particularly Geoffrey Scrimgeour, then Deputy
Clerk and soon to become, in 1932, the first full-time Clerk which the
council had ever had. They had been embarrassed by the indifference
of the leading member of the council to technical detail. The task
of defending the county boundaries would henceforward be entrusted
to more professional hands.

The Manchester Extension Bill of 1930 had other lasting effects.
From 1 April 1931 the three parishes in which Manchester intended
to build the satellite town of Wythenshawe were incorporated in the
city. This was the largest single loss of territory which the county of
Cheshire suffered, and the bitter recriminations which surrounded
its acquisition by Manchester coloured all subsequent negotiations
about 'overspill' in the 1940's and 1950's. Wythenshawe, the brain-
child of the Manchester Labour party, stood out as a tongue of land,
covered with council housing, extending into the new suburban areas
of Altrincham and Cheadle which were being developed predominantly by private enterprise and were largely Conservative-voting.[2] It
became a symbol of Socialist aggression. Manchester had for many
years entertained the idea of developing a satellite town in Cheshire
which would be linked with the city by an express tram-service; a
delegation from the Corporation as early as 1908 had visited Letch-
worth to study the planning of a garden-city.[3] By the end of the First
World War plans were discussed for acquiring Wythenshawe Park,
the country home of T. E. Tatton, county councillor for the Timperley division from 1889 to 1907 and a first cousin of a former chairman of the County Council, Sir George Dixon. But Tatton refused
to sell, and the estate did not come on to the market until his death
in 1924, when the whole project for a Wythenshawe suburb had
become associated with the Labour party. It was an issue in the 1925

[1] Minutes of Evidence before Select Committee (H.L.): Manchester Extension Bill, Q. 2627.   [2] See map at end.
[3] A. Redford, *Local Government in Manchester* (1940), iii. 38.

municipal elections.[1] Alderman W. T. Jackson, who was attracted to Wythenshawe on his visits to Baguley Sanatorium and had himself retired to live deep in the Cheshire countryside at Goostrey, saw in the development of a satellite town a solution to the city's housing problems.[2] In 1920 the Housing Committee had claimed that over 20,000 houses were required in three years if the city was to get rid of its slums.[3] Between 1927 and 1930 the Corporation was building council houses at the rate of 2,500 a year.[4] Jackson achieved his ambition by joining forces with E. D. Simon (later Lord Simon of Wythenshawe) who had been chairman of the Housing Committee from 1919 to 1923. The latter purchased Wythenshawe from Tatton's son, and in 1926 presented it to the Corporation. Although Manchester failed at its first attempt to absorb Wythenshawe into the city in 1927, the success of the Extension Bill in 1930 laid claim to an area of countryside where the local authority, Bucklow Rural District Council, was shown incapable of providing adequate drains and sewers for the building of a large number of council houses. The county of Cheshire lost on a technical argument, and was unable to subsidize the district council from county funds—a point later remembered—except under the insufficient terms of section 57 of the 1929 Act. Wythenshawe also revealed a weakness in the county's legal position in relation to its district councils.

The county boroughs of Chester and Warrington attempted to extend their boundaries into Cheshire by promoting parliamentary Bills in 1931. Flintshire, which stood to lose the parish of East Saltney and part of Sealand under the Bill promoted by Chester, aroused the spirit of Welsh nationalism and lobbied all Welsh M.P.s to resist the claims of an English borough to Welsh soil.[5] The Welsh suggested that Chester was merely trying to acquire population in order to regain the parliamentary representation which it had lost in 1918. The extension proposals were defeated in a town poll of Chester ratepayers in 1932 and the borough was not able to reach a satisfactory agreement with the county until 1936. The corporation of Warrington was concerned to extend its boundaries 'as so many Warrington people had spread over into districts immediately south of the [Manchester Ship] canal' and refused to admit 'that the narrow artificial cutting which now divides Warrington from its people on

---

[1] *Manchester Guardian*, 31 Oct. 1925, p. 15.
[2] Ibid., 6 Aug. 1945. (Obituary notice.)   [3] Ibid., 22 July 1921, p. 6.
[4] E. D. Simon, *The Anti-Slum Campaign* (1933), gives details of Manchester's policy.   [5] *Manchester Guardian*, 4 Jan. 1932, p. 2.

the other side, shall remain a perpetual barrier to the natural growth of the town'.[1] Warrington's ambitions compelled Cheshire County Council to come to an agreement with Lancashire to make the 'narrow artificial cutting' a perpetual boundary between the counties, a proposal which Lancashire had been advocating since 1897.[2]

All the boundaries of the administrative county outside the county boroughs came under revision by the County Council in accordance with section 46 of the Local Government Act (1929). This made the council an arbitrator between a host of conflicting minor authorities which all had the ambition to increase their size and improve their rateable value. Just as the county was engaged in 'jungle warfare' to ward off the piratical attacks of county boroughs, the rural districts and small urban districts were faced with the prospect of covetous neighbours proposing annexation. The *Manchester Guardian* produced a long list of authorities in 1929 which were trying to improve their status.[3] Macclesfield, for example, was anxious to increase its rateable value by absorbing Bollington and other neighbouring parishes. Wilmslow wished to annex the urban district of Handforth; Hazel Grove cast covetous eyes on Poynton and Woodford. Even Crewe, which had ambitions to be a county borough, hoped to acquire part of the Nantwich Rural District. The psychological effects of expanding county boroughs spread throughout the local government hierarchy, and in the political atmosphere of the early 1930's when the increase of private building was altering the distribution of rateable value, it was very hard to secure agreement. The urban districts of Winsford, Middlewich, and Northwich in 1933 passed a resolution that the County Council's proposals 'were contrary to the spirit of the 1929 Act and not in the best interests of local government administration'.[4] Dr. R. S. Hardman, the chairman of the County Local Government Act Committee, had the unenviable task of defending their proposals before conferences of local authorities.

In Cheshire the process of revision was taken in two stages: the Wirral peninsula and the rest. The County Council's solution to the suburbanization of the Wirral was to bring the whole area under urban authorities. Rural district councils were abolished. The chief threats to county territory came from the two county boroughs,

---

[1] *Manchester Guardian*, 19 Nov. 1931, p. 12; 22 Dec. 1931, p. 13.
[2] *County Council Minutes* (1897–8), pp. 304, 305; (1903–4), p. 1077; *Warrington Guardian*, 13 Feb. 1904, p. 3.
[3] *Manchester Guardian*, 25 Nov. 1929, p. 12.
[4] Ibid., 30 Dec. 1933, p. 4.

Birkenhead and Wallasey. The latter, which did not achieve its county borough status until 1913, made an agreement with Birkenhead in 1914 over the division of certain parishes in the event of either borough proposing an extension. The urban authorities of the Wirral were continually demanding living space. Birkenhead and Wallasey successfully extended their boundaries by Act of Parliament in 1927, and the County Council in 1930 conceded further extensions under section 57 of the 1888 Act to Bebington and Ellesmere Port. For several years neighbouring small authorities had been appealing to the county for protection. In October 1923 the Wirral Rural District had written to the County Council about the possibilities of becoming an urban district, and it acquired urban powers for roads, housing, and sewage. In 1926 Moreton Parish Council, adjoining Wallasey, asked for urban powers. As a 'caravan town' for workers in Wallasey which had grown rapidly since 1918, it could not provide the essential services.[1] The County Council therefore decided in revising the boundaries of the Wirral in 1933 to make an area of large urban districts, led by Bebington and Ellesmere Port, each containing a considerable amount of agricultural land.[2]

The boundaries of the rest of Cheshire were not decided until the county review order of 1936.[3] The effect, if not the only purpose of the county's plan, was to create a 'buffer state' of urban districts around Manchester. This intention was even more apparent in the committee report of 1933 which was rejected by the Minister of Health.[4] The committee had proposed to abolish Bucklow and Northwich Rural Districts and substitute for them a much stronger Mid-Cheshire Rural Authority. The county encouraged the strengthening of urban districts in the Manchester conurbation. In 1920 Altrincham was permitted to extend its boundaries to include part of Dunham Massey and Timperley.[5] Sale was strengthened in 1929 by uniting itself with Ashton-upon-Mersey. The chairman of Sale Council admitted that they feared the encroachments of Manchester.[6]

[1] Ibid., 19 Jan. 1926, p. 9; 14 Aug. 1926, p. 14.
[2] The first report of the Local Government Act Committee on the Wirral (17 July 1931) contains interesting historical details, but the map (Cheshire Record Office) accompanying the final order (16 Mar. 1933) is a revised Ordnance Survey, 1909–10, which does not show the extent of suburbanization when the boundaries were redrawn.
[3] Final Order (84,735), 28 Feb. 1936; for a summary, see *Municipal Year Book* (1937), pp. 159–61.
[4] The second report of Local Government Act Committee (23 Nov. 1933); this was well summarized in the *Sale and Stretford Guardian*, 1 Dec. 1933.
[5] *Manchester Guardian*, 13 Feb. 1920, p. 10.   [6] Ibid., 10 Dec. 1929, p. 16.

The strongest protection for the county against the county boroughs was the creation of municipal boroughs which could face Manchester or Birkenhead on an equal footing in the committees of the Association of Municipal Corporations. The county had a considerable amount to gain from the promotion of municipal boroughs in the areas where the new suburbs had been created. On the Wirral, Bebington succeeded in getting its charter in 1937, but Ellesmere Port was not successful until 1955. The urban districts around Manchester had similar ambitions. Sale and Altrincham fulfilled expectation by securing charters in 1935 and 1937 respectively, but not Cheadle and Gatley. The latter, the most rapidly developing urban district in Cheshire, was made the subject of a dispute between Manchester and Stockport in 1933 and 1934.[1] Both these county boroughs promoted Bills for the absorption of Cheadle and Gatley. Stockport's plans, which were so ambitious that Bramhall and Hazel Grove were to be included, provoked Manchester into competition because the county borough authorities between them provided most of the major services in the district. Cheadle and Gatley survived this onslaught, but was not able to acquire municipal status when application was first made in 1937. It is generally supposed that Manchester's acquisition of part of Gatley for its Wythenshawe scheme in 1930 removed the essential piece of population and rateable value which would have been sufficient to establish Cheadle and Gatley as a borough. The urban district had itself in 1930 submitted a scheme to the County Council for taking over Bramhall, Woodford, and Handforth.[2] After the Second World War the urban district in 1946 and 1956 made two further attempts to secure municipal status, but without success.[3] It is ironical that the urban district offices were moved in 1959 to Abney Hall, the former mansion of the Watts family, who were among the first of the Manchester merchant princes to cross the river and settle in Cheshire. An urban district which was the most loyal to Cheshire was administered from a Manchester-made residence.

But the policy of containing the metropolitan areas of Liverpool and Manchester by surrounding them with a chain of lively and independent boroughs or urban districts could not be successful if the latter wished to transfer their allegiance to a new county or by a process of amalgamation wished to become county boroughs. In

---

[1] The dispute lasted from October 1933 to June 1934, see local newspapers, specially *Manchester Guardian*, 20 Mar. 1934, p. 6.
[2] *Manchester Guardian*, 7 Oct. 1930, p. 7.
[3] Ibid., 24 May 1946, p. 8; 31 May 1946, p. 3; 13 June 1956, p. 14.

either case, the county of Cheshire would lose in prestige and prosperity. To remain an effective upper-tier authority within its own historic boundaries, the County Council was compelled to retain the loyalty of the local boroughs and district councils. It could only do so by a system of regular consultations and the delegation of powers, and any development in this direction would inevitably enhance the professional status of the officials who carried out the routine business of administration, particularly the clerks. The threat to county government which was represented in the boundary disputes made the office of Clerk of the County Council into a diplomatic post for the maintenance of good relations between local authorities. Geoffrey Scrimgeour, the first full-time Clerk, who held that office from 1932 until 1952, found himself, consciously or unconsciously, playing a new role in public life.

The greatest danger to the survival of the county's historic boundaries came from various proposals to create new counties. The alternative, a series of contiguous county boroughs in a metropolitan area, was only discussed later as part of the reaction against any increase in the two-tier system of government. Cheshire was threatened by the possible creation of a Merseyside county on the west and a Manchester county on the east, two authorities which would deprive the historic county of all the wealth which had poured into the new suburbs during the 1930's. As outlined above,[1] the most significant expansions in population and prosperity during the twentieth century have all taken place in the regions of the Wirral, Altrincham, and Cheadle. The extreme north-east of the county, the Hyde region, which was likely to be included in any Manchester county, was an area of declining population. The conception of a Merseyside county, comprising Liverpool and other urban authorities on either side of the river, stemmed from the need to co-ordinate local government services following the 'overspill' of Liverpool's working population into the Wirral, a process greatly accelerated by the opening of the Mersey tunnel in 1934. The plan for a Manchester county was much older, and took its origin from the arrangements which were made before the First World War for the city to absorb several adjacent urban districts. Frequent comparisons were made between the problems of local government in the Manchester area and the efficient functioning of the London County Council.[2] The

[1] See above, pp. 104–6.
[2] *Manchester City News*, 26 Sept. 1905; 15 Apr. 1911; 12 Jan. 1940; *Manchester Guardian*, 19 Feb., 5 Mar. 1914.

proposals were then discussed in terms of a 'federation' of local authorities for the district. By the time the Local Government Boundary Commission was appointed in 1945, both the suggested counties on Merseyside and around Manchester were conceived in terms of county government as it had been developed by the 1929 Act.

The problem for Cheshire was whether or not the County Council was to be demoted in the hierarchy of English counties from being tenth on the list (including London) in terms of population to being a poorer and largely rural area, comparable with its neighbours, the counties on the borders of Wales. The county's prestige depended upon a simple matter of financial resources. What was the minimum rateable value necessary for maintaining the existing arrangements? The chief officers of the county recognized that whatever solution was chosen by the Boundary Commission for local government in the Liverpool and Manchester areas, whether it was a new county council or a series of county boroughs (and it was perhaps likely to be the former in the Manchester area), the existing county administration would be deprived of the greater part of its work, the provision of services in suburban areas. The nature of their business was at stake. Furthermore, they realized that if no alterations were made in the metropolitan areas, they would still have to face the demands of expanding cities for more building space. Even if the county had no other county council rivals, it might still suffer from county borough aggression in the demand for sites on which urban dwellers might be re-housed.

The decision in 1933 to make the Wirral a region of urban districts made the proposal to create a Merseyside county or a Wirral county a much less dangerous one than the same plan in the Manchester region. Each authority on the Wirral had sufficient open space within its boundaries for expansion and planned development, and therefore did not display the political 'imperialism' of Manchester and its neighbours.[1] The desire of Manchester to cross the Mersey in its efforts to find more open space on its southern boundary affected all the negotiations on local government reorganization in eastern Cheshire. The discussions which were held in 1946 on the proposed Manchester County Council were coloured by memories of the two Bills which the city promoted for the absorption of Wythenshawe.[2] The Cheshire parishes which the city acquired in 1931 were seen by

[1] See above, pp. 112, 115–16.   [2] *Manchester Evening News*, 1 Aug. 1946.

CHESHIRE INDUSTRIAL SITES AND OPEN SPACES

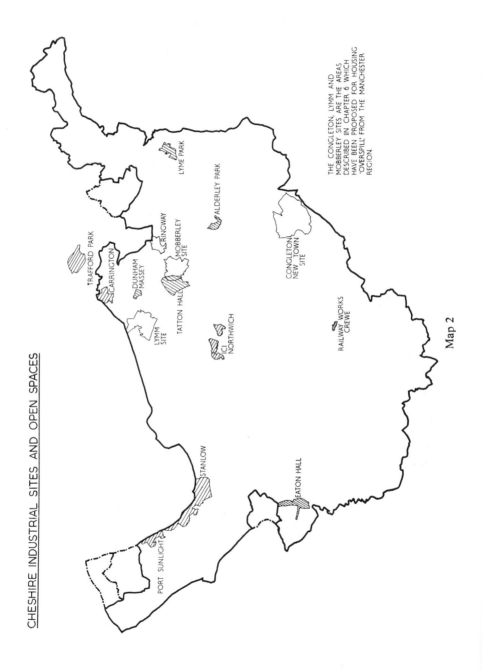

LYME PARK

ALDERLEY PARK

RINGWAY

MOBBERLEY SITE

TRAFFORD PARK

CARRINGTON

DUNHAM MASSEY

TATTON HALL

LYMM SITE

ICI NORTHWICH

CONGLETON NEW TOWN SITE

RAILWAY WORKS CREWE

STANLOW

PORT SUNLIGHT

EATON HALL

THE CONGLETON, LYMM AND MOBBERLEY SITES ARE THE AREAS DESCRIBED IN CHAPTER 6 WHICH HAVE BEEN PROPOSED FOR HOUSING 'OVERSPILL' FROM THE MANCHESTER REGION.

Map 2

county councillors and county officials as the thin edge of an even deeper wedge which it intended to drive into the countryside after the purchase of Wythenshawe Park in 1926. The Park was first used by the city corporation as an airport in 1929, but since it was too small for commercial purposes, in 1934 the city attempted to purchase a large tract of land in the parish of Ringway, immediately south of Wythenshawe. In spite of objections raised by Cheshire County Council and many others, Manchester Airport at Ringway was opened in 1938.[1] When in March 1946, just as all the preparations for the Boundary Commission were in full swing, the city corporation announced that Mobberley would be a suitable place for developing a satellite town outside the city, it looked to Cheshire County Council as another step in the desire to expand southwards. Mobberley is immediately south of Ringway. If the city acquired an estate there, it might claim the right to extend its Wythenshawe boundary to include both these parishes. The attempt to bring Ringway within the city boundary in 1955–6 was unsuccessful, but for ten years and more before that, it had been an open secret that such an attempt might be made.[2]

The county of Cheshire during the period between the Local Government Act of 1929 and that of 1958 succeeded in keeping its historic boundaries intact, except for minor losses already mentioned, because Geoffrey Scrimgeour, the Clerk of the County Council, was adequately prepared for the fight. The loss of Wythenshawe in 1930–1 and the dispute between Manchester and Stockport for the right to absorb Cheadle and Gatley in 1933–4 taught the county its lessons. In 1942 Scrimgeour had the foresight to ask his council to appoint a planning consultant, W. Dobson Chapman, who was commissioned to report on the post-war development of the county.[3] He also followed the example of the West Riding of Yorkshire in 1943 in summoning a conference of all local authorities within the county which nominated a standing committee to discuss the problems of planning and the reorganization of areas.[4] From this arose a body known as the Consultative Committee which is convened whenever representatives of the various local authority associations have a common problem to discuss. From this conference also the suggestion

[1] *Manchester Guardian*, 23 Aug. 1929; 24 Feb. 1936; 9 June 1937; 25 June 1938.
[2] Ibid., 24 Feb. 1954; 16 Nov. 1955; 13 July 1956.
[3] W. D. Chapman, *County Palatine: A Plan for Cheshire* (privately published, 1946; 1st ed., 1948). [4] *County Council Minutes* (1943–4), p. 487.

was first made that the Cheshire branches of local authority associations should nominate their members for co-option to the chief standing committees of the council. The business of planning the machinery of consultation with other local authorities was allocated to a special Post-War Reconstruction Committee appointed by the County Council in 1943.[1] This committee prepared the agenda for a conference with Cheshire authorities and approved the appointment of a Consultative Committee and the various schemes of co-option. It used the device of asking existing local authority associations to nominate their members. The urban authorities in the county had joined together through local initiative. As early as 1910 the contiguous boroughs of Hyde, Dukinfield, and Stalybridge had joined with Crewe, Macclesfield, and Congleton to found the Non-County Boroughs Association,[1] which had nine members by the outbreak of the Second World War. Thirty-three urban districts formed the Cheshire Urban District Council Association in 1929, and the rural districts were persuaded in 1937 by the secretary of the National R.D.C. Association to establish a local branch.[2] The original Standing Committee appointed in 1944 also included one representative from each of the four county boroughs,[3] but this degree of co-operation could not survive the Town and Country Planning Act of 1947 which made counties and county boroughs separate planning authorities. The suggestion that representatives of local authority associations should be co-opted to county committees was first made at a meeting of the Post-War Reconstruction Committee in May 1944 and a draft scheme was approved in January 1945.[4] The only delay in putting the system into immediate operation was caused by the need for securing the approval of the Ministry of Education to a reconstruction of the County Education Committee.[5] But by the end of the Second World War the formal procedures had been established for bringing the County Council into regular consultation with all the local authorities in Cheshire.

The loyalty of the constituent authorities was first put to the test in 1945 when the County Council promoted a local Bill which, if it had been passed, would have authorized the county authority to purchase and develop land for the re-location of population or

[1] *County Council Minutes* (1943–4), p. 437.
[2] Information about local authority associations from their respective secretaries.   [3] *County Council Minutes* (1943–4), p. 623.
[4] Ibid. (1944–5), pp. 306, 703; (1945–6), pp. 151, 363–4.
[5] County Education Committee Records.

industry, and to make annual contributions to county district councils to cover their costs wherever such a scheme might be started. The Bill was in fact defeated on its second reading in March 1946, but the Minister of Health accepted the principle by which the County Council could help county districts and added a clause to this effect in the Housing (Financial and Miscellaneous Powers) Bill.[1] The Cheshire Bill was part of the political game of waiting for Manchester to declare its hand. Scrimgeour co-operated in this with Robert Adcock, the Clerk of Lancashire County Council and formerly Town Clerk of Manchester. The Clerks of Staffordshire, Derbyshire, Nottinghamshire, and the West Riding of Yorkshire were also involved in the preparations for the Bill because they also saw the need for arming the counties with sufficient powers to deal with 'overspill' and the re-location of industry. By the time the Bill had been defeated, Manchester had declared its position—the building of a satellite town at Mobberley at its own expense—but the county had at least shown its willingness to take responsibility itself.

The only reasonable case which the county could present in 1947 to the Boundary Commission for maintaining its present size was to fall in with the plans which Lancashire were making to avoid the creation of a Merseyside county and a Manchester county. Scrimgeour and Adcock were again in close consultation. Lancashire proposed dividing itself, like Yorkshire, into three ridings: a north area centred on Preston; a west area around Liverpool; and an east area around Manchester.[2] The Clerk of Cheshire County Council proposed to complete the pattern by constituting a south area of equal size and rateable value from the existing county of Cheshire.[3] The theoretical advantage of the proposal for four ridings in the north-west was that all existing county boroughs would relinquish their county status! The suggestion represented a final revenge of the counties for the aggression of county boroughs and the glorification of a two-tier system of government. But the dissolution of the Boundary Commission in 1949 made the whole scheme only a theoretical possibility.

The failure of the Boundary Commission to effect any reorganization left the existing authorities to cope with the great increase of work thrust upon them by the Labour government, 1945–51. In spite

[1] 9 & 10 George VI, c. 48, s. 8.
[2] *Manchester Guardian*, 19 May 1947.
[3] Cheshire County Council, Memorandum on the Two-tier System of Local Government (Oct. 1947).

of the creation of the National Health Service which lessened local authority powers, the Acts passed in those years established the county councils as vital organs of local administration. Furthermore, the Education Act of 1944 had greatly enhanced their power and prestige.

The political significance of the boundary disputes, which began in Cheshire in 1927 and lasted until after the Second World War, even until the Act of 1958, lies in the increased strength which they gave to the county. The need to plan and consult with other authorities raised the status of the chief officials, particularly that of the Clerk. The failure to reach any solution left the county with the opportunity to develop professional services and with the organization for consultation and co-option to make use of. Since 1945 the Non-County Boroughs Association, the U.D.C., and R.D.C. Associations in Cheshire have all nominated members for co-option to county committees. The new system of county government was created by professionalizing the relationships of existing authorities. The fact that this had to be done is sure evidence that the informal contacts of social leaders could not be relied upon. In fact, government policy correctly assumed that social leaders, in the sense understood before 1929, no longer existed. The reluctance to reorganize the system of authorities and areas sprang partly from the belief that there were not sufficient councillors of the right quality available. Before the First World War social leaders had created a new local government authority by petitioning for a local board or an urban district, by taking the initiative into their own hands. By the Second World War new authorities could only be created if the established vested interests, the councillors and particularly the chief officials, could be brought into an agreement. The era of the public person had begun.

5

PROFESSIONALIZATION AND BUREAUCRACY

THE process by which the administrative machine of the county of Cheshire had adapted itself to the requirements of new political conditions was completed by the time that the provisions of the Local Government Act of 1958 were brought into force. The latter inaugurated a new local government system, and local events which took place at the same time as this reform played their part in emphasizing that a new pattern of county government had been established. The years after the Second World War were marked by a common agreement that the permanent full-time official or employee of the council was also in some sense a 'public person' with a recognized part to play in the public life of the district. He might be described as a bureaucrat, but no one could deny the need for his professional skill. Government by professional administrators had come to stay, and come to change the function of the elected representatives.

During the 1950's the county was placed on an equal footing with its large urban neighbours. By 1951 the population of the administrative county was greater than that of either Liverpool or Manchester, and as the salaries of chief officers since 1948 have been proportionate to the size of population, the posts which the county could offer were as well paid as those offered by the great county boroughs. When the new valuation lists of rateable property came into force in 1956, Cheshire had for the first time a higher rateable value than either Liverpool or Manchester. Furthermore, in 1957 when the Queen opened the new County Hall in Chester, it possessed for the first time an administrative headquarters which, like any great town hall, had all the chief departments under one roof. By 1957 it had been decided to abandon the tradition of holding all committee meetings in Crewe and hold them all in the new County Hall at Chester. This decision marked a clean break with the methods of the 'social leaders' who had valued Crewe as the railway centre of the county. The Clerk of the County Council, Hugh Carswell, who resigned in 1959, had entered the council's service in 1929 and belonged to the tradition of local family connexion. His brother, Arthur, had been land agent for the Bromley-Davenport family at Capesthorne. His short term of office from 1952 to 1959, which followed a twenty-years' period under Geoffrey Scrimgeour, was filled by many reforms. The new Clerk, A. C. Hetherington, who had been appointed Deputy Clerk just before Carswell's own promotion, took office on 1 April 1959, the beginning of the first financial year to be governed by the Local Government Act of 1958. Aged 43, he faced with vigour the task of formalizing the new pattern of affairs which he had inherited.[1] By 1959, apart from the possibility of boundary changes by the Local Government Commission, the style, methods, and content of county administration in Cheshire had acquired a recognizable form.

What were the chief forces moulding the shape of the new administration? The efforts required to provide adequate local government services, particularly in the suburban and residential parts of the county, have produced a large and reasonably efficient organization, but one which depends for its efficiency upon the professional skill of full-time officials. Behind the whole process of professionalization lie certain legislative landmarks which are common to the history of all county councils. Before 1900 these authorities were primarily concerned with highways and bridges, police, and the administration of justice, but the Education Act of 1902 placed in their hands the responsibility for elementary education which had been to a large degree run by voluntary associations, churches, and chapels. The Local Government Act of 1929 transferred the administration of the poor law from boards of guardians and increased county responsibility for the upkeep of roads. But their most important duties stem from the provisions of the 1944 Education Act and the various enactments of the 1945–51 Labour government, notably the National Health Service Act of 1946, the Town and Country Planning Act of 1947, and the Fire Service, Children's, and National Assistance Acts of 1948. All counties have therefore required an increasing amount of expert advice. The greater significance of the expert has called upon the elected representatives to fulfil a new role in local government. There is one central question which runs through all the debates on bureaucracy: how far do the officials participate in the making of

[1] Hetherington as a young man was articled to the Town Clerk of Peterborough; and before becoming Deputy Clerk of Westmorland County Council at the end of the Second World War, he worked for the Austrian Control Commission.

policy which is supposed to be reserved for councillors alone? This question only has meaning within the context of the new administrative machine.

Training the expert

The extent of the administrative change in Cheshire is well illustrated by the fact that Geoffrey Scrimgeour, who was Clerk of the Council from 1932 until 1952, was the first full-time clerk which the county ever had. Before him, the clerks had been members of the Potts family, a firm of Chester solicitors, who combined the administration of county business with private practice. The family home, Northgate House, in Northgate Street, contained the County Clerk's offices until 1935. Scrimgeour governed the county's fortunes from another eighteenth-century town house, St. John's House, on the site of the Roman amphitheatre, which remained the clerk's office from 1935 until 1956. He had been trained originally as an engineer, but he took a post as assistant solicitor with Lancashire County Council, and after a distinguished Army record in the First World War, became in 1926 the full-time Deputy Clerk of Cheshire.[1] The twenty-five years during which he served the council were taken up by the process of professionalization, which in the first instance was only gradual, but which became much more rapid after 1944, the creation of a large body of people armed with expert knowledge. The extent of this professional expansion can be measured by the increase in the number of pensionable posts which were designated by the County Council under the terms of the Superannuation Act of 1922. When the Act was brought into force in 1924, there were only twenty-seven senior administrative posts, ninety-four clerks, and one hundred and fifty advisers, inspectors, or visitors brought into the scheme.[2] The Clerk's department consisted of three seniors and twenty-five clerks; the Treasurer's (or Accountant's) of three seniors and twenty-nine clerks. When Hetherington assumed the office of Clerk in 1959, the number of whole-time administrative staff in County Hall and other offices was 1,402.[3]

Before 1929 the business of local government in country districts was carried on by the part-time clerk and the part-time unpaid elected representative. The boards of guardians employed about 500 people in full-time positions scattered in the various poor-law and

[1] *Chester Chronicle*, 28 Aug. 1926, p. 12.
[2] *County Council Minutes* (1924), pp. 602–4.
[3] *Cheshire County Finance* (1960).

welfare institutions of the county. But the churchwardens and overseers in each parish, who were elected by the annual vestry meeting,
continued to thumb through their copies of *Knight's Overseers'*
Manual for guidance in the thankless job of assessing and collecting
the rates. The rating and valuation reforms of 1925–9 were an important step in the removal of the 'amateur' administrator from the
local scene. The clerks of boards of guardians and of small urban or
rural district councils were usually local solicitors in private practice,
who like the County Clerk, included the work of the authority with
business brought by private clients. Northwich Rural District, for
instance, employed a local solicitor as clerk until 1949. The number
of other full-time officials in 1930 which it employed was 14. By 1959
the number had risen to 63.[1] The offices were moved from the centre
of Northwich in 1930 and established in a house in Hartford, much
to the regret of several councillors who were farmers, and who combined attendance at council meetings with attendance at the bank in
Northwich on a Friday when they bought and sold their produce or
transacted legal business. The offices of Chester and Tarvin Rural
Districts in Chester continue to have the appearance of premises
occupied by a private solicitor.

The department of the Director of Education established the prototype for the structure of a new career. Teachers became full-time
administrators. Before 1902 the committee of managers for each
village school had performed details of day-to-day administration.
These bodies frequently consisted of 'social leaders' *par excellence*.
In Thelwall, near Warrington, for instance, the owners of two of the
large houses in the village had the right under the terms of the trust
deed to nominate a member of the committee of managers of the
National School.[2] The vicar was *ex officio* chairman. The 1902 Act
established beside bodies like these a group of professional administrators who were responsible for seeing that public money was well
spent in the voluntary schools which were subsidized by the local
authority, and for planning new schools which it established. The
Cheshire Education Committee Official Manual in 1923 listed the
Director, a secretary for higher education, a secretary for elementary
education, two inspectors, the County Librarian and the principals
of Crewe Training College, the School of Agriculture, and the Dairy
Institute as its chief officials. After the 1944 Education Act, which

[1] Information from the Clerk of Northwich R.D.C.
[2] School Minute Book in the possession of Alderman H. J. S. Dewes.

strengthened the powers of the local authority, the size of the county education department was greatly increased. In 1947 a group of advisers to the Director was appointed. Former teachers became experts who toured the county giving advice in their subjects to the teachers employed by the County Council. A professional service had been established.

For promotion in the local government service one had to be geographically mobile. This was already apparent before 1929 in the service of boroughs and urban councils, but after 1929 the ambitious young man who was willing to move from job to job made his appearance in the offices of county and rural councils. Doctors of medicine belong to one of the most mobile professions, and the reorganization of the county health and welfare services encouraged some to make their careers as full-time medical officers of health. The pattern of the transfer of power from private practice to full-time administration was also present in this case. The Local Government Act of 1929 required the County Council to draw up a scheme which would combine county districts in such a way that future medical officers of health could all be whole-time appointments. By 1935 only 20 districts in Cheshire had been combined to provide 7 appointments, and there were still 30 medical officers who were doctors in private practice. The scheme, dated 1937, was delayed by the Second World War, and the new scheme, dated 1948, was not brought into full operation until 1956 when the last medical officer in private practice died. The county was then administered in fifteen separate districts. It is some indication of the mobility of the medical profession that of the 42 medical officers in Cheshire in 1935, 17 had been educated in Scotland. Of the remaining 25, 13 came from the Manchester Medical School, 3 from Liverpool, 3 from Ireland, and 6 from London.[1] This career pattern was soon to become a standard one in the local government service.

Each profession began to raise its standards and to control recruitment by the recommendation that only those who had passed its own recognized examinations should be employed. Several qualifications were used by employees, but only a few of these signified to the profession that the recipient had shown himself competent in an examination. Before the Second World War, membership of the Institution of Municipal Engineers could be secured without holding qualifications from more exclusive bodies such as the Institute of Civil

[1] The Medical Register.

Engineers. The *testamur* of the Institute of Municipal Engineers was gained by examination, but in 1935 only six of the Institute's twenty-two members in Cheshire had secured this distinction. In fact, of the fifty-four engineers and surveyors employed by Cheshire authorities in 1935, only fifteen possessed full professional qualifications.[1] After the Second World War it became more and more essential for all applicants to have passed a recognized examination. John Birtwistle became the first Surveyor to the Northwich Rural District Council in 1911 with only the hard experience behind him of planning water closets and urinals with Harrison's of Newcastle upon Tyne.[2] But before his retirement in 1949 he had himself supervised the building of large numbers of council houses by local builders, and had seen to it that his two sons kept to their books sufficiently to gain the right qualifications, one to succeed him at Hartford and the other to become Surveyor to Congleton R.D.C.

Perhaps the most distinguished qualification was that developed by the Institute of Municipal Treasurers and Accountants. This was distinctly a municipal qualification. While Vincent Williams remained County Accountant and Treasurer from 1915 to 1950, the county council employees stood loyally by the Society of Accountants and Auditors. But the county boroughs and municipal boroughs of Cheshire encouraged the members of their finance departments to take I.M.T.A. exams. In 1935 nearly all the members of the I.M.T.A. in Cheshire were in the four county boroughs, 16 associate members and 25 students; in the other Cheshire authorities there were only 2 associate members and 9 students. But of these 52 people, only 8 in 1960 were still working for the same authority. The 44 others had all received some form of promotion: 18 were chief financial officers to local authorities in all parts of the country, 4 were deputy chief officers, and 7 were the finance officers of other public bodies.[3] An important consequence of the appointment of a new County Treasurer in 1950, R. H. A. Chisholm, who had been made Deputy Treasurer in 1944, was to join the officials of the county finance staff into the I.M.T.A. system. He encouraged them to take the I.M.T.A. exams.

By 1960 the effects of professional mobility and the extended use of examinations were apparent in the composition of the staff in County Hall.[4]

---

[1] *Who's Who in Local Government* (1935); *Institution of Municipal Engineers: List of Members* (1935).   [2] Personal information.
[3] Reports of Proceedings of 50th and 75th Annual General Meetings of I.M.T.A.
[4] The following paragraphs are written from information in the Superannuation Records in the County Treasurer's department.

All the fourteen chief officers and thirteen deputy chief officers at that date, with only a single exception (the Deputy Children's Officer), had worked for one or more other local authorities before entering the service of Cheshire County Council. (See Diagrams IV and V.) The average age at which the fourteen chief officers had been

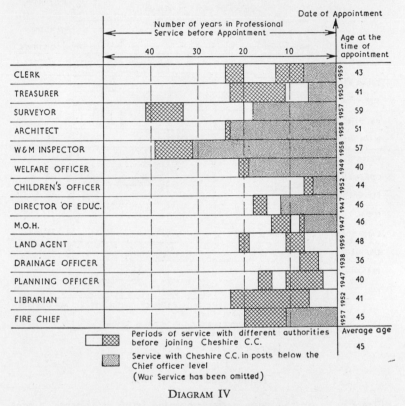

DIAGRAM IV

Cheshire Chief Officers: 1960

appointed was 45, and ten of them had served Cheshire for several years before being promoted. In fact, the convention had been established that a man gains his experience with other authorities before being appointed a deputy, and after he has reached that level, he may reasonably expect promotion to succeed to the chief officer's position. (See Diagram V.) This was in sharp contrast to pre-war conditions. In 1940 there had been signs of this kind of development, but there were few chief officers even then with much experience outside

Cheshire. The Deputy Clerk and Deputy Treasurer, for instance, had been in the same department all their working lives. They represented a former pattern of recruitment by which local boys entered the office on leaving school and secured promotion by seniority. Chief

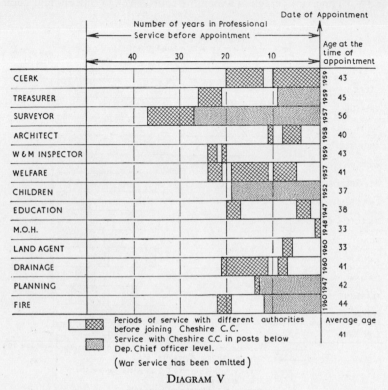

DIAGRAM V
Deputy Chief Officers: 1960

officers were on the same basis appointed from established professional people in the neighbourhood and were not former deputy officers. The records show a tendency for the chief officers in 1930 to have been appointed at a younger age than those in 1960, before their fortieth birthday rather than after it. The strengthening of the new professional structure was exemplified in the expansion of the number of deputy posts and their use as a training ground for future chief officers. In 1920 there were only eight heads of departments and one deputy, the Deputy Surveyor first appointed in 1900. Since that date six new departments have been created: the Librarian in 1922, the Drainage Officer in 1927, the Welfare Officer in 1930, the Children and Planning Officers in 1947, and the Fire Chief in 1948. But the most significant development was the creation of deputy posts:

Architect	1921	Weights and Measures	1936
Education	1922	Drainage	1946
Clerk	1926	Children	1947
Treasurer	1929	Planning	1947
Medical Officer	1932	Fire	1948
Land Agent	1933		

These were the positions to which a man might reasonably aspire in order either to apply for a senior post elsewhere or to be promoted within his own department.

Under the agreements made after 1948 by the Joint Negotiating Committee for Chief Officers of Local Authorities, deputies receive two-thirds of their own chief officer's salary. As Cheshire is one of the most populous counties in England and above the negotiated scales which apply to places with less than 600,000 people, the post of deputy chief officer with the County Council carries considerably more financial reward than the principal posts in many urban authorities. The award made in 1960, for example, gave the County Council of Cheshire the discretionary power to pay salaries of over £4,000 a year to their chief officers, and any deputy chief officer was therefore likely to be drawing between £2,500 and £3,000, which was the recognized minimum salary for chief officers in towns with a population of between 150,000 and 250,000. Cheshire deputies were therefore limited in the number of jobs for which they might apply. It is not surprising that the commonest form of advancement was promotion within the same department!

An important piece of cement in the new professional structure was the work of local professional organizations. These were chiefly of two kinds: first, local branches of national professional bodies, and secondly, associations of the employees of different local authorities within the same area who have professional interests in common. The former were perhaps more important in providing training facilities, while the latter gave the opportunity for informal contacts which smoothed the path of relations between conflicting local authorities. The North-Western branch of the I.M.T.A. although conceived on Cheshire soil in Thelwall at the home of the Borough Treasurer of Warrington in 1893, was to all intents and purposes like its parent body a Lancashire society, dominated by the county boroughs of the Manchester conurbation. This Lancashire predominance was recognized by the fact that the North-Western Students' Society of the I.M.T.A. began its life in 1903 as the Lancashire Students' Society, although the words 'and Cheshire' were added in 1909. Its present name dates from 1921. When the County Treasurer of Cheshire became the president of this society in its fiftieth year, 1952–3, it was the first time a county officer had ever done so—another indication of the break with county tradition represented by his succession to Vincent Williams in 1950.[1] Good examples of the second type of professional body were the Cheshire Surveyors' Association and the Merseyside Surveyors' Association. G. E. Ashforth, Cheshire County Surveyor 1927–42, who entered the council's service as deputy surveyor in 1914, conceived the idea of establishing the former as a sounding-board for professional opinion in the county. Its membership is confined to the surveyors and engineers of Cheshire authorities, and it meets five times a year under the chairmanship of the County Surveyor. The latter association was formed after the Second World War by the City Engineer of Liverpool in order to aid the preparation of a Merseyside Plan.[2]

An interesting side-line in professional activity was the election in 1957 of the Cheshire County Treasurer to be secretary of the Society of County Treasurers. He was formerly in 1954 the honorary co-secretary. Chisholm also served on the Finance Committee of the County Councils Association. Acting in these two capacities he found himself spending a significant proportion of his time on negotiations and committee work with outside bodies. But it was to the advantage of the council to allow its treasurer to develop professional contacts in this manner, because it could then gain immensely from his accumulated experience. It received first-hand accounts of the technical processes involved in the general grant orders made under the 1958 Local Government Act, and the financial statistics for all county services administered by all the counties in England and Wales were produced in its office at Chester. The council had ample opportunity for making the necessary comparisons. Chisholm's work extended its horizons.[3]

---

[1] T. L. Poynton, *I.M.T.A. North-Western Branch* (1956) and *N.W. Students' Society of I.M.T.A.* (1953).
[2] Information from the secretaries of the societies.
[3] Chisholm, born 1909, began local government work at the age of 18 with Middlesex C.C. in 1927. He was with Wiltshire C.C. from 1939 to 1944.

The value of professional contacts of this kind became apparent when chief officers were responsible for making appointments in the offices of their own authority. A man's reputation was known beforehand. The conventions of making appointments in Cheshire County Council varied from department to department. The Finance Committee appointed to the three top posts in the Treasurer's department; the Chairman and the County Treasurer to any post in Scales A to I; but below this, appointments were usually made by the Deputy Treasurer and the Assistant Treasurer. But in other departments the Standing Committee of the council showed more interest in relatively junior appointments. The Medical Officer of Health's department had a staff appointment sub-committee; and the County Welfare Committee itself made the decision about the appointment of a matron in an old people's home. The Staffing and Salaries Committee of the Council made an attempt to control establishments. For instance, whenever a senior post fell vacant, it could not be filled until after the committee had agreed to the necessity.[1] But the greater part of the responsibility for establishments fell on the shoulders of the chief officers themselves, and particularly upon those of the Clerk who as *primus inter pares* had to check the natural 'empire-building' tendencies of his colleagues.

A. C. Hetherington, the Clerk appointed in 1959, in fact placed the final professional touches to the administrative structure. He established the tradition of a regular meeting of chief officers in the County Hall, a 'chief officers' caucus'. Several meetings were held by Geoffrey Scrimgeour, Clerk 1932–52, particularly during the Second World War in connexion with civil defence and air raid precautions, but regular meetings have only been held since 1959. During the first month of his office, Hetherington also established an Organization and Methods team consisting of four men, three recruited internally and one supervisor who had previously worked for London County Council. The reports which this team made on any county department, or the office of a divisional executive, were submitted to the Clerk of the Council and the chief officer of the department concerned, and not direct to the councillors, because it was agreed that the technique derived from the study of 'organization and methods' was primarily a 'tool of management', and not therefore of immediate concern to the elected representatives. In practice, the chief officer sometimes sought the support of his committee in any important

[1] Information from the Deputy Treasurer.

matter which he considered necessary arising from such reports, particularly if further expenditure was involved. The development of management studies represented the new situation in which it was essential to trust the chief officer to carry out the great bulk of the council's work in a responsible manner without interferences. The Clerk himself believed that greater freedom of movement could be developed within the internal structure of a local authority, in contrast with the methods of the Civil Service which was cramped by the doctrine of 'ministerial responsibility'. By 1959 the convention had been accepted in County Hall that only the expert could judge the organizational ability of his colleagues. Training the expert was an expert business.

Working with the councillors

The professionalization of the local government service was a necessary consequence of the great increase of work performed by local authorities after the Act of 1929. It was accompanied by the growth of a very complicated network of formal relationships through committees and working parties where both officers and councillors learnt to co-operate with each other in planning the administrative programme which parliamentary legislation had placed upon their shoulders. The situation called for both officers and councillors to play a new role, and to work out together their respective functions. It blurred the traditional distinction between those who decide policy and those who execute such decisions. There was no real difficulty for councillors to appreciate that the chief officers were also developing the characteristics of public persons; the main trouble arose because some genuine grievances might easily be overlooked if the officers were politically innocent or the councillors administratively inept.

When meetings were first held in the new County Hall in 1958, the arrangements of the seating in the council chamber and in the committee rooms betrayed the informal conventions governing the relationships between councillor and official which had grown up during the previous thirty years. Members were allowed to choose their own seats in the council chamber, wherever they liked, and it was determined that henceforward a newly elected councillor should take the seat of his predecessor. A group of Labour members preferred to take the back row opposite the chair as an 'opposition bench', but otherwise, personal choice produced quite a haphazard scatter

of faces. The exception was in the two halves of the semi-circle on
either side of the chair. Here the chief officers were to sit in front of

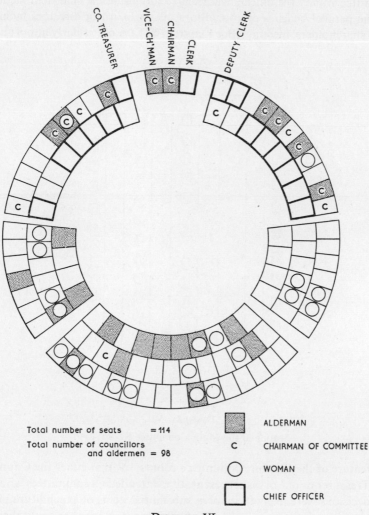

Total number of seats   = 114

Total number of councillors
and aldermen = 98

▓ ALDERMAN

C CHAIRMAN OF COMMITTEE

○ WOMAN

□ CHIEF OFFICER

DIAGRAM VI

Seating in the Council Chamber: 1961

their respective chairmen. (See Diagram VI.) The division of the
council chamber into two, between the 'ministerialist' benches for
chairmen and chief officers, and the 'non-ministerialist' benches for

other councillors, symbolized an important distinction in the workings of the council, described in Chapter 6. Similarly, in the committee rooms the officers were seated alongside the chairman facing
the parallel benches of councillors, like a board of directors facing
a shareholders' meeting. (See Diagram VII.) A particularly important

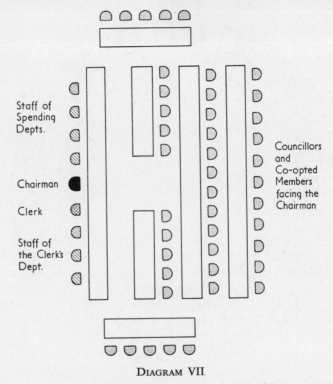

DIAGRAM VII
Seating in the Main Committee Room: 1961

feature of the Cheshire committee rooms was that either the County
Treasurer or one of his representatives attended all committees whose
decisions were likely to involve substantial items of expenditure and
sat with members of the Clerk's Department. No matter could therefore be discussed without reference to financial policy. These seating
arrangements emphasized the fact that officers of the council were to
be encouraged to speak out on behalf of their departments and not
merely to provide information for the chairmen of their respective
committees. The expert was allowed to participate in the council's

deliberations. The only reminder of former practice was that the Clerk or Deputy Clerk continued to attend most of the principal standing committees in person and in the excepted cases his place was taken by a solicitor in his department. The duty of advising the committee was never left to the committee clerk or to the chief or deputy chief officer of another department. The latter were left in charge of most sub-committee meetings.

The committee structure itself developed according to the demands made upon the council by new legislation. Before 1902 only three committees were of real importance: Finance, Parliamentary, and Roads and Bridges. After these came Weights and Measures, and Technical Instruction. The latter was made the most important committee of the council by the Education Act of 1902 and was henceforward called the Education Committee.[1] In 1920 the same pattern was apparent: four committees of the whole council, five principal spending committees, and ten minor committees. The 1929 Local Government Act required the formation of a Public Assistance Committee to do the work of the boards of guardians which in 1948 became the Welfare Committee. But the most important duties of a modern county council stem from the provisions of the 1944 Education Act and various enactments of the 1945–51 Labour government. By the time the Local Government Act of 1958 came into force the council had settled down to work with eighteen principal standing committees including one of the whole council, the General Purposes Committee, which remained the most flexible because any sub-committee made from it could report back to the full council sitting in committee without waiting for the next formal meeting. This formula was especially valuable in receiving reports from committees on Overspill, New Towns, and Rehousing. The principal spending committees were

1. Children	40 members	5. Roads and Bridges	63 members
2. Education	70 ,,	6. Welfare	40 ,,
3. Health	62 ,,	7. Weights and Mea-	31 ,,
4. Planning	30 ,,	sures	

There were also three small committees concerned primarily with agriculture (Diseases of Animals, Small-Holdings, and Land Drainage), the Fire Brigade Committee, and two minor committees for local taxation and civil defence. Above the whole system stood the

[1] Details on committees from annual year books.

guiding hands of two committees composed of the leading politicians on the council, the Finance Committee and the Parliamentary Committee, and two committees composed entirely of chairmen. The latter came into existence as a result of two world wars. The Reconstruction Committee of 1918 for planning the reversion to peacetime methods became in March 1922 the Staffing and Salaries Committee which has since dealt with all administrative appointments. In 1945 the Estates and Works Committee was formed to deal with matters arising from the building of county offices and to consider the applications of all standing committees for the acquisition of property. It was also to act as an arbitrator between the Finance Committee and the Standing Committee concerned, if there were any dispute about cost or purchase; and to manage any newly acquired property which had not been allocated to a particular department. Both the Staffing and Salaries Committee and the Estates and Works Committee have always been composed entirely from the chairmen and vice-chairmen of the principal standing committees.[1]

The evolution of the committee structure brought a corresponding increase in the size of the council's staff, particularly as a result of the Local Government Act of 1929 and the Education Act of 1944. The former added to the employment of the Public Assistance Committee all the existing employees of the guardians. These amounted to about 10 on the staff of the Public Assistance Officer and about 500 scattered in the various poor law and welfare institutions of the county.[2] The expansion of educational services after 1944 was responsible for even larger increases. By 1958 the total number of the council's employees had reached 15,801, of which the largest groups were in the education services: 5,519 teachers, 1,390 caretakers and cleaners, and 2,828 workers in the school meals service. The business of the Education Committee was the chief cause for creating a body of more than 200 professional people in County Hall.

Between 1903 and 1939 the total number of teachers employed in the county schools never exceeded 2,000, whereas in 1959 the number was almost 6,000. The statistics of education services show the same pattern. In 1939 there were 56,500 pupils and 1,888 teachers in 413 elementary schools and departments.[3] In 1959 there were 79,836 pupils and 2,564 teachers in 461 primary schools. The increase in

[1] Their purpose was amply defined in the printed minutes.
[2] *County Council Minutes* (1930), p. 656.
[3] *Jubilee of County Councils* (Evans Bros., 1939).

primary education is slight compared with that in secondary and further education. There were only about 5,000 pupils in 13 secondary schools in 1939. But in 1959 there were 29,903 in secondary modern schools, 15,744 in secondary grammar schools, and 22,705 in technical schools and evening institutes.

In the development of the committee structure and the expansion of numbers on the staff, it was much easier for a particular chief officer to understand his new role than for a councillor, because all the necessary channels of communication were designed primarily for the benefit of the professional expert and not for the part-time politician. How then could the officers work with the councillors? This question involves an examination of the opportunities which were open to councillors in the vast network of relationships which developed after the Second World War. What could a councillor do in the work of a local authority without appearing to be little more than a voluntary helper? A discussion of this subject has two interesting aspects: first, the extension of the system of co-option to various committees so that councillors from different authorities combine to perform co-operative pieces of work; and second, the development of the process by which the councillor himself may become a technical expert by specializing in a certain sphere of administration under the guidance of the permanent officials.

The first aspect, the system of co-option, has an importance both at the county council level and also at the district council level, because it is one of the principal means by which outside help is enlisted and information secured. The origin of the arrangements by which the three local authority associations nominate representatives for co-option to the principal standing committees of the County Council has already been described.[1] Political circumstances compelled the County Council to take other authorities into regular consultation. By 1960 the number of places which could be filled by co-option on the principal committees of the council was more than 140.[2] Those who fill these vacancies constitute a 'second council' which may be larger than the body of elected councillors and aldermen. Theoretically, it is possible for each one of these places to be taken by a separate individual, but because of pluralism and the frequency with which county councillors are invited to represent other associations, it is unlikely that there will ever be more co-opted members of committees than elected members. In 1960 the number of

<hr />

[1] See above, p. 120.   [2] *County Council Year Book* (1960).

each type was about the same—98. Who makes the appointments to these co-opted places? About 45 are made by the local authority associations, but in all the other cases it is possible for chief officers to advise the elected councillors in making the choice. The officers of the Education Department, for instance, suggest the names of teachers for co-option to the Education Committee in the belief that they are in a better position to choose suitable people than the teachers' associations. This committee has one of the longest traditions of co-option. The original committee constituted in 1903 and recon-stituted in 1937 had twelve places for co-opted members. When representation was given to local authority associations in 1945, the number of places was increased to twenty.[1] A conscientious co-opted member of this committee might be far more important in its work than the ordinary elected member.

Co-option is also a feature of the work of district councils when they co-operate with the County Council. Just as the need for estab-lishing a loyalty to the county at the time of the Boundary Commis-sion in 1945 gave a shape and a purpose to the scheme for co-opting district council representatives to the standing committees of the county, so the corresponding need of the district councils to retain some semblance of autonomy encouraged the promotion of schemes for delegating county powers to divisional authorities. After 1945 a fairly complicated division of the county into various divisional executives for particular county services created a new type of local authority in which the public person thrived. Each divisional authority contained three elements: county councillors representing that area, district councillors from the authority or authorities to which powers were delegated, and co-opted members. This system therefore has a considerable similarity to the principle of *ex officio* membership claimed by the magistracy in the nineteenth century on boards of guardians and highway boards.[2] The county councillors and co-opted members of divisional authorities represent links with the central administration and with local specialists just as the magis-trates represented Quarter Sessions and gentry opinion. Delegation agreements made under section 35 of the 1929 Act[3] with individual urban district councils for the latter to maintain the roads and bridges within their areas continued this process of co-operation after the boards of guardians had been abolished. The divisional

[1] Records of the Education Department.   [2] See above, pp. 46-47.
[3] Now replaced by annual agreements under section 45 of the Highways Act, 1959.

administration of education, health, and planning services after the Second World War, which was not based upon piecemeal applications of this kind, in contrast inaugurated a county-wide system of consultation and debate. The schemes drawn up under the Education Act of 1944 and the National Health Act of 1946 grouped local authorities for the purpose of nominating representatives of new joint committees, the divisional education and the divisional health executives, each with their own officer appointed by the county council. The delegation agreements made following the Town and Country Planning Act of 1947 gave individual authorities the right to adjudicate on planning matters but in consultation with the area planning officer, also appointed by the county council. Other services were given a system of administration based on area organizations. For instance, residential establishments run by the County Welfare Committee came under the direct supervision of an area management committee which was composed of the same three elements as other divisional authorities—county councillors, district councillors, and co-opted members.

The role of the county councillor was therefore largely concerned with the business of being a 'go-between', on behalf of divisional authorities and on behalf of the standing committees of the county council. His function was to work with officials at two different levels, and it was sometimes more convenient for the same person to be both a district and a county councillor so that he could act as an advocate for his own particular locality in the deliberations of a county committee.[1] Presenting a case was one of the most important social functions of the 'public person-type' of councillor. His principal weakness was that most of the facts necessary for preparing a brief could only be obtained from the 'public person-type' of official.

The second aspect of the subject, the education of councillors in technical expertise, has a tremendous importance in pointing the contrast between the social leader and the public person among councillors. The former was learned in the law and in the practices of politics from the very nature of his social position because his normal working life brought him into contact with these things; the latter who did not usually have these natural advantages was compelled to learn the job of being a person in public life, almost as a profession, in which an apprenticeship had to be served under the guidance of those who originally professionalized public life, the permanent

[1] See below, pp. 166–7.

officials. The role of the chief officer was largely to educate his committee in the wholly new and complicated apparatus of county administration which developed after the Second World War.

The Education Committee provided its members with the largest number of opportunities for self-education by establishing various working parties which were composed of both councillors and teachers for the study of particular problems. Special drafting sub-committees, for instance, were appointed in 1947–9 to write the Agreed Syllabus of Religious Instruction and in 1960–1 to devise a plan for the Youth Service on lines recommended by the Albemarle Report. The syllabus was to be reviewed regularly by the Standing Advisory Council on Religious Education appointed in 1953, which included councillors, teachers, and ministers of religion; and the youth service was to be supervised by a special sub-committee to which youth leaders could be co-opted. Following the Carr Report, 'Training for Skill', in 1958 five working parties were formed with employers to discuss the apprenticeship system. The Director of Education also encouraged joint-committees of councillors and teachers on specifically educational problems, usually after a conference of head teachers which has been held annually since 1950.[1] The committee on dull children issued its report in 1956, and that on the secondary modern school in 1958.[2]

One of the effects of this specialized study was to make those councillors who participated more appreciative of technical arguments and less inclined to think only of the needs of their particular locality. The officials tended to take into their confidence those who thought on a 'county basis'. This process divided the body of the council into those who participated in general policy-making with the officials and those who confined themselves chiefly to advocating the causes of local interest groups. Pressure groups in local affairs were either rather ephemeral bodies or associations which relied very strongly on the personality of a single person. The Wilmslow and District Society for the parents of mentally handicapped children, for example, received little support because the county officials were able to convince the council that its arguments were based upon an incorrect assessment of the facts. The Cheshire Federation of Ratepayers' Associations revolved around the person of its secretary, L. Beswick, who was sometimes consulted before any action was taken.

---

[1] *Education in Cheshire: 1945–55* (Cheshire Education Committee).
[2] Published by the University of London Press.

The chief officers of the council after 1945 had to work with the councillors in an ever-increasing series of regional authorities and joint committees which constitute the public life of the county. The public person was one who understood his way through the labyrinth in order to lobby or persuade the right official. Many questions were settled 'at officer level' without bringing in too many outsiders, and the whole procedure of interdepartmental discussion among the officers was greatly facilitated by the building of County Hall in Chester, and by the provision of a members' dining room in which the chief officers and their deputies could have continuous daily contact with each other and with the leading councillors. County Hall was to some extent a monument to the fact that most of the leading officials preferred to live in or near Chester rather than in or near Crewe where until 1957 all the regular committee meetings were held. The abandonment of Crewe, the railway centre, symbolized the new régime, because Chester was clearly an attractive city in which to live as a professional officer. The possibility of making Crewe the permanent centre of county administration was precipitated by an offer made in 1931 by the Marquess of Crewe to give his country house, Crewe Hall, to the County Council,[1] and the permanent officials at that date were able to make an effective lobby in favour of Chester because the council itself was divided into two exactly equal groups, almost on strict party lines—Liberals for Crewe and Conservatives for Chester, while the chairman, Sir William Hodgson, refused to use his casting vote, because he was a Crewe man. After almost a year's delay, the vote to reject Lord Crewe's offer was influenced by Councillor Russell Hall, an architect who maintained the house would be extremely expensive to renovate because it had been unoccupied for nearly twenty years.[2] The rumour was of 'dry rot'. In 1934 extra architects were appointed in the County Architect's department to design the present County Hall in Chester, the foundation stone of which had been laid in 1939 when the war put an end to further construction.

Planning the budget

The County Hall, which backed up to Chester Castle on land belonging to the historic precincts, an island of county territory within the city boundary,[3] and which stood on the banks of the

[1] J. Pope-Hennessy, *Lord Crewe* (1955), p. 176.
[2] *Manchester Guardian*, 11 Nov. 1932, p. 10.
[3] Its dust-bins had to be emptied by Chester R.D.C., not Chester City.

River Dee with an excellent view of Handbridge, also symbolized the high degree of professional consultation necessary to the preparation of estimates and the control of expenditure. County officials continued to exchange memoranda between the different departments, although they shared the same building, but the use of the internal telephone and regular conferences between technical advisers made the whole process of planning a much easier operation. After 1945, and particularly after 1949, the scale of the council's activities was increased beyond any measure which had been envisaged when County Hall was designed. The County Architect and his staff architects were called upon to extend the size and scope of the building.

The County Treasurer's department, which occupied the ground floor, was the centre of planning in the new methods of business. Every year the section heads of the Treasurer's staff joined with the finance officers of individual departments in the preparation of estimates for each of the spending committees. The volume of county council business required special vigilance from the Treasurer's staff in the prevention of over-spending and in the calculation of long-term trends. There was a great difference, after making allowances for the effects of inflation, between administering a budget of about £2½ million in the 1930's and one of about £25 million in the 1950's. The latter was presented to the Finance Committee in a document of over 150 pages, which gave the previous year's estimates and actual expenditure, and on the opposite page against every entry listed the main reasons for any changes, whether they were the result of new commitments or of variations in existing commitments.

The Finance Committee and the council itself were unable to find many opportunities for altering the estimates as they were presented to them. The degree of manœuvrability was limited by previous policy decisions which had committed the County Council to certain regular items of expenditure, such as the payment of teachers, and by duties laid upon the council through government policy which brought new commitments, such as the building of schools in rapidly expanding suburban areas. The issue of 'keeping down the rates', which was fiercely debated by many county councillors, frequently resolved itself into either an attempt to eliminate wastage in the current expenses of administration—an attack on the 'bureaucrats' —or a determination to halt the speed of a capital building programme—an attack on 'extravagant schemes'. Neither course of action could reduce the county rate precept by more than a few pence.

The bulk of the budget was determined by the force of circumstances, such as national pay awards, or by the need to maintain standards which had already been agreed by the policy decisions of spending committees in earlier years. Rate-fixing itself was a process of informal negotiation between the Treasurer and the chairman of the Finance Committee which began with a statement of the total net expenditure to be met from rates if the estimates submitted by all departments were accepted. County councillors were chiefly concerned with the burden which the county precept would place upon the rates of the different districts which they represented. The county rate precept after 1950 usually represented about two-thirds of the rate levied by the constituent authorities within the county. Concern for 'keeping down the rates' was naturally expressed in the form of attempts to limit extravagance in County Hall. The Finance Committee and the principal spending committees, particularly the Education Com- mittee, could in theory go back on former policy decision, or resolve to manage with minimum standards, but in practice they were usually compelled by governmental policy and the local climate of opinion to continue to levy an increasing rate precept. Even then, the rate in the pound paid by county ratepayers was usually lower than that paid in adjoining county boroughs. In 1960–1 Manchester ratepayers were faced with 26s. in the pound; those in Cheadle and Gatley, with 21s. The precepting system seemed to inhibit the increase of rates in county areas.

As soon as the policy had been determined, the management of the county finances became a professional task which was carried out independently of political decisions. A distinction was made between the function of the Treasurer in person, and the function of the staff of his department. The latter under the direction of the Deputy Treasurer carried out the routine work of paying wages, salaries, and bills, and the routine management of the accounts. In order to pro- vide an adequate means of budgetary control, weekly statements were produced of spending under each head of the items in committee estimates, and weekly reviews of the capital account were designed to maintain a check upon the building and improvements of schools. The machinery of the Treasurer's department was also placed at the disposal of the Surveyor in order to provide regular fortnightly statements of highways costing. The Loans Fund, recording the authority's dealings in mortgages and short-term loans, also required constant supervision.

The principal function of the County Treasurer in person was that of financial adviser to the council. By a careful husbanding of county resources, making wise investments of money not in use or negotiating short-term loans when money was short, he was able to bring great expertise to the benefit of the ratepayer. Economies might be made more easily by listening to his advice than by cutting down the estimates. He was able, for instance, to advise the council how far it was able to run down the balances during any given financial year in order to meet current expenditure, because his assistants kept a record of seasonal variations in demand by plotting on a graph the weekly balances and the additional revenue arising from new rateable value.

A change in advice was able to produce a striking change of policy. The appointment of R. H. A. Chisholm as County Treasurer in 1950 and the election of Alderman H. J. S. Dewes as chairman of the Finance Committee in 1952 inaugurated a new régime, marked by an extension of publicity methods and the provision of an information service, greatly aided by the improved mechanization of office procedure. The annual report, *Cheshire County Finance*, was first published in 1951. Electronic computing machinery was first installed in 1956. Punched card equipment had been in use since 1946, but the chief value of hiring electronic equipment was that it enabled the Treasurer to bring in new models when they were considered necessary. The I.B.M. 604 electronic calculator of 1956 was exchanged in 1958 for a basic 650. The latter in June 1962 was exchanged for an I.B.M. 1401 with four tape units. But the most revolutionary change of policy was in the method of capital financing. The predecessors of the 'Chisholm–Dewes' régime, Vincent Williams as Treasurer and Sir Otho Glover as chairman,[1] belonged to the school of thought then considered orthodox, which believed that capital development was a burden to be borne by future generations and should therefore be financed by loans. After 1950 the contrary practice was established of financing a large proportion of capital expenditure from revenue. In 1949–50 only 3·8 per cent. of capital came from this source, but in the following year, the first of Chisholm's term of office, 1950–1, the proportion had been increased to over 25 per cent.; by 1959–60 it was as high as 29 per cent. The immense capital development programme during the 1950's, amounting to over £17 million, was financed without increasing the county debt by more than £6¾ million.

[1] Director of Castner, Kellner Alkali Co. Ltd., died 1956.

Planning the budget was to a large extent determined by government policy, particularly that of the Ministry of Education, which decided on questions of priority. The school-building programme, which enjoyed such a predominant position in the County Council's policy for capital investment, was geared by Ministry policy and by

TABLE 6

Capital Expenditure: 1950–60

Year	Education service £	Total £	Percentage of total spent on education
1950–1 . . .	903,000	1,115,000	81·0
1951–2 . . .	1,012,000	1,266,000	79·9
1952–3 . . .	1,065,000	1,329,000	80·1
1953–4 . . .	833,000	1,057,000	78·8
1954–5 . . .	996,000	1,244,000	80·1
1955–6 . . .	1,074,000	1,455,000	73·8
1956–7 . . .	1,565,000	2,290,000	68·3
1957–8 . . .	1,658,000	2,212,000	75·0
1958–9 . . .	1,451,000	2,196,000	66·1
1959–60 . .	1,614,000	2,789,000	57·9

immediate political considerations to provide school places where large numbers of new houses were being built. About 75 per cent. of all capital invested during the decade 1950–60 went on the schools and other educational institutions of the county. (See Table 6.) A considerable proportion of this money was naturally spent in the most populous areas, the divisional executives of Deeside and Chester, of Cheadle and Wilmslow, and of East Cheshire, areas which in the County Development Plan (1952) figured under the headings of sub-region 1 (Wirral), 7 (Altrincham), and 8 (Cheadle), whose importance has already been noted. When presenting his 'budget speech' to the Finance Committee in 1960, the chairman referred to 'the dual problem of extending services to new development areas, while modernizing existing facilities'. He recorded with pride the council's provision of new buildings during the decade, 1950–60:

43 Primary Schools   10 Children's Homes
32 Secondary Schools   8 Clinic Centres
 2 Colleges of Further Education   5 Ambulance Stations
14 Homes for the Aged   4 Fire Stations

This list revealed the importance of the education services, and an examination of the geographical distribution of such buildings, the importance of the suburban areas.

The education services had always after the 1902 Education Act exercised the strongest influence on the fixing of the county rate precept. From the financial year 1903–4 onwards, their cost amounted to half or more than half of the council's total annual expenditure. Government grants in their support were also largely responsible for making the council more dependent on the administrative control of the Ministry. Before the First World War the value of assigned revenues reduced the need for levying a large general rate for county purposes, but throughout the period 1919–39 the council was expected to find between 40 and 50 per cent. of its income from rates. The great changes came after the Second World War when government grants were increased to meet the increasing costs, and after 1949 a pattern was established by which over 50 per cent. of current annual expenditure was met from government grants and about 35 per cent. from the rates. The operations of the block grant formula under the 1958 Act did not alter these proportions. Nevertheless variations in the Education Department's programme had the most influential effect upon the process of rate-fixing. By 1959–60 the maintenance of the education services cost £13½ million or 64 per cent. of the total budget. It was calculated that the weekly cost of county services to the household with a rateable value of £25 was 16s. 6¼d., of which 10s. 11½d. represented the cost of education services. Government grants reduced the total of 16s. 6¼d. to 6s. 5½d., the sum borne by the ratepayer.

The increased rateable value of the county, after the new valuation lists had come into force in 1956 and by the re-rating provisions of the 1958 Act, to some extent shifted the ratepayer's burden from the householder to the owner of a shop or a factory. The rateable value of Cheshire was more than doubled between 1955 and 1960, from £5,900,000 to £12,000,000. But the real significance of this event was for the first time to supply the county with resources equal to those of the great county boroughs like Liverpool and Manchester.

The new suburbs to which people from these boroughs had migrated acquired a new significance. During the 1950's the greatest amount of the County Council's energies went towards fulfilling their needs. Even during the 1930's, the era of boundary revision already described, the county administration recognized the political importance of the residential districts and the relative poverty of agricultural

areas and old industrial towns. The Agricultural Derating Act of
1896 had decreased the rateable value of the county by over 12 per
cent., and the derating provisions of the 1929 Act by over 17 per cent.
Suburban areas demanded the most attention and required the most
money. Many of the political tensions between the various authorities
within the county were caused by the fundamental fact that their
rateable value did not necessarily correspond to their status. The
population of the county was concentrated upon its northern fringes.
There was a natural division between those urban areas where the
rateable value was always increasing and those where it had either
fallen or remained the same. It has always been very hard to demote
a borough once established, and it has been equally difficult to
promote an urban district which has clearly no central core of established industry and commerce. The only urban districts in Cheshire
to receive municipal charters between 1919 and 1939, Altrincham,
Bebington, and Sale, were of the same type, in which residential
development was added to an existing centre. Of the three, only Sale
lacked a long-established market. The political implications of the two
county review orders in 1933 and 1936 were concerned with the possibilities of municipal status. The order of 1933 extended the areas of
Bebington, Ellesmere Port, and Hoylake more than threefold, and
the order of 1936 extended the urban districts around Manchester at
the expense of the rural districts of east Cheshire. The rateable
value of Bucklow Rural District fell from £153,907 to £61,693, and
that of Congleton Rural District from £54,328 to £47,338. But the
anomalies of wealthy urban districts and declining boroughs were
not removed. In 1954, for instance, the rateable value of Hoylake,
a residential urban district in the Wirral, was higher than that of any
of the Cheshire boroughs except Altrincham, Bebington, and Sale,
the new residential boroughs of the 1930's. Similarly, the rateable
value per head of population in Hazel Grove and Bramhall, a residential urban district near Manchester and Stockport, £12. 6s. 10d.,
was more than twice that of any Cheshire borough except Altrincham, Bebington, and Sale, where it was about £8. There were eleven
urban districts with a rateable value higher than that of the two
poorest boroughs, Congleton and Dukinfield. Eight of them, that
is all except Ellesmere Port, Northwich, and Runcorn, were residential districts for workers in the great conurbation areas of Liverpool and Manchester. The history of changing rateable values
illustrates the political importance of the residential areas. Again, the

figures show how important were the three sub-regions Wirral (1), Altrincham (7), and Cheadle (8) delimited by the Development Plan (1952). More than half the rateable value of the whole administrative county lay in these three suburban areas. (See Table 7.)

The political forces generated by the expansion of the new suburbs were to some extent challenged by the official policy in town and country planning which required the definition of a 'Green Belt' around the 'great towns'.[1] The spending of ratepayers' money in

TABLE 7

Percentage of Total Rateable Value in Suburban Areas

	1951	1961
Region 1. Wirral	20·5	22·5
„ 7. Altrincham . . .	21·8	19·3
„ 8. Cheadle . . .	11·8	11·3
Total for 1, 7, & 8. . . .	54·1	53·1
Regions 2–6 and 9 . . .	45·9	46·9
	100·0	100·0

these conditions was likely to acquire a symbolic significance which bore little relation to the technical problems of providing an economic service. The expertise of the Treasurer's department was sometimes called upon to satisfy more subtle demands. In 1960 the County Council was asked to restore and maintain the Mansion House in Tatton Park which the late Lord Egerton of Tatton had devised to the National Trust. The position of Tatton Park, which had even in the 1880's been considered 'ripe for development' by those building villas for Manchester merchants,[2] made it an attractive venture for the General Purposes Committee. The existence of the Egerton estate, which the late Lord Egerton had been disinclined to develop, in fact made it possible for the County Council to maintain a 'Green Belt' against the extension of Altrincham and Bowdon. The opportunity of running a 'stately home' and a large area of parkland as recreational playground close to the new suburbs was not refused. Any proposal which might have been made to take over a park more remote from this area, the south-western part of the county, for example, would not have met with such enthusiastic support. The disputes in the council over the capital expenditure involved for

[1] See below, pp. 191 ff., and map at end.
[2] See above, pp. 26–27, and Map 2, facing p. 119.

the renovation of Tatton Hall, which had been neglected by its former owner, were a reminder of the degree of freedom which members enjoyed to spend money outside the terms of immediate administrative needs, and a reminder of the significance of the Manchester area in planning the county budget. The grand opening of the house at Tatton, after its restoration in 1962, marked an important stage in the development of county administration.[1]

Technical competence

But the needs of the new suburbs after 1945 also drew particular attention to the technical competence of the full-time officials in County Hall and their complete participation in the business of policy making. Officials in the Treasurer's department were able to take the convenient attitude that their work involved the professional management of finances, and not the decision to spend money; but those in the principal spending departments were aware of the degree to which their research and consultation affected policy decisions taken by their own committees. The need to anticipate events, and the preparations necessary for implementing decisions to improve the quality of a particular service, created a situation in which expert guidance was required.

The Education Department provided many good illustrations of the extent to which circumstances demanded a high degree of technical skill from the officials concerned. The Education Act of 1944 raised the whole level of its operations, and produced schemes for planning long-term developments which would provide 'secondary education for all'. The staff of the department of the Director of Education found itself called upon to devise new examinations for selection and new syllabuses, and to stimulate thought on such problems as the education of backward children. The compilation of a development plan for schools and colleges throughout the county brought into being a highly skilled professional service.

The impact of the new suburbs introduced an element of difficulty into long-term planning arrangements. Throughout the country, one of the principal concerns of all education committees was to cater for 'the bulge', an increase in the number of primary school children following an increase in the birth-rate after the Second World War. But Cheshire Education Committee had the added responsibility of providing school places for the children of an immigrant population

[1] *The Guardian*, 30 May 1962.

which entered the county from Manchester, Liverpool, and other large towns and settled in the areas already described. Although the last members of 'the bulge' age-group were admitted in 1952, the number of children in the primary schools of the county continued to rise, from 70,432 in 1951 to 86,502 in 1957.[1] The policy of the Ministry of Education gave considerable priority to the needs of areas where numbers of children were increasing rapidly. Between the issue of Circular 245 in 1951 which limited school-building programmes and the issue of Circular 283 in 1954 which encouraged 'rural reorganization' and lifted controls on minor building projects (under £10,000), the Cheshire Education Committee was to a large extent compelled by the Ministry to erect primary schools in the new suburban areas rather than to improve existing primary schools in other parts of the county. The programme of erecting and improving secondary schools during the same period remained unimpaired. Outside the new suburban areas, some improvements were made within the terms of the Minor Building Programme which did not require the sanction of the Ministry. The plans for the development of further education did not advance so rapidly.

The Ministry required local officials to prepare a brief which argued the case for the building of any new school to be included in the Major Building Programme. The Education Department therefore in all the applications which it made devised its own means of providing all the information necessary to convince the Minister that certain capital expenditure on new schools was thoroughly justified. The siting of such buildings was largely determined by purely technical arguments, and not by the distribution of political favours. The expertise which was applied to these problems illustrated the degree to which education officers were involved in the policymaking process. The bulk of the County Council's capital development programme was planned 'at the officer level', with regular consultations between the Departments of Education, Architect, and Planning. The reputation of the local education authority in the eyes of the staff of the Ministry was either enhanced or discredited according to the skill which the officers applied to their work.

The main aim of the Director of Education in Cheshire was to have a school built or to have extra school places available for the time when increasing numbers of children reached the appropriate age

[1] *Education in Cheshire: 1955–60* (published by Cheshire Education Committee), pp. 11–12.

for admission. The officials in his department based their planning techniques on three separate concepts. First, all surveys of child population were calculated in terms of 'age groups'. The head-teachers who filled in a form three times a year contributed towards the compilation of primary school statistics which were divided into yearly 'age groups'—infants (4–6), juniors (7–10), and seniors (11–14). Second, all new schools which the Education Committee intended to build were zoned to take children from a given 'catchment area'. In 1960 there were 460 primary schools and 73 secondary modern schools. For the purposes of the '11+ examination', an assessment of suitability for grammar school education, the county was divided into 17 areas, each with its own grammar schools, whether they belonged to the 24 maintained by the County Council, or were independent or direct-grant schools providing county places. Third, all schools were classified according to the accommodation provided and the maximum number of children which could be admitted at the appropriate age. This concept required a definition of the size of classes or forms. How many children could conveniently be taught by a single teacher? The answer to this question determined the classification of accommodation into one-form, two-form, or three-form entry. Using these three concepts—'age group', 'catchment area', and 'form-entry'—the officials in County Hall argued the case for a new school by proving a deficiency of accommodation for certain age groups, even after readjustments had been made in the catchment areas. In 1949 they began an annual review of existing school places within each divisional executive. The Planning Department provided figures of the birth-rate to forecast future trends, and local housing authorities submitted the number of houses which it was estimated would be built within each primary school zone. The staff of the Assistant Director for Primary Education then prepared estimates of the total primary school population and subtracted the number which might be expected to attend private or Roman Catholic schools. The Major Building Programme depended on these calculations, and there were only a limited number of possible building sites which the Planning and Architect's Department could accept. The Education Committee itself therefore had little choice of action but to accept the recommendations made by its officers. Any detailed consideration of priorities was left to a few councillors working in close co-operation with the staff of the department, all members of the Education General Purposes Sub-Committee. Plans for building new schools were needed to keep pace with events. In 1961, for instance, a two-form entry primary school at Hazel Grove was placed in the building programme for 1963–4 in order to meet the expected number of children from a private housing estate about to be built. Another one-form entry school at Cheadle Hulme in the 1964–5 programme was designed to meet the needs of Manchester 'overspill' as well as houses built by private enterprise.

The shortage of teachers also increased the importance of the Director of Education's staff in County Hall. The latter assumed responsibility for interviewing and placing newly qualified teachers who had just graduated from training colleges. In 1955 the Education Committee were obliged to ask the managers and governors of Cheshire schools to relinquish their rights so that a 'central pool' of new teachers could be administered from County Hall. In 1959 this arrangement became obligatory. Although the managers and governors continued to appoint teachers with some experience, the county officials interviewed and offered places to training-college students. 'Central pool' arrangements of this kind permitted greater flexibility in planning.

The most delicate task in official enterprise was the administration of the 11+ examination, 'the assessment of children for appropriate education'. Again, the impact of the new suburbs made itself felt. All the county officials were conscious of the fact that the results of the 11+ examination required the authority to provide a higher proportion of grammar school places per head of child population in the 'smarter residential suburbs' than in the old-established towns. The distribution of 'grammar school types' was further complicated by the arrangements for county places to be awarded to those who lived within range of Manchester Grammar School, Stockport Grammar School, Macclesfield King's School, and similar established institutions, and by the need to meet the wishes of Roman Catholic parents. All the social tensions derived from the allocation of grammar school places set a burden on the shoulders of education officers. Certain facts, such as the precise distribution of grammar school places, were not available even to all members of the Education Committee. The latter accepted a policy which confined this information to the 'ministerialists', the leading councillors and chief officers, because it would be unwise to let it become public knowledge. The education officers were therefore required to prepare long, elaborate statements for the press, explaining the committee's policy, but frequently omitting the more interesting sociological facts upon which it was based. Dealing with queries from the public became a task which called for very skilful diplomacy. The tensions which might have been caused by the provision of secondary education in comprehensive schools were avoided. In 1947 and 1948 the Divisional Executives for Wilmslow and for Crewe had asked for the inclusion of comprehensive schools in the Development Plan. The Wilmslow Divisional Executive, perhaps because of the enthusiasm of one of its members, Mrs. Payne, even submitted its own memorandum on the subject to the Ministry of Education, but the County Council rejected these suggestions which were associated in the minds of the majority of councillors with the programme of the Labour party. Selection for secondary education remained a task which the officers had to perform.

How far then did the officials participate in policy-making? This question might best be answered by asking what decisions were left for the councillors to make. The convention of submitting the majority of decisions to a committee or sub-committee in the Education Department produced agenda of tremendous length and complexity and volumes of printed minutes. The most important job of the Director of Education or his assistants in attending a committee meeting was to give advice on the facts, to direct the attention of the councillors to those items where they had a genuine opportunity of deciding an issue of principle, or to persuade them to participate in the studies of a working party, such as those which have already been mentioned. The Cheshire officials have never been shy in debate because they have for a long time been encouraged to participate in committee discussions. There is one difficult question to answer. How far were the committees occupied in merely giving legal sanction to the obvious course of action which had already been determined by the technical competence of full-time professional administrators? Whenever a serious issue was involved, there was likely to be a conflict between those councillors who had participated in the decision-making process of sub-committee work, and those who had not. For the smooth working of committees a lot depended on how far an individual councillor felt that he had the confidence of the officials in the department under consideration. The Director of Education, for example, was frequently better known to the press and to the electorate than the chairman of his committee, and his whole life was involved in a series of public engagements. He was not able to close the office door in the evening and become an ordinary citizen. The county officials and those councillors who enjoyed their confidence had an incomparable advantage over those councillors who felt on the periphery of affairs, by having immediate access to regular sources of information, either direct from the Ministry or through the journals of various professional societies. Any councillor wishing to attack the decisions of the 'inner ring' had to go to the officials for information. County councillors were required to educate themselves in the processes of a department's work before they were able to participate fully in the business of decision-making.

Officials therefore helped to determine the council's policy because only full-time committees could be expected to take collective decisions on the large number of problems which were submitted for their examination. The art of being a councillor was to know how to raise questions on important matters when other members were calling upon the chairman to move to the next item of the agenda. Successful councillors were anyway often more interested in the affairs of their own political party. Officials had more to fear from the consequences of local government reorganization than the leading members of the ruling party. It has already been noted that the Boundary Commission of 1945–9 faced a very different county authority in Cheshire from that meeting the Local Government Commission in 1962. Between these two dates the County Council had extended the number and quality of its professional advisers. In 1962, the professional teams, which had been built up over the years, were faced with the prospect of seeing the more interesting projects of the suburban areas removed from their purview and handed over to newly created authorities for conurbation areas around Liverpool and Manchester. Bodies of technical experts were reluctant to be re-formed, but they recognized the operation of other political forces. Some believed that a Manchester County Council would not be formed by a Conservative government unless it were to the advantage of the Conservative party. Official participation in policy-making was limited to a certain field of action. The activities of councillors were not confined to the committee rooms—they also ran in other corridors of power.

6

PERSONS IN PUBLIC LIFE

No one in the public life of the county attempted to deny the importance of the changes which had taken place inside County Hall, but there was a considerable difference of opinion about the function of elected councillors in the working of the new system. Some observers tended to think that the technical competence of full-time local government officials had outstripped the political acumen of the elected representatives. They were prepared to accept the conclusion that civic pride and a sense of public duty had not survived the 'administrative revolution', just as some bishops regretfully acknowledged the fact that the moral senses of men had not kept pace with their technical achievements. They cultivated a nostalgia for government by social leaders whenever the discussion turned upon the calibre of present-day councillors who could not lay claim to the 'tradition of public service' which belonged to political leadership by virtue of social status. But other observers tended to think that the technical competence of officials was an important challenge to the effectiveness of democratic representation which all political parties were bound to meet. They concentrated their attention upon the need to recruit councillors who were capable of acquiring the technical knowledge necessary for an appreciation of administrative detail, and the political understanding necessary for making sure that the full-time officials provided an efficient service. This difference of opinion was apparent in the selection of the 'right people' at election time. Some hoped to persuade 'the gentry' or 'professional men' to come forward as candidates; others looked for suitable people of ability, regardless of social class.

The central problem of county politics was to reconcile the needs of the new administrative methods of County Hall, which required some degree of specialization from those who were to be chairmen of committees, with the accidents of the processes of election, which supplied the councillors to fill these positions. In the absence of paid political members forming an executive or policy committee, how was it possible to find men and women with sufficient time and sufficient ability to direct the operations of a particular county service? County Hall needed specialists; the political parties needed members with the application necessary to keep in touch with the daily lives of the electors. Both required ability. How far could the practice of nomination and election keep pace with the demands of administrative expertise? Any councillor who possessed the right qualities quickly became an important public person. The business of being a county councillor depended upon securing the nomination of a party in an electoral division or standing as an independent candidate, and then upon winning the election if it were contested. The business of remaining a county councillor depended upon being able to retain the support of the electorate every three years, but the business of becoming an important public person was a function of inclination, stamina, and sheer ability. The County Council ran the risk of functioning only by bringing together in a single place the important people in the public life of the boroughs and district councils, and hoping that from them would emerge suitable leaders and competent chairmen.

The members of Cheshire County Council in 1960 differed from those in 1940 not so much in matters of social class, education, or occupation, although some important comparisons can be made in these fields, but rather in matters of manner and method, in the way they explained their work and in the time they devoted to it. By 1960 the council was reconciled to the absence of 'gentlemen'. It no longer gave the impression of a meeting of county society. There is an obvious contrast to be made between the authority which met the Boundary Commission in 1946–7 and that which met the Local Government Commission in 1962, a contrast in skill and confidence which is not due entirely to the administrative changes of the 1950's. By 1960 there was a nucleus of councillors with fifteen years of practical experience in working the new administrative system. These men, although a minority, represented the new political maturity of the council.

After the Second World War the county of Cheshire became as large a political unit as the great county boroughs. The county council election of 1946, based on the electoral register of 1945, was the first Cheshire election to be fought with an electorate larger than that of either Liverpool or Manchester. Even in 1937, at the last pre-war election which was based on the revision of boundaries made in 1936, Liverpool still had 5,700 more voters than Cheshire. But by the time of the county council elections of 1958, both Liverpool and Manchester had each more than 100,000 voters fewer than the Cheshire electorate of 605,000. Such were the consequences of voluntary migration referred to in Chapter 4.[1] Just as the county increased its rateable value at the expense of the adjacent county boroughs,[2] so it brought more people into the business of county government. There were two obvious differences between political practice in counties and political practice in county boroughs. In the first place, county divisions were more difficult to canvass than borough wards, and tended to have fewer contests. The county electorate was called upon less frequently to exercise its vote, and although, unlike a borough council, the whole county council went out of office at the same time, there was a smaller possibility of a sudden change in party control because of the larger proportion of unopposed returns. In the second place, county hall was much farther from the electorate, in terms of geographical distance, than the town hall was from its citizens; and county meetings are usually held in the day-time, and not in the evening, as in boroughs. The town councillor had a much shorter distance to travel to meetings, and did not need to interrupt his daily work. It was sometimes said that county councils were in danger of being dominated by those who lived closest to the county town. Cheshire did not appear to run this risk. In fact, the attendance registers showed that the poorest attenders at county meetings in Chester were often those representing the rural areas of the south and west which lay within easy access. When comparing county politics with conditions in county boroughs, the most difficult things to understand lay precisely in these two fields, the nature of contested elections and the effects of distance on participation. What kind of people became public persons in county politics? How did they differ from town councillors? What are the special problems caused by the extension of administrative operations over large areas of countryside?

If some symbolic event is needed to represent the arrival of the 'new men' in county politics, those councillors who were to join with the officials and build the complex administrative machine of the 1950's, it might be found in the county council election of 1946. Half the councillors elected in that year for Cheshire, 35 out of 69, were serving for the first time, a change of personnel of such magnitude that it could only be compared with the number of non-magistrates

[1] See above, pp. 104–6.   [2] See above, pp. 107–8.

elected to the first council in 1889. (See Appendix A.) Did this mark
the advent of the public person in the same way as the election of
1889 recognized the existence of social leadership? This question
must be answered in relation to the changing functions of county
councillors after the 1920's. What role did the modern councillor
play in relation to the full-time chief official? Councillor R. H.
Toothill, a retail pharmacist who had been elected for the Timperley
division in 1931 and 1934, and for the Hale division in 1937, wrote
a letter to the *Manchester Guardian* in 1941 expressing his concern
for local democracy:

> The people's elected representatives are losing their power, and the
> ordering of our daily lives is becoming the exclusive privilege of paid
> officials. A commentary on the present tendency was given to me by a
> senior official when he said: 'I have no use for voluntary helpers; give me
> the paid men or women any time.'[1]

What role should the elected representative have played, if it was not
that of a 'voluntary helper' in bureaucracy? Who was prepared to
give up the necessary time for working with the officials? And why?
What motives led one into taking up 'public life' at the county council
level? The election of 1946 might have symbolized the advent of a new
type of councillor, but the whole process of change moved at a much
slower rate than any sudden event may imply. The change developed
out of the social conditions of the inter-war years, and was only
recognized by the jolt given to local institutions by war-time conditions.

It is difficult to describe the work of councillors without becoming
too personal, particularly when local newspapers give the greatest
publicity to their foolishness or occasional acts of indiscretion, and
not to their service on committees. Evidence can only be taken from
records which are normally ignored and from information supplied
by the councillors themselves. There are nevertheless three different
parts of public life which are open to investigation: first, the processes
of nomination and election; second, the selection of leaders and
chairmen; and third, the different levels of administration within the
county council organization upon which councillors can be seen at
work. The selection process tended to divide those who were elected
into two groups, those who worked with the officials and earned
their respect, and those who did not. Within any council there were
different degrees of enlightenment.

[1] *Manchester Guardian*, 1 Mar. 1941, p. 4.

Elections and party politics

How did one become a county councillor? Anybody with ambitions to enter the county council had to stand for election in one of the electoral divisions into which the county was divided. The changes in Cheshire county politics were exemplified by the complete revision of boundaries carried out by the County Review Order of 1936. All the county elections between 1889 and 1934 were fought on the basis of electoral divisions laid down by Quarter Sessions in 1888. But the Local Government Act of 1929 required the authority to review internal county boundaries. The order promulgated in 1936 and first used in the county council election of 1937 increased the number of electoral divisions from 56 to 69, which meant a corresponding increase in the number of aldermen from 19 to 23. The composition of the new County Council in 1937, numbering 92 members instead of 75, reflected accurately the two most important features of this boundary revision. First, the non-borough members were conscious for the first time of representing a specific local authority area, an urban or rural district, and not a haphazard collection of parishes which had been grouped together by the magistrates in 1888. After 1937 the electoral divisions corresponded to other local government areas. The old County Council had been extremely reluctant to interfere with the divisions established in 1888, however disproportionate the electorates of each division had become. Ellesmere Port, for instance, which had been an urban district since 1902, applied to the County Council for a separate representative in 1913,[1] but remained until 1936 in the much larger semi-rural division, called Neston, stretching across the Wirral peninsula. Second, the expansion of numbers in 1937 was largely to the advantage of the new suburban areas around Liverpool and Manchester. Twenty-nine of the sixty-nine elected members were new councillors serving for the first time, the highest proportion of 'new blood' since 1889, twice that of the elections of 1931 or 1934 (see Appendix A), and a record only to be beaten in the remarkable election of 1946 which has already been mentioned. The majority of the new members came from the suburbs of Manchester or from the Wirral. Similarly, the increase of divisions from 68[2] to 74 in 1958 (which meant a total council of 98 members) was to give a more equitable

---

[1] *County Council Minutes* (1913), p. 446.
[2] The loss of one division (69 to 68) was caused by the incorporation of Hoole into Chester City in 1955.

representation in those areas where population was growing (Ellesmere Port, Bramhall, Bredbury, Cheadle, Wilmslow, and Wirral).
The Conservative party in Cheshire County Council has been able
to retain an overall majority of members since the election of 1937
because the new suburban areas which had an increased representation provided fertile ground for its activities. The election of 1937,
even if there had been no war to interrupt and accelerate the process
of change, would have been the starting point for a new system of
politics. Public persons in Cheshire were associated with the representation of local authority areas, with the importance of the new
suburban areas, and with a new kind of Conservatism. All these
features followed the revision of boundaries in 1936.

The aspirant for public office as a county councillor normally
secured the nomination of his own party organization for the division
which he wished to contest. The party committees usually found it
easier to supply candidates in county council than in U.D.C. and
R.D.C. elections. The process of selection was to a large extent
determined by the regular party workers. But occasionally a candidate
who found himself unopposed did not require party support. Anyone who had claims to social leadership was unlikely to be rejected
by his own party, invariably the Conservative party, if he showed
any inclination to stand. A reluctant candidate, a landowner, who
had delayed the acceptance of a seat until his election would be
unopposed, had no difficulty in 1949 to put himself forward for one
of the Bucklow divisions. But otherwise the business of securing a
party nomination was the result of various internal party discussions.
The public person *par excellence* might be the 'dual councillor', the
borough or district councillor who was invited by his local party
organization to represent them 'on the county'. Aldermen Barwood
and Shrigley, for instance, began in public life as distinguished local
councillors who were 'promoted' to the county level.

Having secured a party nomination, what was the likelihood of
the candidate being compelled to fight a contested election? For the
majority of cases in Cheshire, this question resolved itself into the
likelihood of a Conservative candidate being opposed by the Labour
or Liberal parties. After the election of 1937 the proportion of
contests increased. (See Appendix A.) Except for the election of
1931, the proportion before 1937 was consistently lower than that
after it. At the election of 1946 the proportion of seats contested was
the highest ever recorded in the history of the council, almost 74 per

cent. (51 out of 69). Since the Second World War an average of 45 per cent. of the seats have been contested at each election, whereas during the period between the wars, at seven elections, an average of only 24 per cent. were contested. In other words, the party organizers before 1939 expected contests in a quarter of the divisions, but after 1946 they had to be prepared for them in more than a third. But what is more important is the fact that the reasons for causing a contest had also greatly changed. Before 1914 the absence of contests was usually determined by a series of 'gentlemen's agreements', negotiated by the party whips in the council chamber. Contests were then only caused by some local differences of opinion, personal spite, or the rebellion of local party organizations against central control.[1] The Conservative caucus minute book shows that an agreement not to fight existing Liberal and Independent members was still in force in 1936.[2] But the Labour party had to force contests in order to make itself heard; it was not in a position to make 'gentlemen's agreements'. It was not responsible for introducing a 'party' element into the county government of Cheshire for the first time, although it has frequently been blamed for causing strife; but it was instrumental in placing party politics on a new footing. The new Conservatism of the period after 1937 was to a large extent based upon the anti-Labour vote of the new suburbs which cut across the traditional issues dividing Conservative from Liberal. In some places only a pact between the two parties could withstand the challenge of Labour. After 1937 the increase in the proportion of contests was largely caused by the determination of local Labour party constituency organizations to put forward their own candidates.

Many contests provided an opportunity to keep the minority party in fighting trim, and were fought by candidates from outside the divisions concerned. For instance, in 1961 the Knutsford Labour party put forward a lecturer from Salford Technical College as a candidate, although he lived at Bowdon, in order to please Labour supporters who had managed to elect a solitary member on the local council. He lost to the Independent sitting member. In 'safe' Conservative divisions the only other source of strife was the tendency for local Conservative organizations to split into factions. Also in 1961, Lieutenant-Commander Butcher, a former Conservative parliamentary candidate, opposed one of the sitting members for

[1] See above, pp. 61–62.
[2] Minute book in the possession of the Conservative whip.

Wilmslow, W. Grandin Jones, in spite of the fact that the latter was the official Conservative candidate and deputy chairman of the County Finance Committee. Commander Butcher was able to unseat him because he had the support of a personal faction in the Wilmslow Conservative Association. Sometimes a contest between two Conservatives was caused by the local party committee running a candidate against another proposed by the constituency party organization, as for instance in 1958 in Congleton Rural No. 2. In such situations the party whip in Chester might be asked to supply information about a candidate's suitability. The business of becoming a county councillor was largely a matter of receiving or securing a party nomination and being lucky enough to avoid a contest.

Once elected, a new councillor seemed likely to be re-elected almost indefinitely, or until he was promoted to the aldermanic bench. No new councillor could afford to expect that an aldermancy would be an automatic reward for his services, but if he had the staying-power, promotion was likely. It is significant that although the proportion of contests increased after 1937, the proportion of retiring councillors to be defeated on seeking re-election (see Appendix A) did not increase at the same rate. The results of the 1961 election seemed to be a reversal of this general trend—10 out of 49 retiring councillors were defeated—but there was no indication that they represented a new development. Just as in the period before 1937, the sitting member appeared to enjoy an unparalleled advantage over any challenger. This was particularly true in 'safe' Conservative seats where only a serious division of opinion within the local party association caused the sitting member to lose its confidence. Those councillors who were co-opted as members of the County Council during the Second World War when elections were suspended, forty-one in number, stood as good a chance of re-election in 1946 as any of the sitting members who had fought an election before 1939. At the end of the war a large number of the county councillors were in fact war-time nominees; twenty-three of them stood for election in 1946 and only five were defeated. The fact that eighteen members of the new council had originally been co-opted during war-time is sufficient evidence for the predominance of the process of nomination over the process of election. Some of the co-opted councillors were former members who had resigned and were recalled for service; some were the relatives of former members. But they shared a willingness to carry out the necessary duties.

The advantage which the sitting member enjoyed lay in his ability to get his supporters to the polling-booth. The introduction of contests based upon strict party discipline and organization did not increase the proportion of local government electors who bothered to exercise their vote.[1] The remarkable election of 1946 illustrated this point rather ironically. The average proportion of the electorate polling in the 51 contested divisions was only 31·8 per cent., one of the lowest in the history of the council. High polls of over 70 per cent., which were normally expected in contested divisions before 1914, were a function of local society governed by social leaders, just as the low polls of between 35 and 40 per cent., which were recorded between 1919 and 1939, were a function of the process of suburbanization which was taking place. Before 1914, when the total number of qualified electors was between 100,000 and 150,000 in the whole administrative county, the candidates had to consider all the electors; the average division contained between 1,500 and 2,000 voters in 1888 when the boundaries were drawn. After 1919 the candidates were more concerned to discover the number of voters who could be persuaded to go to the poll, in spite of the fact that the total number of qualified electors in the administrative county increased from 287,419 in 1928 to 605,092 in 1958. The extension of the franchise at the local level did not increase the participation of voters. Candidates rightly concentrated on seeing that their immediate supporters went to the poll.

If the apathy of the local electorate was a function of social change, one would have expected greater apathy in areas of rapid change. It is true in Cheshire that the rural areas with a scattered population and those areas which have not borne the brunt of rapid suburbanization tended to record a higher poll in contested county council elections. Movements of population after 1888, when the divisions were first made, made the electorates of different divisions very disproportionate. Between the wars while population was static or declining in the rural divisions like Audlem, Malpas, or Tarporley, in the new urban areas there were many startling increases. In Bebington, for example, the population rose from 14,104 in 1901 to 31,825 in 1931 and the number of local government electors in the Bebington division from 2,611 in 1901 to 18,065 in 1935.[2] The new

---

[1] Before 1946, the total poll has been taken from local newspapers; after 1946, from the Registrar General's Statistical Review. Figures for individual divisions come from the returns kept by the County Registration Office.

[2] The urban district of Bebington was formed from the districts of Lower Bebington, Higher Bebington, and Bromborough.

urban areas were more apathetic. At the election of 1934 the urban district of Ellesmere Port contained more than 48 per cent. of the voters in the Neston division, but only 21 per cent. of these registered their votes, whereas in the rural areas of the same division, like Burton and Little Sutton, there was a poll of over 50 per cent.[1] After 1919 the highest polls were in rural divisions. The only two divisions where the poll exceeded 70 per cent. were Audlem in 1931 and Bollington in 1934. Similarly after 1946 the semi-rural divisions were the only ones to exceed a poll of 55 per cent., except the urban district of Nantwich which polled 59 per cent. in 1952.[2] It is not surprising that the exception was an old market town. Low polls were more likely in areas of rapid industrial change.

But the fact remains that low polls were also a function of lack of interest in county politics. The county councillor still tended to gain his greatest prestige and certainly received the greatest publicity from his work as a borough or district councillor, if he also held that office. For instance, in the boroughs of the extreme north-east of the county, Hyde, Stalybridge, and Dukinfield, which felt very little community of interest with the rest of Cheshire, the county council elections tended to be fought by borough councillors on local borough issues which received a far greater coverage in the *North Cheshire Herald* than any county business. The office of 'dual councillor', one who combined a place on the borough or district council with a seat in the county council, had a very long tradition in this part of the county, but after the end of the Second World War, and particularly after 1937 when for the first time county electoral divisions coincided with local government areas, this office became almost a universal phenomenon. Before 1929 a borough councillor from the north-east who went 'on the county' often resigned his borough seat, or was elected to the county as a compensation for failing in the borough. Sometimes such a 'dual councillor' resigned his borough seat on becoming a county alderman. The increase in the number of 'dual councillors' since 1929 was a direct consequence of the disappearance of social leaders in local politics. The power of the social leader was not entirely dependent upon the number of offices which he held; that of the public person was. In 1935 only thirteen out of the seventy-four members of Cheshire County Council were 'dual councillors'.

---

[1] *Chester Chronicle*, 10 Mar. 1934, p. 2.
[2] The highest percentage poll in 1961 was at Winsford (54·8 per cent.) where the acceptance of Manchester 'overspill' was the main issue.

By 1960 almost half the members enjoyed this distinction. Before the Second World War, probably only one in five county councillors was a district councillor as well; but after the war almost three out of five retained the connection.

The effects of distance from Chester were to concentrate the mind of the elected representative upon events happening in the borough or district council to which he belonged rather than upon events in the county as a whole. In the absence of 'county society', the fellowship of social leaders, the County Council ran the risk of becoming a body of members who represented only an aggregate of different local interests and not a union of similar minds. The reason why the process of nomination was more important to the political maturity of the County Council than the process of election was that the business of the council required members who were capable of looking beyond the boundaries of their own locality, while the business of winning a county election rested upon the haphazard arrangements of local organizations. The functioning of a body of 'public persons' therefore depended upon choice or chance in the process of nomination rather than in the process of election. It did not matter who won the election so much as what kind of people were nominated. Were the successful nominees capable of being educated in the ways of county business? The permanent officials in County Hall tended to divide councillors into those who thought 'in county terms' and those who did not. The two-tier system of county government rested upon the good sense of those who did. The officials relied on those who were willing to educate themselves 'in county ways'.

The responsibility for providing an effective council in Cheshire rested fairly and squarely after 1937 upon the broad shoulders of the local organizations of the Conservative party. The candidates proposed by different local committees who were elected provided the most respected members of the council chamber. This reliance on local committees introduced an element of chance. The party whip in Chester found it difficult to interfere in local decisions because he was no longer capable of reaching a 'gentleman's agreement' with the Liberal party—the challenge came from Labour. The Conservatives were much less amenable to efficient party management in constituency organizations than Labour. The Review Order of 1936, which came into force for the election of 1937, gave the Conservative party in Cheshire County Council an almost unshakeable majority over all its opponents because it added a large number of seats from the 'new suburbs', but at the same time it made the party much more dependent upon the whims of local factions, including the possibility that dissident Conservatives might call themselves Liberals. An effective council depended upon the Conservative party of the 'new suburbs', where the greatest amount of political talent was likely to be found. The anti-Labour voters of the new Conservatism were not interested in agriculture and the small industries which had absorbed the passions of their predecessors.

The Conservative party held an over-all majority of seats in the council after 1937. The only serious challenge to this superiority was the success of the Labour party in the remarkable election of 1946 when fifteen of the fifty Labour candidates were returned. But the inconvenience of a bare working majority in the council chamber, 48 Conservatives out of a total membership of 92, and the political animosity aroused by the Labour government, stimulated the Conservative party organization into making an all-out effort for the county council elections of 1949. The Conservative caucus invited all candidates, their agents, and the officers of the regional organizations to a meeting before polling-day in the Crewe Arms Hotel at which the Conservative leader on the council hazarded the guess that if the party did not win the next General Election, 'it was the last free election we would ever see'.[1] This rousing talk was followed after polling-day by a luncheon to celebrate the victory, at which three Conservative M.P.s and three candidates sat down with the county councillors who represented their respective constituencies in order to symbolize the union which should henceforward exist after the 1948 Act had determined that parliamentary divisions should follow local government boundaries. This Act was expected to foster the links between the County Council and Parliament, just as the Review Order of 1936 which brought county electoral divisions into the same framework had encouraged 'dual councillors'. But in Cheshire the ideal was upset by the creation of the Nantwich constituency in 1955 which disregarded the boundaries of local authorities. At only three county council elections, 1949, 1952, and 1955, have the electoral divisions corresponded exactly with local government and parliamentary arrangements. At each of them, the Conservative party in Cheshire won about two-thirds of the seats. (See Appendix B.) The victory of 1949, when 13 seats were gained for the

[1] Conservative caucus minute book in possession of the Conservative whip.

party, represented the high-water mark of Conservative planning. Although the Labour party fought back, gaining 7 seats in 1952, 1 in 1955, and 5 in 1958, it was not able to shake Conservative confidence. A pattern was established in elections after the war (see Appendix A) that about twenty new members should enter the council every three years, but that the proportion of seats held by the different parties should not vary very much. The Conservatives were equal to the other three parties added together.

This Conservative predominance was the result of two factors: first, that the Liberals failed to maintain their position as the second party after 1937; and second, that the Labour party failed to extend its influence for any distance outside the 'safe' seats in Crewe and Ellesmere Port or the industrial towns of the extreme north-east. The County Review Order of 1936 was also a significant turning-point in the history of the Liberals on the County Council. In the elections of 1937, at which there were 17 new electoral divisions, the Liberal representation on the council dropped by three, from 20 to 17, while the Conservatives increased by fifteen, from 35 to 50. This figure shows the importance of the 17 new divisions to the success of the Conservative party. Although it never won an over-all majority, the Liberal party between 1889 and 1931 always secured more than a third of the number of seats. John Bateman, the Liberal leader who died in 1931, organized a party of between 25 and 30 members with rigorous discipline, but he relied to a large extent upon the Liberal sentiment which survived in the Weaver valley and in the rural areas of the south and west where Protestant Nonconformity was strong, and upon the Liberal social leadership of the Manchester area. This can be seen by examining the geographical distribution of the 32 Liberal members in 1928. Similarly, the rise of the Labour party was associated with certain social conditions— boroughs in which Labour could displace the Liberals. Only the disproportionate electoral divisions which were in force until 1937 retained the traditional battle between Conservative and Liberal. The emphasis given to the 'new suburbs' and the rising industrial towns by the Review Order of 1936, which also ensured a fairer distribution of seats, shifted the social basis of party allegiance. It provided the Labour party with definite objectives; strengthened the new Conservatism of the suburbs; and limited the Independent party to the agricultural interest. The Liberals could only find support in a haphazard manner.

The origin of the Independent party in 1919 as an organized group on the Council lay in a reaction against the party politics of the towns. It was a union between those who believed that national party politics should not play a part in local administration and the farmers who believed that they were getting such a raw deal from the councillors elected in urban areas that they ought to defend their own interests. C. E. Davenport, a civil engineer and architect who had represented Nantwich since 1907, was of the former school of thought; J. O. Garner, the local secretary of the National Farmers' Union, belonged to the latter; and together they organized an independent party inside the council chamber, particularly on behalf of the farmers' interests. In 1919 the contests were largely caused in county council elections by the intervention of Farmers' Union candidates in rural divisions. They fought seven of the ten contested rural divisions and won three of them, Garner himself in Alderley, G. E. Parton in Tarporley, and William Hough, who had been an unsuccessful candidate in 1913, at Weaverham. Garner's own victory had a symbolic significance. Although still absent on active service, he defeated at Alderley a member of a distinguished manufacturing family which had risen to the status of 'county gentry', Alexander Greg, a retired Army officer. Greg was the type of social leader in whom the farmers were ceasing to have confidence. Ten of those returned unopposed, including three farmer councillors, agreed to support the principles of a farmers' party.[1] After the elections of 1922, Garner claimed that he had fifteen supporters on the Council.[2]

The challenge of the Labour party in county politics sprang directly from its tactics in the boroughs. The new and deliberately planned contests were described by Conservative newspapers as 'vexatious'. For instance, in 1928 the Conservative member for the Chester Castle division was compelled to fight a contest for the first time in twenty-one years! His Labour opponent was a clothing manager for the Chester Co-operative Society who was sponsored by the Labour party in Chester.[3] Labour did not win more than two seats on the County Council until 1934, when five members were returned. Four of these came from the boroughs: two from Crewe, one from Macclesfield, and one from Bebington; and one, Miss Lois Bulley, who was returned for Neston, belonged to the tradition of

---

[1] Alfred Ingham, *Cheshire: Its Traditions and History* (1920), p. 183.
[2] *Chester Courant*, 8 Mar. 1922, p. 8.
[3] *Chester Chronicle*, 10 Mar. 1928, p. 5; *Chester Courant*, 29 Feb. 1928, p. 8.

Radical businessmen. Her father, a wealthy Liverpool cotton merchant, had been in his time a Unionist, a Liberal, and a 'Socialist'.[1]
After the First World War the Conservative and Liberal parties in
Cheshire boroughs tended to form 'pacts' not to oppose each other
in contested elections, in order to exclude Labour candidates who
might win in a three-cornered contest. The 'pact' failed most disas-
trously in Crewe where the Labour party won all the contests in the
1919 elections. In October 1920 the Conservatives and the Liberals
formed a 'pact' called the Crewe Progressive Union.[2] The Labour
party in Crewe secured a majority among the 24 councillors after the
elections of 1928, and with the aid of the Mayor's casting vote in
1933 captured the places of all the eight aldermen.[3] Elsewhere the
'pact' was more successful, but tended to favour the Conservatives
rather than the Liberals. When the more militant Liberals strove to
break the 'pacts' in the late 1920's and early 1930's, as in Hyde,
Stalybridge, and Stockport, they tended to lose their advantage to
Labour.[4] After the Second World War, politics in the boroughs
tended to be a fight between Conservative and Labour. In the 1945
elections the only boroughs to return a sizeable number of Liberals
were Chester and Wallasey, and by 1950 Chester stood alone in this
respect. Labour had won the day, wherever it was possible.

The significance of Labour's challenge lay in the fact that a contested election placed some obstacle in the way of Conservative
nominees who might have otherwise become persons in public life
without much effort. Labour aroused a nostalgia for social leadership, for conditions in which 'gentlemen's agreements' were possible.
But the occasional contest was an occupational hazard for the ambitious public person. Once nominated, he had a single duty—to survive
or to resign. Death might remove some from the pleasures of public
life, but survival brought the reward of a seat on the aldermanic
bench. County politics in terms of the electoral process alone were
best understood as a process of nomination and survival in which
the most senior members were important. The proportion of retiring
councillors defeated when standing for re-election was much smaller
than the proportion of new members who resigned or died in office.
The 'casualty' rate was due to death, resignation, or promotion
rather than to defeat at election. Only twice after 1919 did the

[1] N. Ellison, *The Wirral Peninsula* (1955), p. 119.
[2] W. H. Chaloner, *Crewe* (1950), p. 168.
[3] *Manchester Guardian*, 2 Nov. 1928, p. 12; 2 Nov. 1933, p. 13.
[4] Ibid., 31 Oct. 1928, p. 4; 29 Oct. 1932, p. 16.

proportion of retiring councillors defeated when seeking re-election exceed 10 per cent., in 1946 (20·9 per cent.) and in 1961 (15·6 per cent.). (See Appendix A.) Perhaps a good sample of councillors in the process of nomination and survival were the group of new Conservative members returned in 1949, when 13 seats were gained for the party. Of the 18 new Conservatives in 1949, only 3 had survived as councillors in 1960, but only 4 had lost their seats at election time. Eight of the remaining eleven had resigned, and three had died.[1] Three remained after eleven years to expect promotion to the aldermanic bench. The election of councillors as aldermen, which took place after the triennial elections, caused a casual vacancy to be filled at a by-election in the division which the former councillor represented. The importance of the steady process of nomination, survival, and promotion can be seen in the increasing proportion of retiring councillors at each election who began their public careers by stepping into a casual vacancy. (See Table 8 below.)

In fact, the casual vacancy provided the party whip with an opportunity for bringing able candidates on to the council. Particularly in the Conservative party, where the order for promotion to the aldermanic bench had been decided by lot, those divisions in which casual vacancies would occur were known well in advance, and one of the most important functions of the party whip in Chester was to remind constituency organizations of their duty to supply candidates. He worked through the regular meetings at the North Western Regional Office of the party in Manchester. The electoral process of county politics gave the impression of being only a matter of nomination and survival, but the administrative process required something more than mere staying-power. There were important distinctions to be made among those who survived. Which were the most efficient chairmen? Which attended meetings the most regularly for the dispatch of business?

The function of public persons

How effective was a county councillor, once he had been elected? A study of elections alone may tend to overemphasize the importance of seniority within the council, and imply that those who survived as councillors after more than three electoral contests must necessarily be its most influential members. In fact, an individual councillor's

[1] Conservative caucus minute book in the possession of the Conservative whip.

importance to his colleagues and to the chief officers depended upon a delicate process of internal selection by which leaders were chosen. It is much more difficult to investigate the means of promotion than to study the system of election. A natural endeavour to identify the most powerful group within a large organization becomes an even harder task when the members of the body which is to be examined are drawn from many different groups scattered over a

TABLE 8

Analysis of Councillors Standing for Re-election

Year of election	Total no. standing for re-election	Origin: when first elected. Triennial elections							Casual vacancies
		1937	War-time	1946	1949	1952	1955	1958	
1949 .	54	7	15	24	..	..	..	..	8
1952 .	53	..	10	17	16	..	..	..	10
1955 .	58	..	4	13	7	17	..	..	15
1958 .	57	..	2	13	5	14	9	..	14
1961 .	64	..	..	4	3	13	7	14	23

wide area. The County Council was composed of the leading members of different communities living far apart, and they were required to co-operate with a large staff of full-time officials working together every day in the same building. The quest to identify the county *élite* may run into the danger of naming only the leading councillors without reference to the officials, or of concentrating upon the diffusion of power throughout an elaborate network of administrative arrangements and thus ignoring the work of councillors. Another snare is the belief held by some people who are familiar with county council work that a body of people which has little opportunity for meeting together in small groups for informal consultation must necessarily reach its decisions with a greater impartiality than smaller bodies whose members are neighbours, such as town councils, which suffer from the blight of faction and caucus rule. According to this view, county councils are unlikely to develop strong bodies of leaders, but tend to behave like a jury which judges each case presented by the full-time officials on its merits alone. Any theory of *élites* of county government must therefore take into account both the relationships between councillors and officials and the effects upon members of the distance which they live from the county town. Some councillors are clearly more important than others.

Another factor which encourages the refusal to recognize any leading faction is the absence of close divisions of opinion in political party warfare. Cheshire County Council since 1937 has never been forced to depend upon a balance between two evenly balanced parties. Conservative predominance made it possible to entertain very different views about political leadership from those held in adjacent county boroughs where changes of party control were possible. In such conditions differences of ability within one party were as important as those between parties. A successful councillor saw his own rise to position and influence as a result not so much of his loyalty to any party or patron, but of his long familiarity with a given political context, the ward, the division, the constituency committees, the managers of local schools, and of his confidence in public speaking, in being heard by the organized groups of his own locality. The 'public person' *par excellence* was one who enjoyed being in touch with large numbers of different societies and voluntary associations. In theory, the success of any individual member within the County Council might have been measured accurately if it had been possible to represent his political career upon a graph, plotting time against power and producing a curve which rose to a 'plateau of influence', a time when his word was respected, through the sheer persistence and ability of the candidate. Such a mathematical representation would certainly have brought out the fact that a large number of councillors did not stay in office long enough to reach the 'plateau of influence', either through a lack of interest, or through insufficient concentration on the administrative detail of committee work. Those who reached this eminence provided the leaders and chairmen. The existence or absence of a downward curve towards the end of a career might have been as important in this type of analysis as the upward rise. Those whose graph of influence declined very little were the 'elder statesmen' who might have intervened at any stage of the debate and still have been heard with respect, no matter how infrequent was their attendance. Those whose graph fell rapidly were the 'superannuated party servants' who passed their retirement in the restful oblivion of attending committees. Regular attenders were often the least influential. Age and seniority were not the only determinants of success, although there was some evidence in Cheshire to suggest that it was important to begin a career in county politics before the age of forty-five. Not only were such distinguished Liberals as Sir William Hodgson and John

Bateman active in county affairs during the period before the First World War when they were still under the age of thirty-five, but also the chairman and vice-chairman in 1960 had both been originally elected as county councillors before their fortieth birthdays. It was unusual for a councillor elected for the first time when over sixty-five, particularly a 'dual councillor' who had already made a reputation for himself in borough or district council affairs, to make his mark on the County Council. The most able county councillors tended to be those who had moved into county business at an earlier age and acquired the requisite seniority. In the absence of bitter party warfare, the successful councillor was more conscious of those who had entered the business young enough and active enough to get to know how it worked, than of those who had merely served their time.

The only means of reaching some conclusion about the process of selection within the council, which recognizes factors other than age and years of service and which takes into account the peculiar nature of its composition, is to examine the posts which carried the greatest responsibility. The offices of chairman and vice-chairman of the council brought the most burdensome duties. The latter was frequently also elected as chairman of the Finance Committee. The chairmanships of other committees of the council varied considerably in the amount of time which their proper functioning demanded, and they cannot be discussed in isolation from the seats on the aldermanic bench which were frequently taken by the same people. (See Diagram VI, p. 135) The operation of a system which revolved around the chairmen of committees might well produce tendencies in the direction of 'personal rule' or of a 'ruling clique' of senior members who were both aldermen and chairmen.

The principal determinant of the direction in which the council might run was the power of the political party which held a majority in the council chamber. A mark of distinction in the political maturity of Cheshire County Council was that the allocation of committee places had always been determined by a meeting of the party whips who bargained according to the strength of their relative numbers in the council chamber. After each election the whips drew up a treaty or agreement which established the structure of county government. For thirty years, from 1889 to 1919 as already described,[1] the two parties, Conservative and Liberal, held separate caucus meetings

[1] See above, pp. 63–66.

under their respective leaders and elected whips to discipline their members. Each whip met his opposite number at regular intervals to draw up the details of the business which had been delegated to him. This was chiefly concerned with committee places, chairmanships, and the re-election of retiring aldermen. But between the two world wars the development of a four-party system upset the simplicity of these arrangements. After 1922 the whip of the Independent party (or N.F.U. 'farmers' party'), who was making an attempt to discipline all those councillors who were not committed to the major political parties, had to be consulted. The balance between the Liberals and the Conservatives was held by this group, and no fair allocation could be made, which gave each party a number of places on each committee in proportion to its strength on the council, without taking the Independents into consideration. Similarly, the two Labour members elected in 1928 and the five elected in 1934, put the Labour party in a strong bargaining position, and led to the convention that all places should be allocated at a meeting of the four party whips. After the mid-1930's the offices of the four party whips were endowed with a considerable amount of political responsibility.

But the fact that after 1937 the Conservative party enjoyed an absolute majority in the council chamber converted the whips' meeting from an occasion at which each man bargained with his political capital to one at which the Conservative leader and Conservative whips informed their colleagues from the other three parties how far the Conservative party was prepared to allow them to go. The offices of leader and whip in the three minor parties were usually held by the same person, and party organization, particularly among the Independents, was very rudimentary. The significance of all the changes following the County Review Order of 1936 lay in the pre-dominance of the Conservative party organization in the affairs of the council. Any new councillor who became a member of the Conservative party caucus in Chester was more likely to be appointed to the principal committees than other members. As the channels of communication between the Chester caucus and other Conservative organizations within the county were not always very efficient, it was possible for a councillor to accept the Conservative whip in Chester in order to receive a better allocation of committee places, in spite of the fact that he was at loggerheads with his own local association. The means of promotion depended to a great extent upon party agreements.

Before 1935 the positions of chairman and vice-chairman of the council were shared by the Conservative and Liberal parties. When the chairman was a Conservative, the vice-chairman was a Liberal—and vice versa. In fact, the election results only made it possible to promote a Liberal chairmanship once—the period of office held by Sir William Hodgson, 1922–35. (See Table 9, p.179.) The same convention had been followed with committee chairmanships before 1919: a chairman from one party meant the vice-chairman from another.[1] But after 1940 both the chairman and the vice-chairman of the council were Conservatives. By that time it had become almost an 'apostolic succession' that anyone serving in the office of Conservative whip could expect to be elected to one of these positions.[2] Of the five Conservative whips elected between 1911 and 1952, two became both vice-chairmen and chairmen, one a chairman, and two vice-chairmen only. The position of whip provided the greatest opportunities for coming to grips with the very complicated network of political organizations which covered the whole county because it required the holder to familiarize himself with all the regional officers and chairmen of his party. J. W. Emberton and H. J. S. Dewes, during their tenure of the office of Conservative whip, provided models of skilful behaviour, the first training the second to succeed him. The latter was a good example of the public person in the Conservative party. The eldest son of a Tamworth solicitor who had been clerk to various local government authorities, he joined the firm of Edgar Vaughan & Co., oil blenders. In his youth and early manhood he had many opportunities to gain experience in the public life and political party activities of his father's district. Emberton similarly gained experience from his father whom he succeeded as county councillor for Willaston in 1932. Someone who had already gained this experience could be an invaluable addition to the work of the council. Harold Peers, for instance, the chairman of the Conservative Party N.W. Area Advisory Committee on Political Education, and a former parliamentary candidate who was also in business as an actuary, was chosen to be deputy Conservative whip in 1961 although he had been a county councillor for only two years.

[1] See above, p. 65.
[2] The first Conservative whip (1889–92), Dr. James Atkinson (d. 1917), became chairman of the Finance Committee (1889–1910), but his two successors, (1892–1904) John Thompson and (1904–11) C. H. Booth, were not promoted to this office. Booth was chairman of the Parliamentary Committee from 1905 until 1911.

Success within the party was quickly recognized, and an able man did not have to wait until he had acquired the necessary standing of seniority.

The party organization might also have made it possible for a single man to exercise almost 'personal rule'. But Cheshire had no equivalent of the power of the Earl of Macclesfield in Oxfordshire or of the Duke of Northumberland in Northumberland, or even of a triumvirate such as Lord Hazlerigg, Colonel Paget, and Sir Robert Martin in Leicestershire. Although Sir George Dixon was chairman of the council for twenty-nine years, he did not establish a reputation for harsh authoritarianism such as that enjoyed by his successor, Sir William Hodgson, over the Liberal party, or by Hodgson's successor as Liberal Whip, John Bateman. Apart from Dixon and Hodgson and the present holder, all chairmen of the council have served for short periods of time. (See Table 9.) All suggestions of 'personal rule' have been confined to the leadership of the political parties. The chairmen of the council have usually been senior members of the Conservative party, over sixty years of age with twenty or more years of experience as councillors; all except three served as vice-chairman. (See Table 9.) Only Sir George Dixon, whose long period of office was exceptional, corresponded to the traditional image of the Cheshire landed proprietor in local government. The remainder were professional people or *entrepreneurs*, middle class with sometimes a Public School education. Joseph Cooke had never received any schooling outside the Dukinfield National and Technical Schools; Sir Otho Glover had been to Liverpool University; but Sir George Dixon and Major Toler were Etonians and Major Beames had been to Dover College. The present holders of the chairmanship and vice-chairmanship went to Rydal School (Colwyn Bay) and Aldenham respectively.[1] But no single figure, whatever his background and upbringing, made himself predominant in the workings of the County Council.

If the dangers of 'personal rule' were avoided, there was still a considerable risk in a system which encouraged the growth of an oligarchy of aldermen. Only the more enterprising members of the Conservative party organization were in a position to oppose any move towards 'gerontocracy' or the 'rule of old men'. In fact, one important feature of the new system in county government, as it

[1] The Clerk's Department also had minor Public School connexions: Mr. Hetherington at St. Bees and Mr. Bourne, the Deputy Clerk, at Stamford School.

TABLE 9. *Chairmen and Vice-chairmen of Cheshire County Council*

Date of Election	Age at the time of election	No. of years' service as cllr. or alderman	No. of years' service as vice-chairman	No. of years' service as chairman	Party affiliation	Name	Occupation
(a) Chairmen							
1889	65	..	..	4	C.	Duncan Graham	Managing director of Graham, Rowe & Co., S. America merchants in Liverpool
1893	51	4	..	29	C.	Sir George Dixon	Landowner of Astle Hall, Chelford
1922	68	33	13	13	L.	Sir William Hodgson	Doctor and surgeon practising in Crewe
1935	73	28	4	6	C.	Major T. C. Toler	Landowner of Swettenham Hall, Congleton, practising as a land agent
1941	75	37	..	3	C.	Joseph Cooke	Retail grocer and provision dealer in Dukinfield
1944	69	22	4	4	C.	Major H. P. M. Beames	Retired chief mechanical engineer of L.M.S. Railway at Crewe
1948	72	22	4	4	C.	Sir Otho Glover	Managing director of Castner-Kellner Alkali Co. Ltd., Runcorn
1952	56	20	4	Still in office	C.	Sir Wesley Emberton	Cheese factor in a family firm at Crewe
(b) Vice-chairmen not succeeding to the chairmanship							
1889	50	..	4	..	L.	James Tomkinson	Landowner of Willington Hall, Tarporley, and M.P. for the Crewe Division
1893	44	4	8	..	L.	T. W. Killick	Manchester cotton merchant living at Altrincham
1901	68	12	8	..	L.	Thomas Beeley	Head of T. Beeley & Sons, engineers and boilermakers at Hyde
1922	70	24	8	..	C.	R. T. Richardson	Landowner of Capenhurst Hall, Chester, practising as a barrister
1935	c. 75	28	4	..	I.	C. E. Davenport	Architect and engineer practising in Nantwich
1939	..	26	1	..	L.	F. J. Poole	Solicitor and director of Foden's Motor Works, Sandbach
1952	74	24	6	..	C.	Dame Lilian Bromley-Davenport	Widow of W. A. B.-Davenport (d. 1942), landowner of Capesthorne Hall
1958	60	21	Still in office	..	C.	H. J. S. Dewes	Retired engineer living at Thelwall

developed after 1920, was the increasing importance of aldermen. Before the First World War very few aldermen were to be found holding chairmanships or vice-chairmanships of committees, whereas from 1920 onwards an increasing number of aldermen assumed these important posts. The change was wrought, as has been described above,[1] by the councillors themselves who wished to see the office of alderman conferred as a reward for service, and not as a title for a distinguished member of county society. During the 1920's the party whips came to a series of agreements that the aldermanic bench, like the composition of committees, should be divided in proportion to the relative strength of each party. For every three councillors elected, the whip had the right to nominate one alderman. Before the First World War each party caucus meeting had nominated its candidates for promotion by a free vote, but after 1920 there was an increasing pressure from the members of the caucus to permit the privilege to be granted according to seniority alone. All the attempts which have been made from time to time, particularly within the Conservative party to upset the 'gentleman's agreement' of one alderman to every three councillors in each party, have been frustrated by the determination of the party whips to maintain good relations within the council. The five Labour members elected in 1934, who held the balance of votes if the Liberals allied themselves with the Independents against the Conservatives, voted with the Conservatives to retain these conventions. The first Labour alderman, Harold Hodkinson, was elected in 1934; and the second, Frank McLeavy, in 1937, both in accordance with the 'three-to-one' agreement. The latter, coupled with the principle of seniority and the convention that retiring aldermen deserve to be re-elected, tended to produce a situation in which the aldermanic bench was divided between the ambitious and competent members who were at the height of their powers and the weak and failing members who were allowed out of charity to remain at their posts.

The purpose of the aldermanic office was one of the chief sources of dispute within the party caucus. In 1946 the party whips again came to an agreement that the election of aldermen 'should be determined on the basis of seniority and service'. By 1950 several members of the Conservative party caucus, flushed no doubt with their victory in the 1949 elections, were questioning the wisdom of the 'three-to-one' agreement and hoping for a larger number of places

[1] See above, p. 74.

to fill. Similarly in 1958 the Conservative caucus passed a resolution that no alderman over the age of eighty should be re-elected, and that aldermen coming under this ban should be asked to retire not later than the month of December preceding the triennial elections so that it would be possible to fill the aldermanic vacancy without causing a by-election in the division which the successful councillor represented.[1] Several of the Conservative members wished to 'pension off' the aldermen over eighty by making them 'honorary freemen of the County Palatine', but such an honour could not be devised. The minority party whips refused to accept this Conservative resolution, and the Conservative leaders were unwilling to press the matter for fear of offending some of their own members who objected to it. The over-eighties therefore survived. An examination of the division lists of 1958 and 1961 for the election of aldermen reveals that some Conservative members still refused to vote for the most aged retiring aldermen, in spite of a party agreement to do so. Perhaps one cause for dissension within the Conservative party lay in the fact that because a large number of new members were elected every three years, seniority was decided by drawing lots. For instance, in 1957, the Conservatives agreed that, after two members who had originally been co-opted during the war, the party should support the ten Conservative members originally elected in 1946 as the next candidates for the aldermanic bench in an order which had previously been decided by lot. Mrs. Harley became an alderman immediately, but Mrs. Hyde at the bottom of the list had to wait until 1961.

The tensions within the party about aldermanic promotions were similar to those between ambition and sentiment. Public persons were much more sentimental than social leaders. For instance, in 1958 many councillors were prepared to argue that it was cruel to attempt to remove the over-eighties from the aldermanic bench, because they might die of disappointment. Similarly, the chronically ill were permitted to remain elected representatives however infrequently they made an appearance at meetings. The Clerk of the County Council was hardly ever in a position to enforce the 'six-months-rule' by which a member who fails to attend for six months was liable to be removed from office.[2] Capt. W. H. Carter from

---

[1] Under the Local Government Act 1933, S. 67 (3), a casual vacancy caused within less than 6 months before the triennial elections cannot be filled until all the other seats fall vacant.

[2] Ibid., S. 63 (1), failure to attend for a period of six consecutive months disqualified a member 'unless the failure was due to some reason approved by the local authority'.

Bowdon during the early 1940's was supposed to have been carried in on a stretcher in order to sign the attendance register! This again shows a marked contrast with conditions before the First World War. In 1912 William Bromley-Davenport was only nominated as an alderman by the Conservative caucus if he undertook to attend meetings.[1] After the Second World War Alderman Gittins,[2] for example, during the last years of his life was sent copies of the agenda, in spite of the fact that everyone knew he was too ill to attend.

Another contrast between modern conditions and those before 1920 lies in the use of the aldermanic office for retaining the services of members defeated at election time. While the office remained open to any person of worth outside the elected council it could be used for that purpose. But the convention of promoting councillors alone removed this opportunity. Instead, although no formal share-out of co-opted places was determined by the whips, it was possible to co-opt former members to those committees where they had been most useful. Mrs. Madeleine Newell, for example, was defeated at Cheadle in the 1958 elections but was co-opted to the Education Committee because of her considerable experience. She was persuaded to stand again as a candidate, and was re-elected in 1961. Frank Roberts, the former Crewe Labour party agent and county councillor from 1934 to 1937, was the only co-opted member of the Smallholdings Committee to become its chairman. Co-option sometimes allowed the party organization to make some adjustments for the accidents of the electoral system.

Councillors were prepared to treat the office of alderman primarily as an honour rather than a public office. It was clearly associated in their minds with those other distinctions of social worth, a seat on the bench of county magistrates and one of the ranks in the Order of the British Empire. The latter in recent years assumed a new importance almost as rapidly as the Empire itself dissolved away. Councillors expected that the O.B.E. or C.B.E. would be awarded to those whose functions in public life brought them within the channels of communication leading to the desks of the Permanent Secretary of the Ministry of Housing and Local Government and the patronage secretary of the Prime Minister's office. The M.B.E.

[1] See above, p. 74.
[2] He was chairman of the Public Assistance (later Welfare) Committee from 1939 until 1958, and of the Children's Committee from 1948 until 1952. He died in 1960.

was awarded on a different basis through certain advisers. The selection of magistrates was a process shrouded in secrecy by the Lord Chancellor's Department, which remained a mystery even to some leading members of the County Council. Although many councillors were intensely interested in the appointments which were made to the bench, the only formal link between the council and the methods of selection was in the person of the Clerk. The latter was also clerk of the lieutenancy and secretary of the local advisory committee for the selection of magistrates, and of the Magistrates' Courts Committee. He was required to remain silent about all matters concerning selection although the County Hall administrative machine undertook responsibility for Magistrates' Courts, and dealt with costs and claims for expenses. To become a county councillor was one of the means by which a man might attract sufficient attention for him to be considered for appointment to the bench. But in fact the proportion of councillors who were also magistrates seems to have declined. The representatives of the political parties who sat on the local advisory committee tended to avoid the selection of existing councillors. The Lord Chancellor's Department has in recent years adopted a policy of discouraging the appointment to the bench (particularly the borough bench) of more than a certain proportion of local councillors.[1] Before the Second World War the association between the County Council and the bench of magistrates was stronger: 36·9 per cent. of all members of the council in 1939 were also county magistrates.[2] The links between the various rewards for service in the public life of the county, from the aldermanic bench, the Order of the British Empire, to Quarter Sessions, only served to underline the basic truth that the new county society which replaced the gentry had been constituted by a community of public persons, who knew each other not in the country houses but in the committees of the county.

The possibility that power within the council would accrue to a 'ruling clique' of aldermen, who retained the leading committee chairmanships and received honours as the rewards of office, was only removed by the new professional services administered after 1945 which required from each committee chairman a great deal of time and a considerable amount of specialization. Those aldermen

[1] Report of the Royal Commission on Justices of the Peace, 1946–48 (Comd. 7463), para. 129, and the Memorandum prepared for the Royal Commission (1946), p. 13.
[2] Kelly's Directory for Cheshire (1939).

who could not provide either of these commodities, time and skill, were unlikely to be re-elected continuously to the same chairmanships, and those councillors who possessed special qualifications might be chosen in their stead, no matter how new they were to the business of the council. It is significant, from the point of view of Conservative predominance and of the new administrative system, that after 1958 the meeting of party whips at the beginning of each triennial period of office ceased to recommend names for the vacant chairmanships and allowed each committee a greater degree of freedom in using the available talent. The new system called for an *élite* of councillors who were capable of spending a lot of time in careful preparations with the chief officers.

Before this new departure after 1945, the convention of promoting councillors to the aldermanic bench and of party control over chairmanships had tended to encourage a 'ruling clique' of aldermen closely associated with seniority inside each party caucus. This was apparent even at the end of the First World War. A comparison of the leading chairmanships in 1918 and in 1945, at the end of each war, shows how far the process had gone. (See Table 10.) The average length of service performed by each chairman in ten of the principal committees[1] throughout the council's history was nine years. The average for the period before 1914 was a little higher than this, and some of the leading members of the council served for periods of between fifteen and twenty years. The impact of the change which followed the professionalization of county government after 1945 may be represented in the fact that four of the chairmanships of the same ten principal committees in 1960 were held by councillors and not by aldermen. At the same date the council included a high proportion of aldermen who had first joined the council before the election of 1946 and could not easily be removed on reaching an advanced age. (See Table 11.) As soon as the older generation had begun to disappear, there was greater flexibility in appointments. In 1960 only five of the eighteen pre-1946 aldermen held important chairmanships.

This discrepancy between the body of aldermen and the leading chairmen of committees emphasizes an important feature of Cheshire county government which makes it possible to devise some means of

[1] Finance, Education, Roads, Health, Parliamentary, Smallholdings, Weights and Measures, and (established since 1929) Public Assistance (Welfare), Planning, and Children's.

identifying the most important members of the council. The aldermen
and the leading chairmen were not necessarily in regular and constant touch with large numbers of the chief officials. The *élite* of the
County Council consisted of those who were useful and regular

TABLE 10

Chairmanships of Leading Committees 1918 and 1945

Committees	Chairman 1918	Date of election as alderman	No. of years' service as chairman	Chairman 1945	Date of election as alderman	No. of years' service as chairmau
Finance . .	R. T. Richardson	1907	12	E. O. Glover	1940	12
Parliamentary .	,,	..	7	P. Timperley	..	3
Education. .	W. Hodgson	1908	15	L. B. Davenport	1939	16
Roads . .	G. Dixon	1900	4	T. Clayton	1946	16
Health . .	T. R. Bulley	1904	8	J. W. Emberton	1946	6
Smallholdings .	W. McCracken	1899	25	W. A. Gibson	1942	16
Weights and Measures .	G. Wall	1909	23	W. E. Noden	1945	13

TABLE 11

Composition of the Council: 1960

	Numbers elected	(1) Before 1946	(2) In 1946	(3) After 1946
Councillors .	74	0	6	68
Aldermen . .	24	18	6	0
	98	18	12	68

attenders at all committee meetings and who made themselves
familiar with the impact of the day-to-day work of the officials
upon the public at large. Some of these were naturally both aldermen
and chairmen, but by no means all. When aldermen grew older and
began to lose their powers of concentration, their attendance record
declined, although some continued to attend without making any
contribution to debate. Some chairmen were prepared only to put
in a regular appearance at meetings of their own committees,
treating other duties less conscientiously. The members who

constituted an 'inner ring' in county affairs were those on whom the officials could rely for an accurate picture of affairs at many different levels of the administrative hierarchy and in many different places throughout the county.

TABLE 12

Analysis of Committee Membership 1920–60

I. *Attendances* for each of the three-year periods ending:

No. of attendances per member	1920		1940		1960	
	% of total members	% of total atten-dances	% of total members	% of total atten-dances	% of total members	% of total atten-dances
(1) 0–99 . .	38·1	10·6	32·1	9·0	31·3	7·5
(2) 100–199 . .	19·0	14·1	32·1	23·2	26·3	19·0
(3) 200–299 . .	19·0	23·9	14·1	16·6	18·8	22·3
(4) 300–399 . .	9·6	15·6	8·9	13·9	7·5	12·8
(5) 400+ . .	14·3	35·8	12·8	37·3	16·3	38·4
	63	12,681	78	16,835	80	16,569

II. *Committee places* for each of the three-year periods ending:

No. of committees attended by each member	1920		1940		1960	
	% of total members	% of total atten-dances	% of total members	% of total atten-dances	% of total members	% of total atten-dances
(1) less than 3. .	22·2	6·9	23·1	7·7	21·2	8·0
(2) 3–5 . . .	55·6	54·7	55·1	52·8	53·8	48·3
(3) 6–8 . . .	20·6	34·3	19·2	32·8	18·8	29·8
(4) 9+ . . .	1·6	4·1	2·6	6·7	6·2	13·9
	63	245	78	299	80	339

An analysis of the composition of the leading committees and of the attendance registers reveals the existence of this 'inner ring'. Table 12 gives the results for three dates, 1920, 1940, and 1960, the figures in each case covering the three-year period of the council's life. All councillors and aldermen were examined, except the chairman and vice-chairman who were *ex officio* members of all committees, and except all those members who resigned, died, or were elected to fill casual vacancies during the three-year period for which figures were collected—giving totals of 63 in 1920, 78 in 1940, and 80 in 1960. The analysis of committee places excludes all those committees, such as Staffing and Salaries or Estates and Works, which were composed of the chairmen of other committees. It is remarkable that such a regular pattern emerges for the period after 1920 which was not present before that date. Since 1920 over half the number of attendances at committee meetings have been made by less than a quarter of the members of the council; and about forty per cent. of all the committee places have been held by less than a quarter of the members. Less than a quarter of the full council therefore bore the full burden of its work.

An even closer definition of the 'inner ring' is possible. The same pattern is also found in an analysis, not of attendances, but of summonses to meetings. A graph drawn of the number of summonses per member does not show a normal distribution curve. The 'inner ring' who belonged to a larger number of committees received far more summonses than the majority of their colleagues. There were about a dozen councillors who had been summoned to more than 600 committee meetings and had attended more than 300 times during each of the three-year periods ending 1920, 1940, and 1960. Tables 13, 14, and 15 give further details of the career of each of these men, and add to their number those party whips who did not qualify for inclusion on the above definition, and the chairman and vice-chairman. They exclude one member in 1940 and one in 1960 who were both over eighty years old, but who nevertheless had very good attendance records. Such members represented the kind mentioned above who enjoyed passing their retirement in committees without making any contribution to debate, and it would be wrong to include them in any definition of an 'inner ring'. These tables summarize the evolution of the leading group within the council.

An important feature of the 'inner ring' in 1960 which does not appear in these figures or tables was the great extension of work after 1945 in sub-committees and divisional executives. The 'inner ring' in 1920 and 1940 consisted largely of those members who put in an appearance at committee meetings in Crewe and maintained a regular interest in the work of the officials. Their successors in 1960 were really more concerned with a much larger political infrastructure, the extremely complicated pattern of area committees covering the whole county. For instance, to give an example from 1960, John Hollinshead,[1] the chairman of the Welfare Committee

[1] No. 14 on Table 15.

TABLE 13

Leading Members of the Council: 1920

	Party			Aldermen	No. of years' service	Chairmen cttees.	Vice-chairmen cttees.	Occupation	Age
	Cons.	Lib.	Ind.						
(a) Chairman (1)	×	..	..	×	31	(ex officio members of all committees)		Gentleman	78
Vice-chairman (2)	..	×	..	×	31	..	..	Doctor	66
(b) Party whips (3)	×	..	..	×	22	Finance	..	Barrister	68
(4)	..	×	..	..	12	Roads and Bridges	Finance	Auctioneer and valuer	..
(5)	..	..	×	..	23	..	..	Architect	c. 60
(c) Members with best attendance record (6)	×	..	..	×	15	Drainage	..	Gentleman	63
(7)	×	..	..	×	13	Co. Rates	Roads and Bridges	Land agent	58
(8)	×	..	..	..	10	..	..	Clergy (C. of E.)	52
(9)	×	..	..	..	6	..	Small Holdings	Farmer	c. 50
(10)	..	×	..	×	23	Weights and Measures	..	Provision merchant	77
(11)	..	..	×	..	16	Parliamentary	..	Surveyor	69

TABLE 14

Leading Members of the Council: 1940

	Party				Aldermen	No. of years' service	Chairmen cttees.	Vice-chairmen cttees.	Occupation	Age
	Cons.	Lib.	Lab.	Ind.						
(a) Chairman (1)	×	..	..	..	×	33	(ex officio members of all committees)		Land agent	78
Vice-chairman (2)	..	×	..	..	×	27	..	..	Solicitor	..
(b) Party whips (3)	×	..	..	..	×	36	..	..	Grocer	74
(4)	..	×	..	..	..	12	..	..	Miller	59
(5)	..	..	×	..	×	6	..	..	Tramways inspector	41
(6)	..	..	..	×	×	15	..	Milk and Dairy	Farmer	c. 60
(c) Members with best attendance record (7)	..	..	..	×	..	9	..	Finance	Ret. bank manager	72
(8)	×	..	..	..	×	26	..	Local Tax.	Farmer	c. 70
(9)	..	×	..	..	..	11	..	..	Farmer	..
(10)	×	..	..	..	..	6	..	..	Ret. clk. of works	60+
(11)	×	..	..	..	×	30	..	..	Clergy (C. of E.)	72
(12)	..	×	..	..	×	24	Local Tax.	Educ.	Clergy (Congreg.)	c. 80
(13)	..	×	..	..	..	11	..	Pub. Asstnce.	Ret. works manager	72

and deputy chairman of the Local Taxation Committee, two posts which placed him automatically on three other committees composed of chairmen, was on five principal spending committees, positions placing him on fifteen sub-committees which were appointed by them, and on three sub-committees of the General Purposes Com-

TABLE 15

Leading Members of the Council: 1960

	Party				Alder-men	No. of years' service	Chair-men cttees.	Vice-chair-men cttees.	Occupation	Age
	Cons.	Lib.	Lab.	Ind.						
(a) Chairman (1)	×	..	..	..	×	28	(ex officio members of all committees)		Cheese factor	64
Vice-chairman (2)	×	..	..	..	×	23	..	..	Engineer	62
(b) Party whips (3)	×	..	..	..	×	14	Educ.	..	Ret. school-master	75
(4)	..	×	..	..	×	32	Roads and Bridges	..	Miller	79
(5)	..	..	×	..	×	23	Health	..	Insurance agent	58
(6)	..	..	..	×	..	15	..	..	Farmer	67
(c) Members (7)	×	..	..	..	×	16	..	Fire	Ret. draper	78
with best (8)	×	..	..	..	×	14	..	Chn. and Educ.	Solicitor's wife	60
attendance record (9)	×	..	..	..	..	14	..	Health	Ret. pro-vision merchant	71
(10)	×	..	..	..	..	5	..	..	Ret. builder	69
(11)	..	×	..	..	..	14	Planning	..	Ret. builder	77
(12)	..	..	×	..	..	7	..	..	Ret. T.U. official	74
(13)	..	..	×	..	..	5	..	..	Stats. officer	69
(14)	..	..	..	×	..	14	Welfare	Local Tax.	Bus pro-prietor	57
(15)	..	..	..	×	..	6	..	..	Ret. school-mistress	69

mittee, and was also in terms of divisional administration throughout the county a member of the following: the South Area Management Committee for Welfare, the S.E. Cheshire Divisional Health Committee, the South Area Sub-Committee for Children, the S.E. Cheshire Divisional Executive for Education, and the Congleton Area Advisory Sub-Committee for Roads and Bridges. He was also a member of Congleton R.D.C. The significance of an individual member's contribution to the work of the council depended on the degree to which he kept in touch with the administration of county policy as a whole, as well as with its application in the particular district which he represented. One of the main reasons for a fairly clear division between the 'inner ring' and the remainder of the council was the temptation for the majority to concentrate upon their own localities rather than upon the policy being made in County Hall.

The importance of members, as opposed to officials, in the determination of the policy which the County Council was to pursue becomes more apparent in the experience which could be gained from working in the large number of sub-committees and advisory bodies scattered throughout the geographical area of the administrative county. A most valuable function performed by members was their control over the appointments of members of staff in county institutions. This feature of public life, in fact, this activity of public persons —the regular attendance at all bodies making appointments—might easily be ignored in the study of administrative practice at County Hall level. Membership of the boards of governors or body of managers in county schools might well be considered by a councillor who belonged to the 'inner circle' as one of his most valuable contributions to county affairs. It was certainly from his experience in such matters that he acquired the judgement and political acumen which the permanent officials respected.

The means of promotion, the process of selection which determined the *élite* in Cheshire county government, culminated in the appreciation which the officials showed for the skill of certain members. Those who had gone into the business of public life in the county with all seriousness at a reasonably early age, who had served in all the different voluntary and official bodies of their own localities, fitted themselves to use the more expert knowledge which the officials provided. The quest to identify an *élite* in county government depends upon a distinction between councillors receptive to expert advice who saw the implications of official policy and councillors untutored in the new professional skills who were concerned principally with the defence of certain interests. What really distinguished the 'inner ring' of Cheshire County Council from their colleagues, apart from their receptiveness, was their ability to keep the officials informed of possible difficulties. The leading members of the council and the chief officers formed a kind of ministerialist party which was often required to take action against some of their own councillors. The process by which any new councillor entered

the 'inner ring' was largely a matter of self-education, and essentially
a question of being able to emancipate the mind from the confined
views of a particular locality. An understanding of county government requires the application of a well-worn distinction of British
constitutional history, the division between 'court' and 'country',
between 'ministerialists' and 'anti-ministerialists'. To attain the
'plateau of influence' in county affairs was an ambition made possible only by the careful cultivation of many groups in the public
life of the county, the vocation of the public person, which made
a councillor indispensable to the officials, the natural ministerialist.
Those who lacked the talent for this combination of knowledge and
diplomacy formed a permanent body of anti-ministerialists.

The effectiveness of county councillors after 1945 depended more
and more upon their ability to function at the different levels on
which the administrative system worked. The prestige of an individual councillor in County Hall rested upon his ability to handle
problems at both levels in a two-tier system of government, and upon
his familiarity with the organized groups of local society. County
council work had developed into a concern which concentrated its
energies upon planning efficient services and controlling private
development. The real importance of the distinction between the
'inner ring' or ministerialists and the 'country party' or anti-
ministerialists can only be appreciated by examining the principal
subjects for debate in the council's committee rooms.

The politics of controlled development

The committee work of the council consisted largely of defining a
policy which would co-ordinate the activities of district councils and
boroughs within the county and determine the principles of action
to be followed by county officials. The Town and Country Planning
Act of 1947, above all others, inaugurated a system by which the
County Council acted in a quasi-judicial capacity in hearing appeals
from councils which objected to the way in which county policy was
applied by its own officials. The delegation agreements authorizing
district councils to exercise planning powers contained provisions
which permitted the County Planning Committee to hear a case on
'a matter of principle' or to hear about differences of opinion between
district councils and area planning officers. Under the Act, a dis-
satisfied applicant, whether a council or a private individual, was
able to appeal against the County Council to the Ministry of Housing

and Local Government. The two-tier system of county government, as it developed after 1945, was essentially a means of determining where certain developments should be allowed to take place or where certain services should be provided, by the play of forces at three separate levels, district council, county council, and Ministry. The operation of this system was a process of sorting out those cases which aroused local controversies from those which did not. The majority were decided at the district council level; a few reached the County Council when matters of principle were involved; and the rare instances which provoked newspaper comment and concerned issues of major importance, such as the building of new suburbs or the development of new towns, were usually decided only after the Minister's intervention. The education service, the most important function which the County Council performs, did not in theory conform exactly to this three-level system of operation, because the County Council itself, and not the district councils, was responsible directly for providing schools, and it was not under the immediate control of the Ministry of Education. But the administration of the education service in practice followed the three-level pattern. The county officials administered the schools of a given area through a divisional office; the burden of the routine was taken by boards of governors, school managers, and a large number of sub-committees. The sub-committees of the County Education Committee received reports and made such decisions on matters of principle as the officials thought might be necessary. Introducing an item on the agenda, an official would preface it with the opening phrase: 'Your policy on this type of case in the past has been to make . . .' The full Education Committee meeting became a formal session for hearing the work of its various branches, almost as uninformative to the outsider as the County Council meeting itself. But the officials were required to consult the Ministry of Education constantly to secure its approval.

In these circumstances the county councillor was primarily required to make up his mind that he would support a certain policy, after he had considered the technical arguments submitted to the council by the officials whose job was to discover the facts, and the more 'political' arguments submitted by his colleagues or the representatives of borough or district councils. He needed, in order to be successful—to be respected both by the officials and his colleagues —to learn to acquire judgement. Whatever skill and reputation he acquired almost inevitably had a rather restricted publicity. A large part of the County Council's work—fire brigades, ambulances, weights and measures inspectors, surveyors, roadmen, midwives, and nurses—attracted very little public attention. The bulk of routine committee work was not considered to have any 'news' value by the reporters of local newspapers, and few attempts were made to use the techniques of modern advertising in order to familiarize the electors with the work of their county representatives. The result was that Education and Planning were the principal subjects to receive adequate attention because they were the most likely to have 'political' implications. The services administered in these two fields of action, one the most expensive, and the other one of the least expensive—over £14 million on education against £120,000 on planning in the year 1960-1—touched most closely those interests concerned with the economic expansion of certain areas and industries. Where were houses and factories going to be built? Where were the children to be educated? Who was going to have a share in the profits of expansion?

The County Council therefore became a guardian of the public interest which was supposed to defend the principle of planning. But, on occasions, it was likely to be subjected to pressure from various groups and private individuals who objected to the manner in which it exercised control over developments where their interests were involved. The three-level system already described provided various opportunities for accommodating persons who might be injured in any dispute. The organization for the control of development within the county boundaries consisted of three elements which corresponded to the three levels of the system. In the first place, there were the elected representatives, borough or district councillors and county councillors; in the second place, the chief officers of the county council and their representatives in divisional offices, particularly the area planning officers who were the 'eyes and ears of County Hall'; and in the third place, the senior civil servants of the Minister who arranged for public inquiries and took decisions in his name. Of all three elements, the chief officers were the most vulnerable to vulgar abuse because councillors can take shelter behind the shield of collective decision-making, and civil servants behind the discretion of the Minister. The county officials did not enjoy the privilege of anonymity.

The principal difficulty arose when these three elements did not agree on policy. Such disagreements might be comparatively rare, but they illustrated the innate stresses and strains of the system. Some councillors, particularly those with little experience of county affairs and some power in local intrigue, might be interested in trying 'to get round the regulations'. Others might be tempted to treat planning applications, overspill agreements, or the location of in-dustry, primarily as matters which reflected local party warfare, and spend a great deal of time in anticipating the changes in party political control which might follow local district elections. District councillors might find themselves bowing down before the demands of local residents' associations, or listening to complaints about 'sterilization' in the proposed Green Belts. The officials, on the other hand, particularly in the principal spending departments, Education and Roads, might be engrossed in 'getting things through the Minis-try' or in the technique of persuading their own committees to adopt a policy which had a particular appeal 'at officer level'. The civil servants might make judgements which were influenced by politicians, national pressure groups, or the personal prejudices of their Minister. All these possible variations at three different levels demonstrated how disagreements might have taken place and how planning policy was derived from the interplay of all three elements.

The first element, the councillors, were divided into three types: those who were simply county councillors, those who were borough or district councillors, and those who were both county and district, the important group of 'dual councillors'. From the point of view of the senior officials in County Hall, the most important distinction was not whether they were 'county' representatives or 'district' representatives, but whether or not they were capable of thinking 'in county terms'. Those in general who thought 'in county terms' were the 'inner ring' of ministerialists on the council whose activities have already been described. The same distinction could be applied to the officers of borough or district councils. Those working in County Hall were well aware of their privileged position when they compared their lot with their colleagues in district authorities. The latter lived in much closer day-to-day contact with the councillors, and were much more vulnerable to the forces of petty corruption and influence. If the planning regulations were to be ignored, it was much more likely to be done at the district council level. The prestige of the district council in the eyes of County Hall to a large extent depended upon the reputation of its clerk. In any negotiations between county and district councils, the clerk of a district council might be regarded as 'anti-ministerialist' if he caused the county officials what they considered to be needless trouble, or as 'ministerialist' if he pleased them by limiting his council to certain matters of principle. Walter Timperley, Clerk of the Cheadle Urban District from 1925 to 1960, was regarded as a man whose prime concern was to raise the status of his authority to that of borough.

The greatest 'anti-ministerialist' forces were those landowners who with the help of estate agents lobbied district councillors and officials in order to secure planning permission for certain plots of land where houses might be required. The county councillors and county officials who formed the 'ministerialist party' performed their most difficult function in making judgements on applications which involved considerable capital gains for the applicants. It was made more difficult by the fact that the County Council itself might contain strong 'anti-ministerialist' groups. Wayward county councillors might be seduced by the activities of various local pressure groups—veritable phenomena of a 'country party'. One such group which was not very influential, the Cheshire branch of the Council for the Preservation of Rural England, formed before the Second World War in 1930, had an executive committee which was almost entirely composed of people who represented the remnant of social leadership—peers and retired army officers. But by the late 1950's it had acquired a membership more in keeping with the politics of public persons. The more militant groups consisted either of ratepayers or residents, although some, such as the Wirral Green Belt Council, claimed to protect the interests of both by campaigning for amenities which benefited their neighbourhood. The 'ministerialist party' in reply might have to restrain both their own colleagues on the County Council and the district council officials who tended to fear the activities of such groups outside the normal party warfare. The ministerialists might be prepared to use the Minister in Whitehall as a 'long stop' to delay a decision, but even they were sometimes rebuffed by the Minister himself. For instance, the County Council tried to solve the dispute between Manchester and Wilmslow in 1960 over the building of 'point-block' flats at Handforth by giving the Minister an opportunity to intervene by holding a public inquiry, but the suggestion was refused. The second element, the officials, were able to claim that their principal contribution to the building up of a 'ministerialist party' lay in the presentation of 'the facts'. The basis of planned development was that the research performed by officials demonstrated what had been physically possible in the past, and suggested what developments might be possible for the future, while the judgement possessed by the councillors determined what was politically acceptable. Both the leading councillors and leading officials distrusted any intermediate stage placed between the district councils and themselves. In 1954 the Cheshire Planning Committee abolished the area advisory committees, based on the pre-war planning arrangements, which dealt with all appeals in the first instance before they were sent up to the County Council, because such bodies were found to be in the hands of 'anti-ministerialists', district councillors who were guided too much by local considerations. The judicial functions could only be properly performed at the county level. The county planning officers concentrated on their main task of presenting 'the facts'. They calculated in 1950 that it would be possible to build houses at the rate of about 5,000 a year for the whole county during the next twenty years, and that during this period between 80,000 and 90,000 people would enter the county voluntarily from Lancashire, and between 156,000 and 166,000 in planned overspill arrangements. But the decision where a quarter of a million people should live could not be made entirely on 'planning grounds'. The plan to locate the largest number of migrants by planned overspill in a New Town at Congleton involved important political considerations. This particular project was abandoned after several Ministers had taken it to the highest levels of negotiation.[1] After all the calculations for any project had been made by the officials and plans approved by the Minister, the 'ministerialists' then had a blue-print for action, a map indicating where development would be allowed. The greatest pressure on planning authorities arose wherever the 'white land', marked on the map for use only after 1970, was not considered sufficient, and where a Green Belt limited the spread of residential housing.

The third element, the civil servants, was primarily required to keep a check upon the 'ministerialists' in County Hall. The latter enjoyed a reputation in Whitehall according to the degree of understanding which they were considered to possess about 'the mind of the Minister' or 'the view of the Ministry'. There was always a possibility that the ministerialist party in County Hall would not accept a Ministry decision. Councillors could listen to the 'country party' voices of the opposition, and attempt to gain access to the

[1] See below, pp. 208–9.

private office of the Minister through the political party organization. A great deal in the smooth working of the system depended upon mutual respect and trust between civil servants and county officials. Each could inform the other of impending crises. The civil servants were required to make sure that county officials understood and obeyed the regulations which were made under various statutes to govern all aspects of the control which the Minister exercised. The Minister's decision was final, and in any serious dispute he would himself decide what to do. The civil servants made only the routine decisions on his behalf.

The maintenance of a policy controlling development required techniques for dealing with pressures from three separate sources. First of all, various private interests, landowners, industrialists, builders, were competing for permission to use certain stretches of land. Secondly, other public bodies, central departments, local authorities, or nationalized industries, expected their needs to be accommodated. Thirdly, various *ad hoc* groups in local society such as residents' or ratepayers' associations, staged campaigns for the promotion of certain county services. The pressure from all three sources had to be met by the 'ministerialists', a combination of the first two elements, councillors and officials, leaning on the statutory powers of the third element, the civil servants.

Estate agents were often in the vanguard of organized pressure from the first source, private enterprise. They provided the necessary technical arguments to any landowner who wished to augment the capital value of his possessions, and were prepared to appear as witnesses at any public inquiry. The increasing price of land in some areas stimulated competition. In 1961 an estate agent on behalf of some clients even approached the rector of Cheadle to see whether he was willing to sell the site of Cheadle parish church.[1] Those who hoped to make money by land speculation were faced with opposition from two quarters: first, the planning authority itself which might have scheduled the land for some other use, either industrial or agricultural; and secondly other public authorities which might claim priority for the service of the 'public interest'.

Disputes between the planning authority and private interests wishing to build houses were concentrated in those three areas of Cheshire, the Wirral, Altrincham, and Cheadle (designated sub-regions 1, 7, and 8 in the County Development Plan) which have

[1] *The Guardian*, 7 June 1961.

played such an important part in the county's political development.[1]
Land in these areas increased in value wherever the planning authority
gave permission for houses to be built, because these regions included the more fashionable residential places for people in the
business life of Liverpool and Manchester. The over-all increase in
the number of planning applications from these regions dealt with
by the County Planning Office reflected their relative importance over
the remainder of the county. (See Table 16.)

TABLE 16

Applications for Private Development: 1948–61

*Regional Totals as Percentages of the Number for the Whole County
for Two Consecutive Periods of Six Years:*

Economic Sub-Region	1948–54	1955–61
1. Wirral . . .	16·3	15·9
7. Altrincham . . .	19·5	17·7
8. Cheadle . . .	12·9	12·0
Sub-Total	48·7	45·6
2. Chester . . .	6·6	5·5
3. Runcorn . . .	5·8	7·7
4. Northwich . . .	7·8	9·4
5. Crewe . . .	9·3	9·6
6. Macclesfield[2] . .	15·8	15·0
9. Hyde . . .	6·0	7·2
	100·0	100·0

The planning authority, aided by the Ministry, attempted to enforce
a policy of encircling both the Birkenhead and the Manchester
urban areas with a Green Belt, but many strong political forces
pressed upon the county officials so that they would not draw the
boundaries of limited development too tightly, and the Ministry
itself was very vulnerable to Conservative party interests which
feared the political consequences of 'sterilization'. The final drafts
for the Wirral and North Cheshire Green Belts were not placed in
the hands of the Minister until 1960–61.[3] Certain decisions, however,
which were taken in the middle of the 1950's laid down the chief

---

[1] See above, pp. 104–6.
[2] The high proportion from this region was due to the large number of
applications from private individuals wishing to build a single house at one of the
villages within reach of Manchester.   [3] See map at end.

points of dispute which were likely to arise. For instance, in 1955 the Ministry, in judging an appeal submitted by B.C.D. Estates Ltd. against the planning authority, refused to allow as much as thirty acres of the proposed Wirral Green Belt at Hooton to be developed as a residential area. The firm were only allowed to complete one side of Vernon Avenue which it had laid down before 1939. No further large-scale schemes in this area were likely to succeed. Another decision made in 1956 established the principle that some limitations must be set to the expansion of Cheadle and Gatley. It concerned a narrow strip of country separating Cheadle Hulme from Handforth and Wilmslow which was described as 'the first clearly defined break south of Manchester'. Although the local district council supported their application against the wishes of the County Council, Messrs. John Gerrard & Son Ltd., the builders, were refused permission by the Ministry to erect houses on 57 acres lying to the north side of Stanley Road. The County Planning Officer defended his case for preserving a Green Belt by demonstrating that there was no real shortage of building land: planning permission for 3,000 houses, then un-built, had already been given. The planning authority was also able to prevent, through a decision of the Minister, the development of 70 acres at Nether Alderley in 1957, in spite of the fact that the local district council was supporting this scheme and providing technical arguments based upon the need to improve water supplies. By 1960 the North Cheshire Green Belt had survived such onslaughts, but only after many adjustments. A decision of the Ministry in March 1961 which dealt with ten appeals from the Cheadle and Wilmslow areas revealed how many compromises were considered to be necessary in order to provide 'a steady and well-distributed supply of sites to serve the needs of the Manchester conurbation'. Permission to develop within the inner boundary of the proposed Green Belt was allowed in some cases, but not in others.

The new system of controlled development in many cases frustrated the completion of projects which had been sanctioned under the former planning laws before 1939. The County Development Plan of 1952 envisaged a limited amount of 'in-filling', the process of closing the gaps left in eertain pieces of pre-1939 'ribbon development'. But the planning authority received a considerable number of applications which expected the term 'in-filling' to be interpreted in a very generous manner. For instance, the Caldy Manor Estate in 1953 applied for permission to continue the 'ribbon development' of Telegraph Road, Caldy, which had been begun before 1939, in spite of the fact that the existing houses were far apart. This was refused. Similarly all the arguments about A. S. Eden's application in 1959 to develop 23 acres at Woodlands farm on the south side of Hall Lane at Mobberley were based upon the possibility of 'in-filling' upon this site after a new sewer had been laid. The Ministry found the fact that part of the proposed estate had been planned before 1939 was no valid reason for permitting further development.

The most embarrassing situations arose from the conflict between private interests and the schemes promoted by local authorities or the County Council itself. Sometimes one of the County Council's own departments seemed to be at variance with its own planning policy. The County Education Department in its search for suitable sites on which new schools might be built occasionally felt bound to ask for concessions from its colleagues in the County Planning Department. The long and rather tedious controversy about the siting of the proposed College of Further Education at Hyde, for example, illustrated the persistence of the Education Committee in defying the Ministry to allow another large building within the pro-posed North Cheshire Green Belt. Although the County Council's first application for 12 acres at Bowlacre, Hilda Road, was turned down by the Ministry in 1958, its second application for 6 acres on the same site in 1960 was accepted. The only loss was the playing-field. Sometimes a private interest which came into conflict with the County Council's school-building programme was able to reach an agreement with the Education Department without taking the matter on appeal to the Ministry. In 1957 a site at Bredbury Green was shared between the County Council, which wished to use part of it for a school, and Maurice Mason, who had originally applied for permission to develop the whole. At other times the Ministry, on an appeal from the County Council, permitted it to erect a school, but rejected all other applications for the same site. District councils also found great difficulty in promoting some of their own schemes. In 1957 Disley Rural District Council, which included a member of the committee of the National Playing Fields Association, was involved in a very acrimonious dispute to preserve an area on Jacksons Edge Road, which was part of the view enjoyed by visitors to Lyme Park, for use as playing-fields. The appeal of Mrs. Duck and Mrs. Simpson to build an estate on the same land was dismissed. Perhaps the siting of council houses produced the greatest anxieties for district councils.

Northwich Urban District Council, for instance, was refused permission in 1957 by the Ministry to build council houses on the west side of London Road, Leftwich; but struggled in the following year to gain permission for developing part of a site at Thorn Farm, Hartford, against rival private interests.

Landowners were occasionally capable of making considerable gains by putting in an application for the private development of a site which was known to be the subject of local authority negotiations. Until 1961 such anticipations of public policy by private interests, if taken on appeal to the Ministry, could frustrate local authority schemes because the law made it difficult to prescribe that certain sites could be developed only by local councils. The Ministry worked on the general rule that planning control was not concerned with the person or agency who used the land but simply with its appropriate use. Cheshire County Council ran up against the consequences of this policy in its attempts to find suitable sites for the housing of 'overspill' from Liverpool and Manchester, although the most important case concerned the housing programme of Chester County Borough. The latter in 1957 found itself obliged to share a site at Plas Newton with the owner, A. E. C. L. Jones-Lloyd, who had applied for permission to develop as soon as he heard of the borough's intentions. The Clerk of the County Council protested against this decision of the Ministry in a strongly worded letter pointing out that such a precedent would make it very difficult to find sites suitable for overspill housing. If the owner of a possible site put in an application on his own behalf which was then taken on appeal to the Minister, the Jones-Lloyd decision guaranteed him a share in the right to develop, and compelled the exporting authority to look for another site on which to complete its quota of council houses. This case was a good illustration of the way in which the opinion of local government officers could bring to the attention of the Ministry important faults in its own interpretation of the public interest.

The second source of pressure in the politics of controlled development, public authorities which sought permission to develop, was usually dominated by local councils themselves. The Cheshire County Council was primarily concerned with the 'overspill' requirements of the Merseyside and Manchester regions. The great county boroughs of Liverpool and Manchester, whose inhabitants were responsible for the pressure from private interests in the Wirral, Altrincham, and Cheadle areas already described, asked for their needs in council housing to be met on Cheshire soil. Geographical factors, the position of the Mersey and the grouping of urban authorities on Manchester's north and west, tended to draw more attention to the needs of Manchester rather than those of Liverpool. The Manchester authority was constrained to look southwards for a satellite town rather than northwards into Lancashire. This is the 'Wythenshawe psychology', already described.[1] The chief difference between Manchester and Cheshire was on the subject of 'concentration', whether or not Manchester emigrants should be placed together in a new town close to their native city. Cheshire has always been able to argue that it could provide sufficient space by dispersing Manchester overspill in several 'block sites' attached to existing settlements, and was at one time willing to develop Congleton as a New Town. The siting of new towns and large estates required the arbitration of the Minister himself because the local authorities concerned were not able to agree.[2] But in 1954 Cheshire was able to begin a series of negotiations with Manchester for 'block sites' or for places to be expanded under the provisions of the Town Development Act (1952). The County Council found various sites which would accommodate houses for Manchester 'overspill', at places already in the Manchester 'suburbs'—Cheadle, Bredbury, Hazel Grove, Marple, Knutsford, and Wilmslow. The greatest success and the greatest trouble over 'block sites' were geographically fairly close to each other. The development of the village of Partington, beside the petro-chemical works which lies west of Sale and is separated from it by a Green Belt, provided a project which was politically acceptable to local opinion. But a site within Sale itself was the source of some dispute because local councillors knew that the land could be quickly developed by private builders if it were not handed over to the Manchester council, and if they could obtain planning permission against the opposition of the Ministry of Agriculture. 'Block sites' were usually acceptable where they did not interfere with private development. The Hyde region, which was under less pressure from private interests, was therefore selected for 'overspill' prospecting. Sites at Hattersley and Hollingworth were chosen, and although the idea of developing the latter was abandoned because it would have extended the continuous building of the conurbation area, the former received a proportion of 'Manchester houses'. Consideration of these matters involved so many political forces that not a single 'overspill'

[1] See above, pp. 112–13.   [2] See below, pp. 205 ff.

house had been built by Manchester in Cheshire by 1957, although various Cheshire authorities with the aid of grants from the County Council had provided some 2,000 houses for Salford, Stretford, Manchester, and Stockport.

The other principal cause of friction between the Manchester and Cheshire authorities was the former's proposals to make various extensions of Ringway Airport.[1] Aeroplanes required so much land and made so much noise that they were likely to be considered offensive in residential areas, and Ringway lies close to the more 'desirable' new suburbs.

Other public bodies which required land or wished to develop existing property tended to avoid getting themselves involved in the competition between rival local authorities, because they were able to settle their affairs in direct consultation with the Ministry concerned. Under the cover of security regulations for example, the Atomic Energy Authority in 1949 was able to go ahead with its plans for building a plant at Capenhurst without having its application openly considered by the planning committees of the district. County officials were apparently placed in the embarrassing position of being informed of these developments but being forbidden to disclose them even to their own councillors. Nationalized industries have not benefited so much from the powers of ministerial discretion. The North-Western Gas Board was subject to constant complaints about its gasometer at Winsford and its staff college at Mere. The most persistent central department in planning matters has been the Ministry of Agriculture. The latter was particularly active in proposing alternative sites of a lower agricultural value when any valuable farm was in danger of being used for building development. The Ministry's assessment of agricultural value might have some serious political consequences. It certainly frustrated such schemes as the Halton Lodge Farm housing scheme in 1952–3. The Ministry was one of the strongest forces limiting the expansion of urban areas.

The third source of pressure came from *ad hoc* groups in local society which were usually formed to fight one particular issue, and which, once that issue had been decided, tended to lose their impact in local affairs, in spite of the fact that their names might be perpetuated and their officers elected for year after year. Ratepayers' and residents' associations were so ephemeral and depended so heavily for their effectiveness on one or two people who brought

---

[1] *The Guardian*, 14 July 1961, p. 18.

them into existence that the County Council could usually afford to let the brunt of their attacks fall upon the district councils. Many such associations appear to have taken their origin from disputes within such councils. Marple Ratepayers' Association was apparently created after a dispute about council-house tenancies in the 1930's. The Winsford Association was constructed by those voters who objected to their own council's plans for building a New Town; it had merely the negative purpose of 'keeping out Manchester'. But the most powerful kind of local pressure group was that which gained the support of the district council and the local M.P. Manchester's housing programme at Outwood Road, Heald Green, provoked the creation of a Residents' Association in 1955 which staged a campaign against the three-storey flats of the borough's 'overspill' design. This body quickly secured the support of Cheadle and Gatley Urban District Council and was able to persuade the local M.P. that it represented the wishes of a large number of his constituents. Although the County Planning Officer approved of the design which Manchester hoped to use for flats and shops, he was required to take into account other factors which influenced decisions of county planning policy.

National organizations also brought pressure to bear through their local branches. The Cheshire branch of the National Farmers' Union was extremely active in opposing the building of 'overspill' houses on good agricultural land. In 1951 it even went as far as finding a site at Newchurch Common, an infertile heath, on which a New Town could be built with the minimum amount of damage to agriculture. Similarly, the County Council received representations from Ramblers' Associations about footpaths, from Caravan Associations about caravan sites, and from the Inland Waterways Association about canals.

It is significant that those *ad hoc* groups which received the most attention in county council discussions were those which originated within the ministerialist party itself. The Chester University Promotion Committee, which in 1961 received the promise of financial aid from the County Council, arose out of a chance conversation between the council's chairman and the Bishop of Chester. The Clerk of the council himself took charge of the negotiations which followed the formation of this committee. Any local group was always in a stronger position if it could call upon someone from within the ministerialist party to argue its case. Otherwise, the county officials might merely be explaining their policy to organized groups which had not had a sympathetic hearing from members of the council. The Education Department was frequently called upon to pacify harassed parents who organized themselves into an association to agitate on behalf of their children. One of the most notable features of the politics of controlled development, perhaps a consequence of the distance which separated County Hall from the majority of the electorate, was that some issues received a great deal of violent and wrong-headed publicity in local newspapers while others were scarcely mentioned. There were no newspapers which thought in 'county terms'—no county society existed to buy them—and a considerable amount of anti-ministerialist feeling directed against the county officials sprang from the ignorance occasioned by this lack of publicity. The strength of the ministerialist party lay in its access to the principal sources of information.

The arbitration of the Minister

But the ministerialists of County Hall were not politically self-sufficient. They were occasionally required to submit their plans for the consideration of Ministry officials in Whitehall. The senior civil servants of the Ministry of Housing and Local Government and the Ministry of Education, in particular, were called upon regularly to make some assessment of the activities of Cheshire's chief officers and leading councillors. The decisions made by the Minister were based to a large extent upon the opinions formed by his advisers. Because the Ministry of Housing and Local Government had direct contacts with the boroughs and district councils which made up the county, as well as with the County Council itself, its officials were well placed to view the working of the two-tier system of government. Those in the Planning Division which dealt with the provinces maintained their principal contacts with the County Planning Office, but the assistant secretary and heads of sections in the Housing Division which dealt with the North-Western Region considered matters arising from all authorities within the county. The inspectors sent to hear public inquiries about planning permission also came away with an assessment of the 'political feeling' in the area. Therefore, in various different ways, Whitehall formed an impression of County Hall.

It is hard to make an accurate assessment of the informal contacts which took place between the two sets of professionals, those in the

Civil Service, and those chief officers who bore the brunt of the council's negotiations with central departments, the Clerk, the Treasurer, the Chief Education Officer, and the County Planning Officer. An increasing number of decisions on general lines of policy appear to have been made at unofficial meetings between the leading officers of the council with their chairmen and vice-chairmen on one side, and on the other side civil servants or parliamentary secretaries. Of course, opportunities for such meetings were increased by the holding of conferences by professional associations and by the regular committee work of such bodies as the County Councils Association. The Clerk and the Treasurer in particular, had many chances of establishing informal contacts with other persons in public life. One post-war institution which strengthened their position was the 'business men's lunch'. Although until 1957 various county council committees met regularly at the Crewe Arms Hotel by Crewe Railway station,[1] they never had any formal arrangements with the hotel manager for having lunch together. Eating in company was reserved for occasions organized by the 'party caucus'. Otherwise, some members had a private lunch at the hotel; some ate sandwiches in the station refreshment room. The abandonment of Crewe and the opening of the members' dining room in Chester made day-to-day contact over lunch a possibility and provided a more relaxed atmosphere for assessing the political potentiality of all concerned in the business of county administration. War-time rationing seems to have encouraged the habit of communal feeding. After 1958 the business of county administration was aided by a tradition of hospitality under which both officers and councillors could invite friends to lunch.

The most important informal contacts were probably those between the chief officers of different authorities before an approach was made to the Ministry. Some of the most far-reaching decisions in 1946 about Cheshire's attitude to the Boundary Commission and to Manchester's claims for 'overspill' seem to have been made over dinner by the Clerks of Cheshire and Lancashire at the former's London club. Food rationing compelled the club to limit its members to entertaining only one guest each—an excellent pattern for intrigue! In fact, one of the chief difficulties experienced by civil servants was to assess how far the chief officers of local authorities were prepared to work in harmony with others, and how far their public

[1] See above, pp. 15, 123, 143.

pronouncements were made to give the semblance of antagonism between their own authority and another, without intending to 'fight a campaign' against any ministerial decision. The chief function of the Minister was to arbitrate between antagonistic authorities, but only his advisers could provide him with an accurate assessment of the strength of feeling involved.

Informal discussions sometimes prevented disputes from breaking out, and some Ministers were reluctant to impose a settlement upon warring parties. No case illustrates the nature of ministerial action better than the long and rather complicated history of Manchester's search for a site in Cheshire on which a satellite town could be built. The places which Manchester City Council wished to develop lay in an area close to the new suburbs of the 1930's and therefore subject to the County Council's policy of maintaining a Green Belt around the conurbation. Only the intervention of the Minister could lead to a solution of such a direct conflict of aims, but even in 1961 Manchester City Council was still complaining that Cheshire's Green Belt plans 'were designed not to give expression to the needs of the public but to justify the County Council's opposition to the legitimate desires of Manchester to rehouse Manchester people on larger sites in Cheshire'.[1] In 1946 Manchester City Council proposed building a new satellite town at the village of Mobberley on the north-east side of Knutsford and on the main railway line from Manchester Central Station.[2] The Minister of Town and Country Planning at first approved of the plan and sanctioned the creation of a Development Corporation for the purpose of completing it, but then withdrew his approval and only later, in 1949, agreed to let Manchester City Council develop the same site on a smaller scale from its own resources.[3] Cheshire County Council had meanwhile in 1947 gained the Minister's interest in the development of Congleton as a New Town, which was far enough away from Manchester for 'overspill' population to be able to break their ties with their native town, but delay in reaching a decision, as in the case of Mobberley, was caused by the discovery of salt deposits which might cause subsidence.[4] Even in 1950 it was still considered likely that a Development Corporation would be created for Congleton by the Minister, and it was not until 1952 (after the General Election), when the Town Development

[1] *The Guardian*, 28 Oct. 1961, p. 12.
[2] See Map 2, facing p. 119.
[3] *Manchester Guardian*, 26 Apr. 1949.
[4] Ibid., 7 Dec. 1946, 27 Apr., 27 July, 1949.

Act provided an alternative form of administration, that the project for extending the town on a large scale was dropped. Manchester City Council was also interested in a site at Lymm which like Mobberley enjoyed the possibility of good railway communication with Manchester, particularly with the Trafford Park Industrial Estate. It pushed its claim for both Mobberley and Lymm to a public inquiry in 1953, but had to wait for over a year before the Minister issued an adverse decision. This failure did not daunt the City Council, which continued putting forward its arguments in favour of satellite residential settlements at Lymm and Mobberley. In 1955 the Minister in person again investigated the sites on the ground, and many thought that he would be compelled to permit some limited form of development. Finally, in 1957 the Minister of Housing and Local Government, Henry Brooke, decided to allow the dispute to be settled by an impartial observer, and he appointed J. Ramsay Willis, Q.C., to hold an inquiry in January 1958 at Chester and to publish his opinion.[1] The latter was also to reject Manchester's case.

The arbitration of the Minister was sometimes an attempt to force a decision without being compelled to issue a set of precise regulations. Civil servants in the Ministry were concerned to ensure that all parties in any dispute should, wherever possible, settle their differences with the aid of the local planning authority. The Minister's power represented an ultimate sanction which was used as a constant threat to speed the business of negotiation. For example, in 1951 a conflict arose between those planning the development of Congleton New Town and those seeking permission to build a steerable radio telescope for Manchester University at Jodrell Bank Experimental Station. In order to avoid excessive electrical interference, the latter project required some limitation of housing and industrial development within a zone which extended over the whole area for a radius of six miles and included the northern outskirts of Congleton borough. Although the scheme for a New Town under the 1946 Act was abandoned in 1952, the ambitions of the borough council to press forward with plans for receiving Manchester 'overspill' under the terms of the Town Development Act led the Director of Jodrell Bank, Professor Lovell, to seek assurances that those parts of Congleton which lay closest to the telescope would not be expanded. The representations which he made to the Department of

[1] *Report of Inquiry into the Proposed Development of Land at Lymm for Manchester Overspill* (1958).

Scientific and Industrial Research, sponsor of the project, brought the dispute into central departments for ministerial consideration. A reply to a question in the House of Commons in 1953 was construed as a guarantee that the claims of the telescope would be respected.[1] The details of negotiating which areas on Congleton Town Map could be developed without interfering with the operations of the telescope were worked out at a series of rather acrimonious meetings in 1954 and 1955. Officials in the Ministry of Housing and Local Government persuaded Professor Lovell to make various concessions, and played the role of expert mediators who reconciled conflicting claims. But the presence of the Parliamentary Secretary was necessary at the final meeting before agreement could be reached. No other interest outside Congleton made effective objections to the restriction of development within the zone which surrounded the telescope. Jodrell Bank was obliged to agree to the electrification of the Manchester–Birmingham railway, but received assurances that electrical interference would be reduced to a minimum. It was successful in asking for the diversion of several high voltage lines, including the super-grid line from Drakelow to Carrington. The meeting with the Parliamentary Secretary led to a request that arrangements for restricting development should be formalized in a 'private treaty' between the Experimental Station and the Planning Authority, Cheshire County Council. From 1957 onwards, it was agreed that applications received by the County Planning Department for development within the inner zone around the telescope should be submitted to the staff of Jodrell Bank for their comments. Applicants who were refused permission by the joint agreement of these two authorities could still, in theory, appeal to the Minister for a reversal of the decision, but were unlikely to succeed while the 'private treaty' retained ministerial approval. Professor Lovell, the Director of Jodrell Bank, had an unusual status on the local committee of the Council for the Preservation of Rural England! The Minister's power, which produced such strange consequences, could be exercised through other bodies which were not formally instructed to act on his behalf.

On the vexed question of local government boundaries, the Minister's discretionary power has frequently been delegated to other bodies. The Commissions of 1888 and 1945 have already been mentioned.[2] The Local Government Commission for England

[1] Hansard, 5th ser., vol. 520 (written answers), cols. 148–9.
[2] See above, pp. 72, 121.

appointed in 1958 faced the problem of advising the Minister to adopt a certain course of action after it had heard the evidence from various local authorities which it knew very well had for a long time been in constant discussion with each other. The clerks of borough and district councils were in the habit of having several informal meetings to relate their own points of view to those of other authorities. The Minister was expected to be aware of various intrigues. In 1960 the clerks of several county boroughs issued a report proposing that the best form of government for the Manchester region was to partition all the existing authorities and absorb them into a pattern of contiguous county boroughs.[1] This report was followed by the announcement that two urban district councils which feared that they would be absorbed into the county borough of Stockport, Cheadle & Gatley and Hazel Grove & Bramhall, had decided 'in principle' to amalgamate in order to form a single, and therefore stronger, authority.[2] This proposed amalgamation had the approval of the County Council. In all the debates which preceded the arrival of the Commission, the Clerk of the County Council was involved in a whole series of informal meetings with officers and councillors from authorities which feared extinction.

The Minister's occasional attempts to remove a particular issue from the inter-play of local forces, so that it might be settled in consultation with his civil servants and not left to the informal agreements of local officials, serve as a reminder that the ministerialists of County Hall did not always agree with those of Whitehall. Those councillors and officials who understood each level of the administrative system were few in number, and naturally proud of their own authority. The Minister's arbitration might be a *deus ex machina* necessary for the removal of tensions which involved more than the future of the County Council. There were many weaknesses within a two-tier system of government.

The difficulty of reconciling the needs of the new county services, which had been established after 1945, with the products of the triennial elections for councillors, which continued along the lines laid down before 1914, was only met by the willingness of certain successful candidates to perform the diplomatic functions of elected representatives at the local level, and to learn from full-time

[1] *The Times*, 18 July 1960; *The Guardian*, 18 May 1960.
[2] *The Guardian*, 17 Sept. 1960; county councillors recognized this as another move towards borough status, see above, p. 116.

officials how standards might be improved and how policy might be altered. It is hard to determine the motives which influenced part-time councillors to spend their time in the very complex business of a large administrative machine, and harder still to explain why certain members were more successful than others. There were tangible rewards in the form of titles and honours, but these were normally given only to those who had played an important part in local public life over a period of years. The greatest reward lay in the successful accomplishment of playing the role of a public person. Much depended upon co-operation between councillors and officials who were both public persons in the eyes of the electorate. The leading councillors and officials enjoyed the privilege of sharing 'ministerial responsibility' for the direction of policy within the 'collective responsibility' of the committee system. This form of government rested on the availability of a few able elected representatives who could afford the time to make what was originally an occasional public service into almost a full-time occupation.

CONCLUSION

THE main thesis of Part III is that the county society of social leaders was replaced by a community of public persons in which the leading members and the chief officers of the County Council were the principal personalities. Those who retained any sense of belonging to 'county society' were either surviving families of gentry and successful industrialists with strong local ties who were linked together largely by various personal and economic interests in London, or families of business and professional people who dominated the organizations of the wealthier suburban areas. But nobody believed that 'county society' was in any way responsible for the public welfare. The process by which 'county society' had grown away from the responsibilities of county administration was completed by the end of the Second World War. The remnant of county pride, loyalty, and devotion, and the sense of social obligation which these induced, which the first County Council had to some extent inherited from the magistrates in Quarter Sessions and had fostered by the tradition of social leadership, were represented under the new system by the technical competence of the full-time officials of the County Council. The informal relations between the great patrons of the shire, such as the Duke of Westminster and Lord Tollemache, and members of the lesser gentry which had given a political significance to hunting meets or winter assemblies were replaced by a vast network of committee meetings, informal lunches, conferences, and even telephone conversations which joined together the community of public persons and which occupied the full-time officials of all the local authorities in the county.

County government depended upon professional guidance. The building of new suburbs and the expansion of existing towns was accompanied by a great increase in the number of services which the County Council was expected to provide. Parliamentary legislation transformed the task which county authorities were required to do. Only professional local government officers had the time to cope with the necessary pieces of social research and the application of specialized knowledge which the duty of planning for the whole county placed upon the County Council. The Town and Country Planning Act of 1947 symbolized the need for introducing special

CONCLUSION   213

techniques into county administration. The authority became responsible for controlling development.

Those areas of the county which attracted the most professional
attention were precisely those in which the tradition of social leadership had been destroyed by the sudden influx of population, those
places in which the 'new suburbs' had been built, Wirral, Altrincham, and Cheadle. Local government services in those areas could
not be provided by a group of social leaders petitioning for the
creation of new urban district councils, as would have happened
before the First World War, but only by adjacent boroughs and the
County Council. The boundary disputes which were such an important feature of local politics between 1926 and 1936 represented the
need of rural areas to submit to urban forms of government where-
ever great social change took place. The prototypes of all public
persons, both official and lay, were evolved in the conditions of
borough politics where social leaders had tended to disappear.

The County Council therefore gradually became a body of elected
representatives, each of whom was primarily a person in the public
life of his own local town or community, and each of whom
was dependent for his position not on his social standing but on his
experience in public service. In county council affairs the 'dual
councillor', one who remained a borough or district councillor in the
place where he had gained his experience after his election 'on to
the county', became almost the norm among elected representatives.
A large number of such councillors saw themselves as the representatives of local interest groups at the county council level, but they
quickly found it hard to press for services to be improved in their
own areas unless they could convince their colleagues of the fairness
of their case. Committees of the County Council took on a quasi-
judicial role when they were deciding the merits of claims from
different areas. It was difficult for councillors themselves to arrange
deals by which one councillor would support another if the latter
returned the compliment on another occasion, because the chief
officers of the County Council constituted a body of permanent
'ministers' who had almost an absolute control over the chief sources
of information. Furthermore, the party whips disciplined members
of the council in such a way that chairmanships and the places on the
aldermanic bench, the principal positions of influence, were under
the control of the majority party caucus.

In these conditions, the leading councillors were those who learned to acquire the art of understanding discussions 'at officer level' and who thereby gained the confidence of the chief officers. Such men, if they were also respected by the organizations of the political parties, and had the necessary ability to grasp the intricacies of the administrative detail involved, constituted an informal group of 'ministers', the 'inner ring'. They in alliance with the chief officers constituted a kind of ministerialist party, grouped around the persons of the chairman and vice-chairman of the Council. The other councillors constituted a kind of permanent 'country party' or group of anti-ministerialists. Promotion into the 'inner ring' depended upon making an impression upon not only one's immediate colleagues but also upon the chief officers and chairmen of the principal committees.

The autonomy of the County Council rested upon the ability of the ministerialists to maintain good relations with, on the one hand, borough and district councils which might exercise delegated powers under county supervision, and on the other, the senior civil servants of central departments which were required to approve its schemes. The Minister of each department was sometimes called upon to arbitrate between antagonistic authorities, particularly between the County Council and hostile county boroughs, but he frequently left the burden of reaching a decision to an independent body.

It is therefore misleading to think of the County Council primarily as a body of elected representatives who make decisions of policy and then order officials to execute them. Although such a view constitutes the theory, the reality is vastly different. It is better to regard the system of county government as a body of professional people, placed together in a large office at County Hall, who can call upon the services of representatives from all places throughout the area which they administer. Some of these representatives by sheer ability and drive make themselves indispensable to the successful working of the machine; others merely represent points of view which come into conflict with it. County Hall is therefore a meeting-place for a community of persons in public life, formed partly of local government officers, who enjoy the privileges of various professional associations, and partly of elected representatives whose main job, either through a party organization or independently, is to keep in touch with all the interests which are affected.

PART IV

CONCLUSION

7

THE EVOLUTION OF COUNTY GOVERNMENT

How far have the other counties of England and Wales followed the same pattern of development as Cheshire? There are still very obvious contrasts between different county councils. On the one hand, Durham has come so completely under the sway of the Labour party that its councillors can only achieve the status of being public persons through local Labour organizations; while on the other hand, Oxfordshire in spite of iron-stone mining and the consequences of re-settling its villages with small colonies of 'dons', remains obstinately loyal to the principles of social leadership embodied in the activities of the Duke of Marlborough and the Earl of Macclesfield. But may Durham be taken as an example of the likely evolution to be followed by any county council which finds its territory becoming urbanized? Does Cheshire's development represent a stage in the pattern which others will follow? Economists have in recent years been concerned with theories of economic growth which postulate a point in time at which a country's economy 'takes off' into a new era of affluence. Is there a similar phenomenon in county administration, a point of growth from which there is no return, marked by a certain degree of urbanization? Must all social leaders be eventually displaced by public persons? It is not easy to make generalizations about the possible evolution of county councils when so many different local factors, both historical and geographical, have influenced the way in which political conventions were determined. A study of Cheshire emphasizes the unity of the period between the two Local Government Acts of 1888 and 1958, seventy years during which each county council struggled to carry out its administrative duties within the confines of its ancient boundaries. The recommendations of the Local Government Commissions established by the 1958 Act will bring into being a new administrative map and a new pattern of authority.

The basic difficulty in generalizing about the political evolution of county councils arises from the fact that even in 1889 there was a division of opinion about their purpose. The Conservatives maintained that they were purely executive bodies to take over the administrative functions of Quarter Sessions, while the Radicals were prepared to argue that they were small legislatures in embryo which could be expanded in order to decentralize the sovereignty of Parliament. *The County Council Magazine* congratulated the chairman of Buckinghamshire County Council for grasping the principle that his council was only an executive,[1] but at the same time the Radicals in Northamptonshire were making enthusiastic speeches in favour of local parliaments, and attacking the Act of 1888 for introducing a political assembly no more vigorous than 'Quarter Sessions white-washed with a public vote'.[2] The Conservative Cabinet had itself been split in 1886 on the issue whether or not to introduce a measure of local government reform which would have included an overhaul of the poor-law system. Lord Randolph Churchill who had established himself as the leading agitator on behalf of 'Tory democracy' proposed making the poor-law unions the most important local authorities in rural areas, and was supported outside the government by Joseph Chamberlain, then the leading Liberal to have broken with Gladstone. There was for a moment the possibility that smaller administrative units might be created, but Churchill's resignation and Goschen's introduction into the Cabinet, together with the pressure placed upon the Prime Minister, Lord Salisbury, by large numbers of Conservative magistrates, committed the government to accepting the outlines of Ritchie's Local Government Bill which established the dual system of county councils and county boroughs, leaving untouched the boards of guardians and poor-law unions. As explained above, the latter were abolished in 1929 and their duties shared between county and district councils. The original purpose of county councils was in dispute because the opponents upheld different ideals. Those who cherished the notion of local self-government by small legislatures elected on a wide franchise found little

---

[1] *County Council Magazine*, ii. 266.
[2] F. A. Channing, *Memories of Midland Politics* (1918), p. 89.

satisfaction in the Act of 1888. Redlich and Hirst came to the conclusion that county councils could only be transformed into local parliaments 'as the result of a profound and comprehensive change in the distribution of landed property'.[1] All agreed that the political evolution of local authorities depended on social change.

Working out the different types of development which county councils have experienced may in fact be largely a question of finding a satisfactory index of social change within their boundaries. If it were possible to collect sufficient data on the change in the distribution of landed property since 1888, the degree of change might have a high correlation with the degree to which the principles of social leadership had been abandoned. The Act of 1888 imposed upon each geographical county the form of municipal government, a body of aldermen and councillors, without any regard for the specific needs of rural areas, and the recommendations of the Boundary Commission of 1888, which proposed various alterations of county boundaries, were almost totally ignored. It is not surprising that county authorities have evolved in different ways. The form of government for a county borough was at least defined by a common standard, the number of people living in any given town, and county boroughs were therefore to some extent comparable units. The size and population of administrative counties have always varied enormously.

One factor which may allow some discussion of the typology of county development is the extent to which agricultural land has been covered with large numbers of housing estates which constitute the suburbs of great towns or the extent to which existing towns have expanded. Some index of urbanization is necessary. London County Council was established in 1889 to administer a wholly urban county, and therefore is exceptional. Middlesex was divided into two parts in 1889, the 'urbanized' part which was included in the new county of London, and the remainder which became a new administrative county. The latter has by now become equally 'urbanized', and should also be classed with London as an exceptional county. In the following paragraphs therefore, any reference to London and Middlesex has been deliberately excluded. It only makes sense to deal with Cheshire as one of the sixty remaining counties in England and Wales (12 Welsh counties, Monmouthshire,[2] and 47 English

---

[1] J. Redlich and F. W. Hirst, *Local Government in England* (1903), ii. 50.
[2] For the dispute whether or not Monmouthshire belongs to Wales, see *The Times*, 10 Mar. 1961, and subsequent correspondence on 16 Mar. and 20 Mar.

counties) which contain the largest proportion of the nation's population. At the time of the National Census in 1961, while there were
13,600,000 people living in county boroughs and 5,400,000 in the
counties of London and Middlesex, 27 million out of 46 million
in England and Wales lived in the remaining sixty administrative
counties.

The degree of urbanization can be measured by the density of
population to the acre in each administrative county (figures given
in detail in Appendix D from the estimates of the Registrar-General
for mid-1960). County boroughs which lie outside administrative
counties frequently attract population to the adjacent county districts. But only in the Midlands, and in the North and North Midlands,
does a large proportion of the inhabitants live in county boroughs (see
Table 17, p. 229). In the Home Counties around London and Middlesex
in 1961 over ninety per cent. of the population lived in the administrative counties, and of these, more than forty-seven per cent. lived in
towns with 50,000 or more inhabitants (see Table 17). In the North
and North Midlands, although only fifty-three per cent. lived in the
administrative counties, sixty per cent. of these were in towns of less
than 50,000. The distribution of population between administrative
counties and county boroughs is a deceptive index of urbanization.
A study made at the Census of 1951 revealed that of the $31\frac{1}{2}$ million
living in 'built-up' areas in England and Wales, more than half a
million lived in rural administrative areas, while of the 12 million
living in non-urbanized districts, nearly four and a half million lived
in urban administrative areas.[1] A distribution based on administrative
areas within each county is therefore equally deceptive. Nevertheless
it remains true that the majority of the one hundred and thirty towns
with a population of more than 50,000 listed in the National Census
of 1961,[2] were in the London Region or in the industrial areas of the
Midlands and the North. These basic demographic facts provide a
starting-point for studying the evolution of county councils. Those
administrative counties with a density of less than 0·5 per cent. to the
acre, chiefly in Wales, the South-West, and Eastern England, might be
expected to develop a different political tradition from those with
a higher density. (See map facing p. 229.) The development of the
latter depended upon the type of urban settlement outside the county
boroughs.

An indication of the effects of different types of social environment

[1] *National Census: 1961* (Preliminary Report), p. 8.   [2] Ibid., pp. 72–73.

was the extent to which each administrative county became dependent upon subsidies from the central government for its financial resources. Radnorshire, for instance, was hardly comparable as an administrative county with Essex. The Local Government Act of 1958 contained financial provisions which were designed to compensate those authorities which had the least income from the product of a penny rate by providing rate deficiency grants from central funds. During the first financial year for the operation of this system, 1959–60, the percentage of expenditure in all the counties of England and Wales met from this source of income, as an average for all counties, was 22·25 per cent., but this figure was obtained from a considerable range of subsidies, from counties such as Surrey and Hertfordshire which received no rate deficiency grants to counties such as Radnor and Montgomery which relied on them for more than 60 per cent. of their income.[1] The proportion of expenditure met by rate deficiency grants therefore provides a valuable index of the resources available for the administration of each county. There are three broad categories:

Proportion of Expenditure met by Rate Deficiency Grants:
1959–60[2]

1. Less than 15 per cent. .   .   . 12 counties in S.E. England.
6 others.
2. Between 15 and 25 per cent. .   . 14 counties, mainly in the Midlands and West.
3. More than 25 per cent. .   .   . 28 counties in the North, Wales, and E. Anglia.

Total   60 administrative counties.

The most remarkable features of this analysis provide ample material for a commentary upon the social geography of England and Wales. The wealthy counties of S.E. England are predominant in the first category—all twelve counties closest to London and Middlesex, the most urbanized counties in the country, share the privilege of requiring the least amount of subsidy from central funds. Similarly, Cheshire and Warwickshire, which are close to other great conurbations, enjoy a similar standing by virtue of the affluence in which they can stake a claim. Urbanization, it seems, is

[1] All figures in this and following paragraphs taken from *Financial and General Statistics of County Councils* issued by the Society of County Treasurers (January 1961).
[2] See Appendix C, pp. 234–8.

the principal factor in differentiating one county from another. The third category, in complete contrast, includes all the least urbanized counties in the country and also some urban areas, such as Durham and the West Riding of Yorkshire, which contain large tracts of old-established industrial towns. This suggests that urbanization alone is not the principal factor, but urbanization of a more recent date. Cornwall and all Wales, except Caernarvon and Flint, and the four most northern counties come into the third category. The second category consists of those fourteen counties which lie between comparative affluence and comparative poverty. Ten of them lie literally as border counties in a geographical sense, following the line of the Cotswolds and other limestone hills, between the independence of the South and East and the dependence of the North and West. The only exceptions to this distribution are the counties of the Fenland and East Anglia which belong to the poorest or third category. This analysis of counties corresponds very closely to an analysis of social geography made by studying towns. The latter approach also leads to a division of the country into the North and West and the South and East,[1] but at the same time it runs the risk of all typological studies in the absurdity of placing two dissimilar towns within the same category. The above analysis requires Cheshire to be considered beside the Soke of Peterborough and the Isle of Wight! Such are the dangers of placing too much reliance on one set of figures.

But an analysis based on any other factor still tends to show the same three-fold division between the suburban counties of the South and East, the agricultural and ancient industrial counties of the North and West, and finally those lying in between. An elementary exercise in county typology (see Appendix C) was based on three other factors which help to measure the degree of urbanization and its nature:

1. The percentage increase in private dwellings 1951–61:
    (i) Over 35 per cent.
    (ii) 25–35 per cent.
    (iii) Less than 25 per cent.
2. The number of primary and secondary school children per 1,000 population:
    (i) 100–139.
    (ii) 140–155.
    (iii) More than 155.

[1] C. A. Moser and Wolf Scott, *British Towns* (1961).

3. The mileage of county roads per 1,000 population:
  (i) Less than 5 miles.
  (ii) 5–10 miles.
  (iii) More than 10 miles.

The first category of county, those meeting less than 15 per cent. of their expenditure from rate deficiency grants, numbered eighteen; they included:

(a) 7 out of the 8 counties with a percentage increase in private dwellings, 1951–61, of over 35.
(b) 5 out of the 6 counties with less than 140 schoolchildren per 1,000 population, and
(c) 16 out of the 24 counties with less than 5 miles of county road per 1,000 population.

The third category of county, those meeting more than 25 per cent. of their expenditure from these grants, numbered twenty-eight; they included:

(a) 26 out of the 36 counties with a percentage increase in private dwellings, 1951–61, of less than 25.
(b) 20 out of the 32 counties with more than 155 schoolchildren per 1,000 population, and
(c) 18 out of the 19 counties with more than 10 miles of county road per 1,000 population.

Therefore, in very broad terms, the wealthier counties of the South and East have more new dwellings, fewer schoolchildren per head of population, and shorter lengths of road per head of population than the poorer counties of the North and West. Perhaps the most significant statistics are those relating to the increase in the number of private dwellings (or habitable units recorded by census enumerators) between 1951 and 1961. West Sussex, Berkshire, and Hertfordshire increased by more than 50 per cent., while the average rate of increase in private dwellings for the twelve Welsh counties was only 16·4 per cent.

But this broad classification of counties according to their resources is not sufficient to describe the differences of political evolution in terms of parties and selection of leaders. What can be done in the absence of evidence on such factors as the change in landownership? Of the sixty administrative counties already analysed, there is no significant difference between the first and third categories, the rich and poor counties, in terms of acknowledged party activities. Both categories contain roughly the same proportion of those county councils, which were twenty-five in number, publishing their political party composition in the *Municipal Year Book*.[1] Cheshire is clearly in the first category from the point of view of administrative resources; it stands eighth in the list of counties in order of total population;[2] and, like Warwickshire, it benefits from its proximity to great towns, although it is naturally more vulnerable to the latter's ambitions. But where does it stand in relation to the development of party politics in county affairs? A remarkable feature of the history of Cheshire County Council is its political maturity. Although the officers and leading councillors may be reluctant to confess its importance, the business of the council and the composition of the committees have always, since the beginning in 1889, been determined by the political party caucus. Cheshire has a very honourable tradition of party political activity.

The majority of county councils still prefer to be called 'nonpolitical' when they are pressed to declare the nature of their internal organization. Even Cheshire made this reply to a circular from the *Municipal Year Book* in 1958, when only fifteen counties were willing to give any details to that journal. The latter was more successful at its second attempt in 1961 when twenty-five replied. But there are still many county councillors who entertain the idea that the introduction of party politics is a retrograde step, and who accept the myth that the Labour party alone was responsible for introducing party politics wherever that step has been taken. It remains true that county council election results are now generally published in party terms only where there is a body of Labour members. The Labour party forces other members to commit themselves, or the very presence of Labour members introduces a party system in spite of the fact that the others are unorganized. Election results from Cumberland, Dorset, Lincolnshire (Lindsey), Northumberland, and East and West Suffolk usually appear in the form of two groups, Labour members and the rest. Rutland in 1961 elected 27 Independents and 1 Labour member! But the publicity given to Labour party defeats or victories disguises the much more ancient tradition of county politics, a contest of Conservative versus Liberal, in which social leaders were ranged on both sides. The gradual

[1] *Municipal Year Book* (1962), p. 1885.
[2] Excluding London and Middlesex.

disappearance of social leaders has permitted the opponents of the Labour party in some places to wish to be regarded as 'non-political', whatever that term may mean.

The political evolution of county councils has largely been determined by the rate at which leadership by social leaders has been transformed into leadership by public persons, and this rate itself has been governed by a variety of different social conditions, particularly the extent of suburbanization or urbanization. The number of Labour councillors is to some extent an index of the politics of public persons, because it corresponds fairly closely to the distribution of industrial urban areas. The only counties in which Labour has made considerable headway against the parties united against it are Northumberland and Durham, Lancashire and the West Riding of Yorkshire, Nottinghamshire and Derbyshire, Glamorgan and Essex. But there are many other county councils which now prefer to label themselves as 'non-political', but in which the Liberal party was strongly represented. Sir Robert Martin, for instance, the former chairman of Leicestershire County Council, used to pride himself upon the way in which his authority avoided serious party strife, but was perfectly willing to confess that his own entry into county politics was occasioned by the necessity of finding a suitable local Conservative to fight a Liberal division. The Labour party's success in county elections may sometimes appear to be simply an extension of its control over certain boroughs. But what factors determined the evolution of party politics in county councils before Labour issued its challenge?

The first factor was the degree to which local society tolerated the principles of social leadership and elected representatives from the class of gentlemen, both businessmen and landowners, who predominated in Quarter Sessions. Where an executive body of 'gentlemen amateurs' was not acceptable to the majority of electors, the group of families which constituted 'county society' would find an outlet for their energies elsewhere than in the service of a local authority. In 1889 the Holland division of Lincolnshire, a society of Fenland farmers, elected a county council which consisted largely of tenant farmers and rejected the services of the squirearchy.[1] Similarly the first county council elections in Wales resulted in a defeat of the resident Conservative and Anglican gentry by the Liberal and Nonconformist tradespeople. Almost two-thirds of the Welsh county

[1] *County Council Magazine*, ii. 135–40.

councillors in thirteen counties were Liberals.[1] It is significant that the Welsh electors, following the campaign of Stuart Rendel in favour of Welsh Home Rule, thought of the new county councils as legislative bodies which would act as small parliaments for Welsh affairs. Wales did not accept the principle that they were purely executive. A letter to *The Times* from a 'disgusted ratepayer' expressed his horror at the choice of aldermen in Denbighshire where several prominent magistrates and members of Parliament were passed over in favour of 'several village shop-keepers, two timber dealers, and a phalanx of the officials of the so-called Land League'.[2] The Welsh councils were unwilling to elect 'social leaders' as aldermen. The same letter warned that the upper classes might therefore migrate. 'It is quite within the bounds of possibility that many country gentlemen with no public duties to detain them at home may seek brighter wintry skies and more congenial surroundings.'[3]

Another important factor was the willingness of the great landowners, the magnates and important political patrons, to participate in the business of local elected councils. Wherever a peer and landowner wished to stand for election, he was usually successful. At the first county council elections, a few peers were defeated, such as the Earl of Kimberley in Norfolk or Lord Kesteven in the Holland division of Lincolnshire, the latter by only seven votes; but the majority of the peerage who wished to maintain their connexion with county administration were successfully chosen as either councillors or aldermen (131 peers in England and Wales).[4] Several local leaders were unwilling to allow themselves to be elected as chairmen of the first councils, such as the Duke of Buckingham in Buckinghamshire and W. H. Gladstone in Flint, but a far greater number of local leaders holding the offices of lord-lieutenant and chairman of Quarter Sessions did not share this reluctance to undertake the duties of another post.

The majority of county councils began their lives with a large complement of social leaders from the aristocracy and gentry. Only

[1] H. J. Hanham, *Politics and Party Management in the Age of Gladstone and Disraeli* (1959), p. 179; cf. *Manchester Guardian*, 31 Jan. 1889, p. 8; *County Council Magazine*, i. 216–19.

[2] *The Times*, 5 Feb. 1889, p. 7.

[3] *County Council Magazine*, i. 68 adds to this sentence the phrase 'in places where they will not have social life poisoned by narrow-minded provincialism or sectarian jealousy'.

[4] J. Redlich, *Local Government in England* (1958 ed. by B. Keith-Lucas), p. 235; cf. three articles on 'M.P.s Experience of Local Government' in *Public Administration* (1953) p. 46; (1954) p. 409; (1955) p. 207.

nineteen English counties in 1890 had chosen a fresh person to be the first chairman of the county council. Of the remaining number, twenty-six councils had elected the chairman of Quarter Sessions for this office, and three, the lord-lieutenant (Cornwall, Northampton-shire, and Oxfordshire). The 'landed interest' in English political life lived on into the twentieth century by this form of social leader-ship. The fifth Marquess of Bath (1862-1946) was both chairman of Wiltshire County Council and lord-lieutenant of Somerset. The principles of social leadership have survived in those parts of the country where members of the aristocracy and gentry were willing to take up 'public service' with conscious deliberation. Just as public persons might be viewed as professional social leaders, so those aristocrats who continued to participate in local government work might be regarded as self-conscious public servants who had taken the ideal of *noblesse oblige* and rationalized it to their own satisfac-tion. After the first county council elections in Staffordshire, the Earl of Harrowby wrote to the Prime Minister, Lord Salisbury: 'Our rural society here is convulsed by the County Council business: we shall all have to live in the country for the next three years, to keep things straight.'[1] Such men were 'country' politicians by definition, willing to forgo the pleasures of foreign travel and the London season, and such sentiments might well have been expressed by later public servants such as the fifth Marquess of Exeter in the Soke of Peter-borough or the seventh Duke of Northumberland in Northumber-land. But their devotion was only made possible in areas where there was a minimum amount of social and industrial change.

The political evolution of the county councils near London has been different from that of many provincial councils, not only be-cause the area around London has undergone a tremendous amount of social and industrial change, but also because the proximity of the capital meant that any peer or landed gentleman who was concerned with local government work was not compelled to make the choice between 'living in the country' and 'enjoying the season'. The two could be combined. Perhaps the distinction between social leader and public person is essentially a provincial one. Hampshire, for instance, in 1955, was still electing councillors of the 'squire' type to its county council.[2] The county councils around London have always

---

[1] Salisbury Papers.
[2] P. R. G. Hornsby, *Party Politics and Local Government in Hampshire* (unpublished M.Sc. (Econ.) thesis, Southampton, pp. 93–94).

contained representatives from the business world of the City and the Law Courts. The first county council of East Sussex included two former Presidents of the Local Government Board (Lord Monk Bretton and James Stansfeld), four peers, two baronets, nine barristers, and five solicitors.[1] In 1894 some residents of Brighton asked that the polling-booths in municipal elections should be opened from 12 noon to 8 p.m. in order to enable those working in London during the day to cast their vote in the evening.[2] The attraction of London was also apparent in the choice of meeting-places in 1889. Middlesex and Surrey councils continued to meet in the Old Guildhall, Westminster, and the Newington Sessions House respectively, although these buildings now lay outside their jurisdiction, and Hertfordshire agreed to hold all committee meetings in London, leaving Hertford and St. Albans for alternate quarterly meetings of the full council. Essex County Council has maintained the custom of printing the time-table of trains from Liverpool Street Station to Chelmsford at the beginning of its agenda.

The only attempt to maintain political influence through social leaders, which was not directly affected by urban developments, was the policy of Conservative governments in appointing lord-lieutenants between 1886 and 1906, twenty years of Conservative predominance interrupted only by the short ministries of Gladstone and Rosebery. All the English lieutenancies except six[3] fell vacant during this period and the appointments came into the gift of a Conservative Prime Minister, Salisbury or Balfour. This patronage was less important in England where the majority of Liberal lieutenants became Unionists after 1886, but it was responsible in Wales for securing Conservative lieutenants in every county except Caernarvonshire. The first Marquess of Abergavenny urged upon Lord Salisbury the idea of appointing young lieutenants so that the Conservative party should have some influence in the counties if there were another Liberal government, and went so far as to persuade the older generation, like the Earl of Verulam in Hertfordshire, to resign in order to allow young men to be appointed. He set the example himself by resigning the lieutenancy of Sussex in 1905 just before a Liberal government came into office. This policy had several spectacular successes: the fourth Earl of Powis was lieutenant of Shropshire from

---

[1] *County Council Magazine*, ii. 257.
[2] *County Council Times*, 12 Oct. 1894, p. 229.
[3] Cambs., Durham, Gloucs., Northants., Rutland, and Westmorland.

1896 to 1951; Sir R. H. Williams Bulkeley, lieutenant of Anglesey from 1896 to 1942.[1] Its intention was to place a Conservative political patron at the head of 'county society' in each shire, but by the 1920's and 1930's various changes in the manner of parliamentary electioneering made this of doubtful advantage to the party. The longest reigning social leader and political patron was neither a lord-lieutenant nor a Conservative. Sir Godfrey Baring who was chairman of the Isle of Wight County Council for almost sixty years, from 1898 to 1957, had been elected chairman of the Isle of Wight Liberal Union at the age of twenty-three!

A good indication of differences in county politics, emphasizing the amount of political influence enjoyed by social leaders from the 'landed interest', was the manner in which aldermen were elected in 1889. Changing attitudes to the function of aldermen may reveal the extent to which a particular county was emancipated from the principles of social leadership. Should a newly elected council in 1889 have chosen the chairmen of Quarter Sessions committees who were experienced in county administration to be the first aldermen, if they had not submitted themselves for election? In a speech at Potterne in Wiltshire, the Parliamentary Secretary of the Local Government Board, Walter Long, gave it as his considered opinion that all the aldermen should be chosen from outside the council, and not from the newly elected councillors.[2] This provoked a letter to *The Times* from Lord Brabourne who claimed it was tantamount to saying that the people have failed to elect the best men and that there was a class of 'superior persons' too noble and too good to be exposed to the rough test of popular elections.[3] Wherever there was a strong party feeling, as in the three divisions of Lincolnshire,[4] the majority of aldermen were chosen from the body of the council itself. Where there was a complete deadlock between the parties, as in Northamptonshire (24 Liberals versus 25 Conservatives with an independent councillor who refused to mediate),[5] the aldermen were chosen 'by lot'. It was some measure of party feeling, to count the number of councillors who were promoted to be aldermen. In 1889 by-elections caused by the promotion of councillors put the counties

---

[1] Periods of office of more than 25 years were also served by Lord Ashcombe (Surrey), the Marquess of Bath (Som.), J. H. Benyon (Berks.) Lord Camden (Kent), Sir John Cotterell (Heref.), the Earl of Dartmouth (Staffs.), and the Duke of Portland (Notts.).

[2] *The Times*, 19 Jan. 1889, p. 12; cf. *Local Government Chronicle* (1889), pp. 72, 75.

[3] *The Times*, 29 Jan. 1889, p. 7.

[4] Ibid., 11 Feb. 1889, p. 7.

[5] *County Council Magazine*, i. 321.

to the expense of a contested election in seventy-seven cases. Apart from Middlesex, the only English counties to follow Walter Long's advice completely were six of the most 'feudal' and Conservative-dominated, Oxfordshire, Hertfordshire, and Leicestershire in the Midlands, Norfolk in the east, and Gloucestershire and Somerset in the west country. All these counties chose their aldermen from the most distinguished members of 'county society' and on this basis provided themselves with important links between the county council and Parliament. County M.P.s were invited to serve as aldermen, and some counties were able to make use of retired Cabinet Ministers. Gloucestershire, for instance, in 1908 invited Sir Michael Hicks-Beach (Lord St. Aldwyn) to be an alderman. As a former Chancellor of the Exchequer, he rose quickly to be President of the County Councils Association.[1]

The proportion of seats contested in county council elections provides an indication of the degree to which social leaders have been replaced, and a more accurate definition of the regions in which public persons have made their mark. On the first two occasions, in 1889 and 1892, for which parliamentary returns were made, the elections in Cheshire corresponded very closely to the national average. The average percentage of seats contested in all the counties of England and Wales for these two years was 56·3 per cent. and 23·9 per cent. respectively, but there was a considerable range in the degree of political activity. In 1889, for instance, more than 60 per cent. of the seats were contested in all the Welsh counties except Radnor, while the proportion in England ranged from 76 per cent. in the Holland division of Lincolnshire to 28 per cent. in Huntingdonshire. These differences to some extent represent the different degrees of support received by the Radical wing of the Liberal party. There is some correlation between the pattern of party allegiance in county councils and the pattern of Liberal voting in county parliamentary divisions before 1910.[2] In fact, the Liberal party's declining influence in rural areas after 1910 was largely responsible for a diminution in the number of contests and for the growth of the 'non-political' ideal in county politics.

The Labour party was able to issue a more effective challenge to the 'non-political' ideal in those administrative counties which

    [1] Lady Victoria Hicks-Beach, *Life of Lord St. Aldwyn* (1932), ii. 275, 279.
    [2] Edward Krehbiel, 'Geographical Influences in British Elections' in *Geographical Review* (American Geog. Soc.), Dec. 1916, pp. 419 ff.

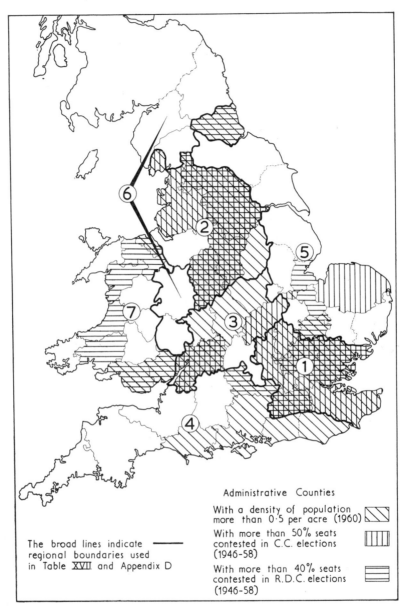

Administrative Counties

With a density of population
more than 0·5 per acre (1960)

With more than 50% seats
contested in C.C. elections
(1946-58)

With more than 40% seats
contested in R.D.C. elections
(1946-58)

The broad lines indicate ——
regional boundaries used
in Table XVII. and Appendix D

Map 3. Regional Characteristics of County Government

were the most urbanized, perhaps best defined as the broad band of country stretching from London and the Home Counties in the south-east to the industrial counties of Lancashire and the West Riding of Yorkshire in the north-west (see map) which had a density of population of more than 0·5 persons per acre. There were points of Labour support concentrated in certain parts of Northumberland, Cumber-

TABLE 17

Analysis of Counties by Regions

(A summary of Appendix D)

Region	No. of counties	Average for counties included in each region			% of total pop. living in county boroughs	Population 1961		
		(1) Density of pop. per acre	(2) % of seats contested elections 1946–1958 C.C.	(3) R.D.C.		Admin. County % of population living in:		
						(1) Boroughs or U.D.C.s above 50,000	(2) less than 50,000	(3) R.D.C.s
1. Home Counties	6	1·84	72	41	9·57	47·84	31·07	21·09
2. N. and N. Midlands	7	1·40	56	36	46·97	13·76	60·03	26·21
3. Midlands	6	0·73	44	31	51·16	16·39	35·93	47·68
4. South West	10	0·67	34	28	24·50	15·67	38·12	46·21
5. Eastern England	13	0·42	33	27	27·89	9·38	35·48	55·13
6. Border Counties	5	0·27	39	22	25·53	..	59·03	40·97
7. Wales and Mon.	13	0·42	27	36	22·41	9·79	50·86	39·35

land, and Durham, but the party's success in local elections after 1945 was largely confined to this area. An analysis of the proportion of seats contested at the five county council elections held between 1946 and 1958, and at the rural district council elections held in the same five years, provides the basis of Appendix D in which details have been given to make possible some study of regional characteristics.[1] Table 17 gives a summary of this information. The average of five separate occasions gives a relatively good index of the degree of party political activity in the proportion of seats contested, and the average for all the counties in each region gives some indication of marked regional differences. The proportion of seats contested at the county council elections of 1946 in England was uniformly high: only fourteen out of the forty-seven English counties witnessed contests in less

[1] The figures for these calculations have been taken from the *Registrar-General's Statistical Review*, Table VV. Where the latter is defective or obviously misprinted, some estimates have been made.

than 50 per cent. of the electoral divisions. But after this initial sally into the 'non-political' areas, the Labour party seems to have limited its activities to the urbanized regions already described. The number of contests and the type of political system were to some extent functions of the type of urban development.

It is easy, on this basis, to divide England into six regions, three where contests are common and three where they are not. Wales forms an entirely separate region of its own because of the wide variations in the support of Welsh Nationalist candidates at the local elections, in spite of the fact that Glamorgan, Monmouthshire, and Flint enjoy certain features in common with their English neighbours.[1] On the evidence already cited, one would expect local authorities which depended chiefly on the services of public persons, such as Cheshire County Council, to be regularly found within the three regions of political activity, the Home Counties, the North and North Midlands, and the Midlands. Any remnant of the politics of social leadership is more likely to have survived in the three other regions, the South-West, Eastern England, and the Border Counties. Table 17, summarizing Appendix D, shows how marked were the regional differences. In the South-West, Eastern England, and the Border Counties, little more than a quarter of the population lived in county boroughs, and of the remainder almost half lived in rural districts. The majority of towns had less than 50,000 inhabitants. They were the regions *par excellence* of county council government for rural areas, as it was intended to be in 1888, and also the regions where, outside the towns, contests were fought at election time in barely a third of the electoral divisions. In this part of England, an uncontested election was almost the norm.

Cheshire, which has been the subject of this book, on the basis of such a regional analysis lies in the political tradition of the other three regions. It may not be so firmly attached as its neighbours, Lancashire, the West Riding of Yorkshire, Derbyshire, and Staffordshire, but it nevertheless shows all the tendencies which appear to have shaped their development. How far does it represent a model to be followed by any county which undergoes concentrated industrial development in certain areas and experiences the building of dormitory suburbs to serve them? In other words, how far has political development been influenced by the accidents of economic growth and social change which have taken place within the county's

[1] *Working for Wales*, the report presented to the Plaid Cymru Conference in 1961, gives some information on local elections.

historic boundaries? When the Local Government Commissions established under the 1958 Act have completed their work and submitted their recommendations to the Minister of Housing and Local Government, the new pattern of county authorities which is about to be established will have been governed largely by the adjustments which social change has made necessary. But the legacy of the old régime is likely to remain in the administrative machines of those authorities which survive. Social leadership really depended on the historic boundaries which defined 'county society', and as soon as these boundaries are destroyed, government by public persons is likely to become part of the accepted tradition of political behaviour. Such a transfer of power will be more than necessary. The gentry, which constituted 'county society' and provided the backbone of the 'country party' in English constitutional history, has not survived.

APPENDIXES

APPENDIX A

CHESHIRE COUNTY COUNCIL ELECTIONS: 1889–1961

	Number of county councillors	Number of contests	% of electors polled in contested divisions	Number of retiring councillors				New councillors	
				Not returned		Re-elected			
				Did not stand	Defeated at contest	Un-opposed	After contest	Un-opposed	After contest
1889	57	35	75	..	6*	13*	15*	9	20
1892	58	14	72	5	4	40	8	4	6
1895	59	8	..	5	3	47	3	4	5
1898	59	5	..	9	2	45	3	9	2
1901	59	1	..	6	..	52	1	6	..
1904	59	14	67	13	3	38	5	7	9
1907	61	14	..	15	3	36	5	11	9
1910	61	12	..	14	3	41	3	8	9
1913	56	4	..	15	..	44	2	8	2
			(First World War: 8 nominations)						
1919	56	12	25	14	3	34	5	10	7
1922	56	7	51	13	2	38	3	11	4
1925	56	12	44	12	4	36	4	8	8
1928	56	10	46	8	3	42	3	4	7
1931	56	22	42	8	4	33	11	1	11
1934	56	10	34	8	4	41	3	5	7
1937	69	26	36	12	4	33	7	10	19
			(Second World War: 41 nominations)						
1946	69	51	32	26	9	13	21	5	30
1949	69	35	42	15	6	32	16	2	19
1952	69	26	40	16	5	35	13	8	13
1955	68	26	31	11	3	37	18	5	8
1958	74	28	34	11	4	39	14	7	14
1961	74	33	34	10	10	39	15	2	18

* J.P.s who stood for election as county councillors in 1889.

APPENDIX B

CHESHIRE COUNTY COUNCIL:
PARTY COMPOSITION: 1889–1961

The columns show the strength of each party after each triennial election and the subsequent election of aldermen, and the percentages which each party holds of the total membership:

Date of election	Total no.	Conservative	% of total	Independent	% of total	Liberal	% of total	Labour	% of total
1889	76	35	46·1	9	11·8	32	42·1	..	..
1892	77	38	49·4	7	9·1	32	41·5	..	..
1895	78	42	53·8	6	7·7	30	38·5	..	..
1898	78	41	52·6	6	7·7	31	39·7	..	..
1901	78	40	51·3	5	6·4	33	42·3	..	..
1904	78	37	47·4	3	3·9	37	47·4	1	1·3
1907	81	43	53·1	2	2·5	36	44·4	..	..
1910	81	44	54·3	5	6·2	32	39·5	..	..
1913	75	41	54·7	3	4·0	31	41·3	..	..
1919	75	39	52·0	9	12·0	27	36·0	..	..
1922	75	33	44·1	16	21·3	25	33·3	1	1·3
1925	75	35	46·7	12	16·0	28	37·3	..	..
1928	75	31	41·3	10	13·3	32	42·7	2	2·7
1931	75	33	44·1	13	17·3	28	37·3	1	1·3
1934	75	35	46·7	15	20·0	20	26·7	5	6·6
1937	92	50	54·3	17	18·5	17	18·5	8	8·7
1946	92	48	52·2	18	19·6	11	11·9	15	16·3
1949	92	61	66·3	15	16·3	10	10·9	6	6·5
1952	92	62	67·5	12	13·0	5	5·4	13	14·1
1955	91	60	65·9	12	13·2	5	5·5	14	15·4
1958	98	56	57·1	15	15·3	8	8·2	19	19·4
1961	98	58	59·2	16	16·3	9	9·2	15	15·3

APPENDIX C

TYPOLOGY OF COUNTIES IN ENGLAND AND WALES: 1959-60

The following broad classification in three categories according to the proportion of county council income derived from rate deficiency grants has been subdivided into types, according to three other factors, in columns B-D:

Column B. Percentage increase in number of private dwellings 1951-61*

(1) Over 35 per cent.
(2) 25-35   „
(3) Under 25 „

Column C. Number of primary and secondary schoolchildren per 1,000 population.

(1) 100-139.
(2) 140-155.
(3) More than 155.

Column D. Mileage of county roads per 1,000 population.

(1) Less than 5 miles.
(2) 5-10 miles.
(3) More than 10 miles.

* This represents a net increase in the number of habitable units visited by National Census enumerators. See *National Census: 1961 (Preliminary Report),* Table 3.

(1) FIRST CATEGORY

	A. Less than 15% income from R.D.G.	B. Percentage increase in private dwellings 1951–61			C. No. of schoolchildren per 1,000 population			D. Mileage of county roads per 1,000 population		
		(1)	(2)	(3)	(1)	(2)	(3)	(1)	(2)	(3)
Hants	6·90	46·5	..	..	..	148	..	4·47	..	..
Sussex W.	..	50·3	..	24·6	138	..	..	3·34	..	..
Surrey	..	..	34·3	..	131	..	..	1·05	..	..
Sussex E.	11·99	..	..	24·5	118	..	..	4·29	..	..
Cambs.	3·91	37·3	..	..	139	..	..	4·01	..	..
Beds.	8·17	52·8	..	..	..	155	..	2·40	..	..
Berks.	..	39·7	..	..	..	151	..	4·20	..	..
Bucks.	..	50·2	..	..	..	155	..	3·44	..	..
Herts.	..	40·6	..	..	..	..	165	1·89	..	..
War.	6·90	..	32·4	..	..	..	163	2·98	..	..
Essex	5·66	..	..	24·7	..	..	162	1·72	..	..
Kent	2·26	..	..	19·5	..	151	..	2·39	..	..
I.O.W.	..	..	..	..	..	141	174	3·69	..	..
Peterb.	1·68	..	30·5	..	..	..	174	2·26	..	..
Ches.	11·60	..	26·4	..	..	153	..	2·38	..	..
Flint.	..	..	..	23·8	128	..	171	4·71	..	..
Devon	10·37	..	..	23·9	..	..	..	..	8·03	12·64
Lincs. (L)	8·24	..	..	23·7	..	..	170	..	..	..

(2) SECOND CATEGORY

	A 15–20% income from R.D.G.	B Percentage increase in private dwellings 1951–61			C No. of schoolchildren per 1,000 population			D Mileage of county roads per 1,000 population		
		(1)	(2)	(3)	(1)	(2)	(3)	(1)	(2)	(3)
Hunts.	23·59		29·7			151			6·34	
Dorset	16·65		26·1			140			6·31	
Yorks. N.	16·21		27·9			153			7·72	
Som.	20·20		25·7			143			8·76	
Oxon.	23·81	35·8				149			7·53	
Yorks. E.	23·97			23·2		153			9·41	
Glos.	19·29		33·0				158		6·44	
Wilts.	19·89		31·3				159		5·57	
Leics.	23·93		32·7				161		4·58	
Northants.	21·46		26·6				162		5·56	
Notts.	22·58		27·1				162	2·47		
Worcs.	18·90		26·1			153		4·27		
Lancs.	24·80			20·5			162	1·44		
Caernarvon	24·00			16·2			157		8·59	

(3) THIRD CATEGORY

	A 25%+ income from R.D.G.	B Percentage increase in private dwellings 1951-61			C No. of schoolchildren per 1,000 population			D Mileage of county roads per 1,000 population		
		(1)	(2)	(3)	(1)	(2)	(3)	(1)	(2)	(3)
A. England										
Salop	29·21			22·6			155			10·71
Cumb.	34·96			17·6			172			10·38
Lincs. (K)	33·32			23·3			162			11·37
„ (H)	39·53			15·8			167			10·78
Hereford	37·98			18·9			157			13·98
Yorks. (W)	37·53			17·0			165	2·46		
Durham	34·06			19·5			174	1·87		
Northumb	29·84			22·8			163		5·38	
Derby	27·92			24·8			165	3·27		
Ely	30·33			12·0			162		6·78	
Suffolk E.	29·99			21·1	139				8·35	
„ W.	36·97			23·9		142			9·26	
Cornwall	28·52			15·6		141				11·39
Westm.	27·02			15·5		149				13·88
Norfolk	41·97			22·1		146				11·71
Rut.	29·19		32·6			153				12·30
Staffs.	27·38		32·5				163	2·58		

(3) THIRD CATEGORY

	A 25%+ income from R.D.G.	B Percentage increase in private dwellings 1951–61			C No. of schoolchildren per 1,000 population			D Mileage of county roads per 1,000 population		
		(1)	(2)	(3)	(1)	(2)	(3)	(1)	(2)	(3)
B. *Wales**										
Anglesey	42·86	:	:	22·7	:	:	164	:	:	12·52
Brecon	51·02	:	:	13·2	:	:	169	:	:	19·52
Carmarthen	37·08	:	:	12·9	:	:	161	:	:	11·76
Denbigh	29·14	:	:	18·5	:	:	169	:	:	10·34
Merioneth	55·94	:	:	16·3	:	:	164	:	:	21·11
Montgy.	68·07	:	:	11·7	:	:	161	:	:	31·45
Pembroke	44·33	:	:	21·0	:	:	169	:	:	13·82
Cardigan	61·55	:	:	14·3	:	154	:	:	:	23·01
Radnor	63·55	:	:	8·6	:	140	:	:	:	51·35
Glam.	34·86	:	:	17·7	:	:	174	:1·84	:	:
Mon.	41·00	:	:	20·1	:	:	177	3·51	:	:

* Except Caernarvon and Flint.

APPENDIX D

REGIONAL ANALYSIS

(1) HOME COUNTIES

	Classification in Appendix C	Density of population per acre	Elections 1946–58		Population 1961 in 000's				
			% contests in C.C. elections	% contests in R.D.C. elections	Total for whole county	Total for county boroughs in that county	Administrative county		
							Total in M.B. & U.D.C. above 50,000	Total in M.B. & U.D.C. less than 50,000	Total in R.D.C.
Surrey . . .	1	3·25	75	53	1733	252	769	534	178
Essex . . .	1	1·92	88	42	2286	427	1299	305	255
Kent . . .	1	1·70	85	34	1701	31	635	668	367
Herts. . . .	1	1·99	71	53	832	..	181	404	247
Beds. . . .	1	1·19	60	26	380	..	194	63	123
Bucks. . .	1	0·98	51	36	486	..	131	110	245
Average . .	..	1·84	72	41	..	..	..	..	..
Percentage of population in C.B.s .	..	..	..	..	..	9·57	..	..	..
Percentage of population in areas of admin. county .	..	..	..	..	..	..	47·84	31·07	21·09

(2) NORTH & N. MIDLANDS

	Classification in Appendix C	Density of population per acre	Elections 1946–58		Population 1961 in 000's				
			% contests in C.C. elections	% contests in R.D.C. elections	Total for whole county	Administrative county			
						Total for county boroughs in that county	Total in M.B. & U.D.C. above 50,000	Total in M.B. & U.D.C. less than 50,000	Total in R.D.C.
Lancs. . . .	2	2·11	62	28	5131	2930	394	1484	323
Yorks. (W.R.) .	3	1·03	56	42	3641	1992	112	1073	464
Ches. . . .	1	1·45	48	29	1367	446	158	555	208
Staffs. . . .	3	1·42	74	43	1733	748	184	553	248
Derbys. . .	3	1·17	55	42	877	132	68	298	379
Notts. . . .	2	1·12	47	27	902	312	110	296	184
Durham . .	3	1·53	48	41	1517	564	81	570	302
Average . .	..	1·40	56	36	..	..	..	..	..
Percentage of population in C.B.s .	..	..	..	..	..	46·97	..	..	..
Percentage of population in areas of admin. county .	..	..	..	..	..	..	13·76	60·03	26·21

(3) MIDLANDS

| | Classification in Appendix C | Density of population per acre | Elections 1946–58 | | Population 1961 in 000's | | | | |
| | | | % contests in C.C. elections | % contests in R.D.C. elections | Total for whole county | Total for county boroughs in that county | Administrative county | | |
							Total in M.B. & U.D.C. above 50,000	Total in M.B. & U.D.C. less than 50,000	Total in R.D.C.
Glos. . .	2	0·62	52	47	1000	506	72	96	326
Leics. . . .	2	0·77	37	27	682	273	..	185	224
Northants. . .	2	0·51	50	31	398	105	..	162	131
Oxon. . . .	2	0·43	39	22	309	106	..	55	148
War. . . .	1	1·06	39	39	2023	1411	276	123	213
Worcs. . . .	2	1·00	47	22	568	127	54	260	127
Average . .	..	0·73	44	31	..	..	..	..	..
Percentage of population in C.B.s .	..	..	..	..	..	51·16	..	..	..
Percentage of population in areas of admin. county .	..	..	..	..	..	..	16·39	35·93	47·68

(4) SOUTH WEST

	Classification in Appendix C	Density of population per acre	Elections 1946–58		Population 1961 in 000's				
			% contests in C.C. elections	% contests in R.D.C. elections	Total for whole county	Total for county boroughs in that county	Administrative county		
							Total in M.B. & U.D.C. above 50,000	Total in M.B. & U.D.C. less than 50,000	Total in R.D.C.
Cornwall	3	0·39	21	35	341	..	..	188	153
Devon .	1	0·32	29	24	822	284	54	226	258
Somerset	2	0·49	34	24	598	80	..	251	267
Wilts. .	2	0·49	38	26	422	..	92	124	206
Dorset .	2	0·50	31	14	309	..	103	88	118
I.O.W..	1	0·99	30	29	95	..	..	77	18
Berks. .	1	0·83	45	40	503	120	..	119	264
Hants .	1	0·82	40	37	1336	574	195	262	305
Sussex E.	1	0·94	34	27	664	290	73	131	170
Sussex W.	1	0·98	44	26	411	..	134	117	160
Average	..	0·67	34	28	..	..	..	..	..
Percentage of population in C.B.s	..	..	..	..	..	24·50	..	..	..
Percentage of population in areas of admin. county. .	..	..	..	..	..	..	15·67	38·12	46·21

(5) EASTERN ENGLAND

| | Classification in Appendix C | Density of population per acre | Elections 1946–58 | | Population 1961 in 000's | | | | |
| | | | % contests in C.C. elections | % contests in R.D.C. elections | Total for whole county | Administrative county | | | |
						Total for county boroughs in that county	Total in M.B. & U.D.C. above 50,000	Total in M.B. & U.D.C. less than 50,000	Total in R.D.C.
Yorks. (N.R.) .	2	0·30	34	25	554	157	..	220	177
Yorks. (E.R.) .	2	0·30	28	20	527	303	..	114	110
Lincs. (H) . .	3	0·38	22	44	103	..	..	40	63
„ (K) . .	3	0·29	26	20	135	..	..	50	85
„ (L) . .	1	0·34	42	21	504	174	67	101	162
Rut. . . .	3	0·20	22	15	23	..	..	4	19
Hunts. . . .	2	0·35	19	13	79	..	..	35	44
Ely . . .	3	0·37	29	47	89	..	..	55	34
Peterb. . .	1	1·32	53	27	74	..	62	..	12
Cambs. . .	1	0·59	25	44	189	..	95	..	94
Norfolk . .	3	0·30	65	26	561	172	..	78	311
Suff. E. . .	3	0·42	28	20	342	117	..	102	123
Suff. W. . .	3	0·34	36	23	130	..	..	48	82
Average . .	..	0·42	33	27	..	..	..	..	..
Percentage of population in C.B.s .	..	..	..	..	..	27·89	..	..	..
Percentage of population in areas of admin. county .	..	..	..	..	..	..	9·38	35·48	55·13

APPENDIX D

(6) BORDER COUNTIES

| | Classification in Appendix C | Density of population per acre | Elections 1946–58 | | Population 1961 in 000's | | | | |
| | | | % contests in C.C. elections | % contests in R.D.C. elections | Total for whole county | Total for county boroughs in that county | Administrative county | | |
							Total in M.B. & U.D.C. above 50,000	Total in M.B. & U.D.C. less than 50,000	Total in R.D.C.
Northumb. . .	3	0·38	46	24	818	339	..	371	108
Cumb. . . .	3	0·23	39	36	294	71	..	91	132
Westm. . .	3	0·13	46	12	67	..	..	33	34
Salop . . .	3	0·35	38	25	297	..	..	152	145
Hereford. . .	3	0·24	26	10	130	..	..	59	71
Average . .	..	0·27	39	22	..	..	..	..	..
Percentage of population in C.B.s .	..	..	..	..	..	25·53	..	..	..
Percentage of population in areas of admin. county .	..	..	..	..	..	..	..	59·03	40·97

(7) WALES & MONMOUTH

	Classification in Appendix C	Density of population per acre	Elections 1946–58 % contests in C.C. elections	Elections 1946–58 % contests in R.D.C. elections	Population 1961 in 000's Total for whole county	Population 1961 in 000's Total for county boroughs in that county	Population 1961 in 000's Administrative county Total in M.B. & U.D.C. above 50,000	Population 1961 in 000's Administrative county Total in M.B. & U.D.C. less than 50,000	Population 1961 in 000's Administrative county Total in R.D.C.
Anglesey . .	3	0·29	22	27	51	..	..	21	30
Brecon . . .	3	0·12	29	23	55	..	..	15	40
Caernarvon . .	2	0·33	20	27	121	..	..	72	49
Cardigan . .	3	0·12	30	41	53	..	..	18	35
Carmarthen . .	3	0·29	40	44	167	..	..	66	101
Denbigh . .	3	0·40	38	46	173	..	..	83	90
Flint . . .	1	0·90	42	46	149	..	..	77	72
Glam. . . .	3	1·59	30	66	1227	482	200	323	222
Merioneth . .	3	0·09	23	48	39	..	..	17	22
Monmouth . .	3	0·98	31	44	443	108	..	276	59
Montgomery .	3	0·09	13	9	44	..	..	18	26
Pembroke . .	3	0·24	23	26	93	..	..	47	46
Radnor . .	3	0·06	13	25	18	..	..	6	12
Average . .	..	0·42	27	36	..	..	..	..	..
Percentage of population in C.B.s .	..	..	..	..	..	22·41	..	..	..
Percentage of population in areas of admin. county .	..	..	..	..	..	..	9·79	50·86	39·35

APPENDIX E

NOTE ON SOURCES: BIBLIOGRAPHY

There is no more recent bibliography for the county of Cheshire than J. H. Cooke, *Bibliotheca Cestriensis* (Warrington, 1904), and the volumes published by the Lancashire and Cheshire Antiquarian Society and Chetham Society rarely give references to modern administrative or social history. The numerous town-guides or the Robert Hale Regional Books, such as F. H. Crossley, *Cheshire* (1949) and N. Ellison, *The Wirral Peninsula* (1955), do not attempt to give the origins of most of their information. The manuscript *Cheshire Index* (1915), compiled by H. Hulme and deposited in Manchester Central Reference Library, is designed chiefly to help the genealogist looking through town histories. There is a short bibliography which is relevant to the theme of this book in *The Historical Atlas of Cheshire* (Chester, 1958), eds. Dorothy Sylvester and Geoffrey Nulty, but it is necessary to add the following notes if the reader is to understand the kind of material at the moment available. These notes, which are by no means exhaustive, are in five sections:

1. Newspapers and Magazines.
2. Reference Works and Directories.
3. Parliamentary Papers and Government Publications.
4. Local Printed Works.
5. Original Local Sources.

(1) *Newspapers and Magazines*

National: *The Times.*
County Council Magazine, ed. C. E. Baker (1889).
County Council Times.
Local Government Chronicle.
County Councils Gazette.

Local: (*a*) for N.E. and E. Cheshire:
Manchester Guardian (known as *The Guardian* after 24.8.59): index before 1914 in Manchester Central Reference Library, after 1914 at the Guardian Offices.
Ashton Reporter: available at Ashton, Stalybridge, and Dukinfield Public Libraries.
North Cheshire Herald and Hyde Reporter: formerly two papers, an index in Hyde Public Library.

(b) for N. and Central Cheshire:

Warrington Guardian: no index, and available on microfilm at Warrington Public Library.

(c) for W., S.W., and Central Cheshire:

Chester Chronicle: at offices in Bridge Street, Chester.
Chester Courant ⎱ at Courant offices, also in Bridge
Cheshire Observer ⎰ Street, Chester.
The holding of Chester Public Library for these three papers is poor before 1900.

(d) for the whole county:

Cheshire Life (pub. by the Philips Park Press, Manchester), a monthly magazine.

Cuttings: Manchester Central Reference Library (Local History) has a good set of newspaper cuttings, biographical and topographical. There are smaller sets elsewhere, e.g. Brunner Public Library, Northwich.

(2) *Reference Works and Directories*

National: (a) for statistical information:

County Councils and Municipal Corporations Companion, ed. J. R. S. Vine, from 1890 onwards.
Local Government Annual and Official Directory (L. G. Jnl. Ltd.).
Municipal Year Book (Municipal Jnl. Ltd.).
Financial and General Statistics (Society of County Treasurers).
Debrett's House of Commons and Judicial Bench.
Haydn's Book of Dates (2nd ed.).
Constitutional Year Books, 1885–1939.
Jubilee of County Councils (Evans Bros., 1939).

(b) for biographical information:

Directory of Directors, from 1880 onwards.
Who's Who in Local Government (Municipal Jnl. Ltd.), 1931, 1935, and 1961.

Local: (a) for statistical information:

Kelly's Directories of Cheshire, 1906, 1914, 1923, 1928, 1934, 1939.
Various smaller directories, such as *Directory and Gazetteer of Cheshire Towns* (1880), Morris & Co., Nottingham; *Postal Directory for Crewe, Congleton and Middlewich* (1913), Staffordshire Sentinel Ltd.

(b) for biographical information:

Cheshire Leaders: Social and Political (Will. Pollard & Co., Exeter, 1896).

Robert Head, *Contemporary Biographies: Cheshire at the Opening of 20th Century* (ed. W. T. Pike), Pike's New Century Series, No. 11 (1904).

Ernest Gaskell, *Cheshire Leaders: Social and Political* (priv. print., London, 1909).

Who's Who in Cheshire (E. Baylis & Co., Worcester, 1935).

Various local year books are also useful, e.g. those for Warrington and for Stalybridge, and *Manchester Faces and Places*.

(3) *Parliamentary Papers and Government Publications*

Local financial statistics before 1937 are available from the *Local Taxation Returns* made to Parliament under Acts of 1860 and 1877, and details of population and boundary changes can be obtained from the *National Census* volumes and from the *Registrar General's Statistical Review*.

Some indication of the state of Cheshire politics can be gained from the reports of inquiries into the petitions against two elections:

North Cheshire: H.C. 567 (1847–8), xi.

Chester: (C. 2824) (1881), xl.

The following parliamentary papers contain interesting Cheshire material:

Report of Select Committee on Co. Rates Bill, H.C. 468 (1850), xiii (evidence of J. Sadler, Chief Constable of Stockport).

Report of Select Committee on Local Taxation, H.C. 353 (1870), viii (evidence of J. May, Clerk of Macclesfield Union).

Report of Royal Commission on Noxious Vapours (C. 2159) (1878), xliv (evidence of landowners and businessmen).

Report of Royal Commission on Agriculture (C. 3096) (1881), xvii (evidence of Thomas Rigby).

Report of Select Committee on Highway Acts, H.C. 371 (1881), x (evidence of W. Egerton).

Report of Royal Commission on the Housing of the Working Classes (C. 4402–1) (1884–5), xxxi (evidence of F. Impey).

(4) *Local Printed Works*

The best collection of printed books and pamphlets on Cheshire is in the Chester City Library. The County Library has also been

building up an important local collection. Some towns, like Stalybridge and Altrincham, have made similar efforts. Manchester
Central Reference Library has a particularly valuable collection for
the Manchester region. In a brief note it is only possible to point
out the main types of work available.

Plans and Surveys:

S. Reece and A. E. Smith, *Industrial Cheshire: A Survey* (Man-
chester, 1940).
W. Dobson Chapman, *A Plan for Cheshire* (London, 1948).
R. Nicholas and M. J. Hellier, *An Advisory Plan: S. Lancs. and
N.E. Ches.* (Manchester, 1947).
British Association, *Survey of Merseyside* (London, 1953).

Towns:

William Lowndes, *The Story of Bebington* (Liverpool, 1953).
H. K. Aspinall, *Birkenhead and Its Surroundings* (Liverpool, 1903).
James Williams, *The Story of Chester* (Chester, 1907).
W. H. Chaloner, *Social and Economic Development of Crewe*
(Manchester, 1950).
Thomas Middleton, *Annals of Hyde* (Manchester, 1899). *The
History of Hyde* (Manchester, 1932).
C. F. Lawrence, *The Annals of Middlewich* (Stockport, 1911).

Firms:

J. F. Gibson, *Brocklebanks: 1770–1950* (Liverpool, 1953, 2 vols.).
W. J. Crosland-Taylor, *Crosville: the Sowing and the Harvest*
(Liverpool, 1948). *State-Owned without Tears* (Liverpool, 1954).
Mary Crozier, *An Old Silk Family: 1745–1945* (the Brocklehursts)
(Aberdeen, 1947).
T. E. Gregory, *Westminster Bank through a Century* (Oxford, 1936,
2 vols.) (for details of Parr's Bank, Warrington, see Chapter ix,
vol. 2).
W. H. Scott and others, *Technical Change and Industrial Relations*
(Liverpool, 1956), for John Summers & Co.
Charles Wilson, *History of Unilever* (London, 1954, 2 vols.)
ed. H. D. Willcock, *Browns and Chester: Portrait of a Shop:
1780–1946* (Mass Observation, London, 1947).

Biography:

Walter Lewin, *Clarke Aspinall* (Liverpool, 1893).
Katherine Chorley, *Manchester Made Them* (London, 1950).
J. M. Cohen, *Ludwig Mond* (London, 1956).
T. W. Legh, Lord Newton, *Retrospection* (London, 1941).

Elma K. Paget, *Henry Luke Paget: Portrait and Frame* (London 1939).

F. F. Potter, *Educational Journey* (London, 1949).

George Slater, *Chronicles of Lives and Religion in Cheshire* (London, 1891).

'*Fasciculus Cestriensis*' *in honour of Sir William Hodgson* (published by the Cheshire Medical Panel Committee, 1934).

Miscellaneous:

F. Leary, *History of Earl of Chester's Yeomanry Cavalry, 1797–1897* (priv. print., Edinb., 1898).

E. J. W. Disbrowe, *History of Volunteer Movement in Cheshire.* (Stockport, 1920).

John Brunner and T. E. Ellis, *History of Public Education in Cheshire* (Manchester, 1890).

J. H. Cooke, *Diamond Jubilee in Cheshire* (Warrington, 1899).

John Armstrong, *History of Freemasonry in Cheshire* (Liverpool, 1901).

A. F. Calvert, *Salt in Cheshire* (London, 1915, 2 vols.).

(5) *Original Local Sources*

The County Record Office in Chester Castle contains all the Quarter Sessions records as well as the printed minutes of the County Council, its year books, and the triennial speeches of the chairmen. There is also a large quantity of uncatalogued family papers which may contain some relevant material. The files of the Clerk's Department in County Hall were used in the second part of the book, but they are not available for inspection by the public.

The archives of Eaton Hall (Duke of Westminster) at the Eccleston Estate Office are disappointingly small because of the large-scale destruction which took place on the death of the first Duke, and consist mainly of eighteenth-century letters and papers with some valuable poll books for Chester City. John Rylands Library in Manchester possesses some catalogued collections of family papers, e.g. Bromley-Davenport, Legh of High Legh.

THEHESHIRE

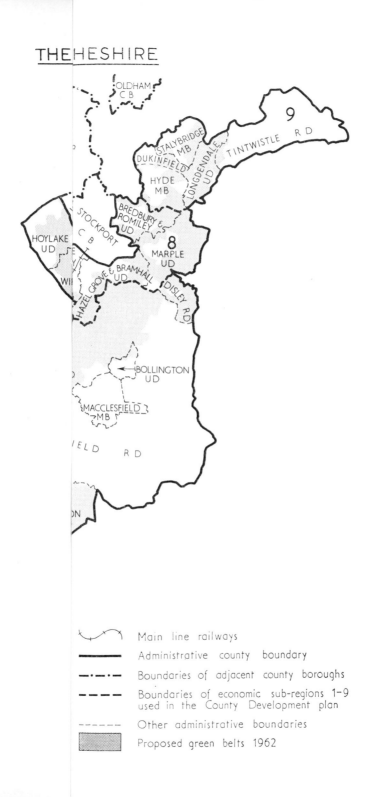

OLDHAM
C B

STALYBRIDGE
MB

DUKINFIELD

LONGDENDALE UD

TINTWISTLE R D

9

HYDE
MB

BREDBURY &
ROMILEY
UD

STOCKPORT
C B

HOYLAKE
UD

8
MARPLE
UD

HAZEL GROVE & BRAMHALL
UD

WIL

DISLEY RD

BOLLINGTON
UD

MACCLESFIELD
MB

IELD   R D

ON

Main line railways

Administrative county boundary

Boundaries of adjacent county boroughs

Boundaries of economic sub-regions 1–9
used in the County Development plan

Other administrative boundaries

Proposed green belts 1962

INDEX OF PERSONS AND PLACES

INDEX OF SUBJECTS

PRINTED IN GREAT BRITAIN
AT THE UNIVERSITY PRESS, OXFORD
BY VIVIAN RIDLER
PRINTER TO THE UNIVERSITY